ReFocus: The Films of Jane Campion

ReFocus: The International Directors Series

Series Editors: Robert Singer, Stefanie Van de Peer and Gary D. Rhodes

Board of advisors:
Lizelle Bisschoff (Glasgow University)
Stephanie Hemelryck Donald (University of Lincoln)
Anna Misiak (Falmouth University)
Des O'Rawe (Queen's University Belfast)

ReFocus is a series of contemporary methodological and theoretical approaches to the interdisciplinary analyses and interpretations of international film directors, from the celebrated to the ignored, in direct relationship to their respective culture – its myths, values, and historical precepts – and the broader parameters of international film history and theory.

Titles in the series include:

ReFocus: The Films of Susanne Bier
Edited by Missy Molloy, Mimi Nielsen and Meryl Shriver-Rice

ReFocus: The Films of Francis Veber
Keith Corson

ReFocus: The Films of Jia Zhangke
Maureen Turim

ReFocus: The Films of Xavier Dolan
Edited by Andrée Lafontaine

ReFocus: The Films of Pedro Costa: Producing and Consuming Contemporary Art Cinema
Nuno Barradas Jorge

ReFocus: The Films of Sohrab Shahid Saless: Exile, Displacement and the Stateless Moving Image
Edited by Azadeh Fatehrad

ReFocus: The Films of Pablo Larraín
Edited by Laura Hatry

ReFocus: The Films of Michel Gondry
Edited by Marcelline Block and Jennifer Kirby

ReFocus: The Films of Rachid Bouchareb
Edited by Michael Gott and Leslie Kealhofer-Kemp

ReFocus: The Films of Andrei Tarkovsky
Edited by Sergey Toymentsev

ReFocus: The Films of Paul Leni
Edited by Erica Tortolani and Martin F. Norden

ReFocus: The Films of Rakhshan Banietemad
Edited by Maryam Ghorbankarimi

ReFocus: The Films of Jocelyn Saab: Films, Artworks and Cultural Events for the Arab World
Edited by Mathilde Rouxel and Stefanie Van de Peer

ReFocus: The Films of François Ozon
Edited by Loïc Bourdeau

ReFocus: The Films of Teuvo Tulio
Henry Bacon, Kimmo Laine and Jaakko Seppälä

ReFocus: The Films of João Pedro Rodrigues and João Rui Guerra da Mata
Edited by José Duarte and Filipa Rosário

ReFocus: The Films of Lucrecia Martel
Edited by Natalia Christofoletti Barrenha, Julia Kratje and Paul Merchant

ReFocus: The Films of Shyam Benegal
Edited by Sneha Kar Chaudhuri and Ramit Samaddar

ReFocus: The Films of Denis Villeneuve
Edited by Jeri English and Marie Pascal

ReFocus: The Films of Antoinetta Angelidi
Edited by Penny Bouska and Sotiris Petridis

ReFocus: The Films of Ken Russell
Edited by Matthew Melia

ReFocus: The Films of Kim Ki-young
Edited by Chung-kang Kim

ReFocus: The Films of Jane Campion
Edited by Alexia L. Bowler and Adele Jones

edinburghuniversitypress.com/series/refocint

ReFocus:
The Films of Jane Campion

Edited by Alexia L. Bowler and Adele Jones

© Edinburgh University Press is one of the leading university presses in the UK. We publish academic books and journals in our selected subject areas across the humanities and social sciences, combining cutting-edge scholarship with high editorial and production values to produce academic works of lasting importance. For more information visit our website: edinburghuniversitypress.com

© editorial matter and organisation, Alexia L. Bowler and Adele Jones, 2023 ,2024
© the chapters their several authors, 2023,2024

Edinburgh University Press Ltd
13 Infirmary Street, Edinburgh, EH1 1LT

First published in hardback by Edinburgh University Press 2023

Typeset in 11/13 Ehrhardt MT by
IDSUK (DataConnection) Ltd

A CIP record for this book is available from the British Library

ISBN 978 1 3995 0026 5 (hardback)
ISBN 978 1 3995 0027 2 (paperback)
ISBN 978 1 3995 0029 6 (webready PDF)
ISBN 978 1 3995 0028 9 (epub)

The right of Alexia L. Bowler and Adele Jones to be identified as editors of this work has been asserted in accordance with the Copyright, Designs and Patents Act 1988 and the Copyright and Related Rights Regulations 2003 (SI No. 2498).

Contents

List of Figures vii
Acknowledgements viii
Notes on Contributors ix

    Introduction: Unruly Filmmaker, Fellow Traveller 1
    Alexia L. Bowler and Adele Jones

Part One
1 Claiming Campion: The Question of Jane Campion's Politics Revisited 19
    Stephen Kuster
2 *Two Friends*: Circumstances of a Historic Feminist Collaboration 37
    Zachary Zahos

Part Two
3 Unsettling Presences: Agentic Embodiment in Jane Campion's Films 57
    Catherine Fowler
4 'The mood that passes through you': Reverberations of Music and Meaning in *The Piano* 73
    Leanne Weston
5 'Only another man': Homosociality in Jane Campion's *Bright Star* and *The Power of the Dog* 91
    Alexia L. Bowler
6 'I don't think so, Jan, that's just another fantasy': Practice, Paratext and the Power of Women's Talk in Jane Campion's Filmmaking 108
    Rona Murray

Part Three

7 Articulating Feminism(s): Voicelessness, (In)Visibility and Agency in *Top of the Lake*   129
   Adele Jones

8 Jane Campion's Palimpsestuous Gothic: Kinship in *Top of the Lake: China Girl*   144
   Johanna Schmertz

9 Photosensitive Primetime: Race and Recovery in *Top of the Lake: China Girl*   160
   Blythe Worthy

Afterword: Unsettling Feminism   178
Annabel Cooper

Bibliography   185
Filmography   198
Index   200

Figures

1.1	Angela, mouth wide open, in 'Angela Eats Meat', *Passionless Moments*	26
1.2	Rufus the pig in 'Angela Eats Meat', *Passionless Moments*	26
2.1	Auteurist touches in *Two Friends*	46
2.2	Campion's unusual framing in *Two Friends*	47
4.1	Ada enters the sea	74
4.2	Ada watches over her piano on the beach	79
4.3	Texture	81
4.4	Ada's prosthetic finger	87
8.1	Family in focus, in *Top of the Lake: China Girl*	151
8.2	Puss in focus, in *Top of the Lake: China Girl*	151
9.1	From a 35mm print of Masahiro Shinoda's film *Pale Flower*	160
9.2	Brett Iles and Cinnamon	165
9.3	Stally Watkins, Robin Griffin, Miranda Hilmarson and Mo	167
9.4	Robin Griffin and the panda	176

Acknowledgements

We would like to thank our contributors for their work during the strangest of times. In addition, the series editors, and Gillian Leslie and Sam Johnson at EUP, have provided invaluable guidance and reassurance. Amy Heller at Milestone Films put us in contact with Isabella Del Grande from Australian Broadcasting Corporation, who provided access to *Two Friends* – thanks to both. Hilary Radner gave us sound advice: with thanks.

Alexia would like to thank her family, Nora, Allen and Victoria Bowler, and her partner, Richard Jones, for their unfailing support.

Adele thanks Harper for not caring about writing and requiring regular (long!) walks.

Notes on Contributors

Alexia L. Bowler is a senior lecturer in the School of Culture and Communication at Swansea University. Alexia has published on science fiction cinema, postfeminism and romantic comedy. She co-edited, with Dr Jess Cox, a special issue of *Journal of Neo-Victorian Studies* (2009/10) on adaptation. Her most recent article on Jane Campion and *In the Cut* (2003) was published in *Feminist Theory* (2018).

Annabel Cooper retired from the University of Otago's Gender Studies programme in 2021. Her research covers cultural history and cultural politics, including publications on gender, media, and colonial culture. Her book *Filming the Colonial Past: The New Zealand Wars on Screen* (2018) is the basis for an exhibition she is developing with Ariana Tikao. He Riri Awatea/Filming the New Zealand Wars will show at the New Zealand Portrait Gallery in late 2022.

Catherine Fowler is Professor of Film and Media at Otago University, New Zealand. Her research has focused on women filmmakers, avant-garde, experimental artists' practices, and European cinema. She is the author of a BFI Classic: *Jeanne Dielman 23, quai du Commerce, 1080 Bruxelles* (2021), a book on *Sally Potter* (2009), and is editor of *The European Cinema Reader* (2002) and co-editor with Gillian Helfield of *Representing the Rural: Space, Place, and Identity in Films about the Land* (2006).

Adele Jones teaches in the Centre for Academic Success at Swansea University, where she has also taught across a range of courses in English Literature. Adele has published on Sarah Waters, Michèle Roberts, and neo-Victorianism, and she co-edited *Sarah Waters and Contemporary Feminisms* (2016, with Dr

Claire O'Callaghan). Her most recent publication on Margaret Atwood and Naomi Alderman is forthcoming in *Legacies and Lifespans in Contemporary Women's Writing* (2023).

Stephen Kuster is a graduate student at Freie Universität Berlin, studying North American Studies. Outside of the academy, he also works in independent film production and film festival programming.

Rona Murray's PhD, received from Lancaster University, was a comparative study of female filmmakers' authorship agency across different cultural and institutional contexts. She has published on questions of authorship relating to Kim Longinotto and Agnès Varda. She lives in Germany and continues to teach film studies.

Johanna Schmertz is Professor of English at the University of Houston-Downtown, where she teaches courses in film theory, gender studies and composition. Her work on writing, film and feminist theory has appeared in *Rhetoric Review*, *Postscript* and *Pedagogy*. She has also published several book chapters.

Leanne Weston is an Institute of Advanced Study Early Career Fellow at the University of Warwick. Her doctoral thesis on music programming, memory, and materiality in post-broadcast screen culture forms part of ongoing work in the Centre for Television Histories. Leanne has published work in *Velvet Light Trap* on televised music histories and recently co-edited a special dossier on BBC Four for *Critical Studies in Television* with Dr Michael Samuel.

Blythe Worthy is a sessional academic at the University of Sydney, conducting research into serial narratives and adaptation. They teach in Writing Studies, Film Studies, American Studies and English Literature, and have been published by Springer and University of California Press. Blythe is currently coediting a collection on television adaptations to be published in 2023 and is the Documentary, Film and Television Editor for the *Australian Journal of American Studies*.

Zachary Zahos is a PhD candidate studying film in University of Wisconsin–Madison's Department of Communication Arts. His research focus includes art cinema distribution and exhibition in the United States, avant-garde film and video, histories of film style and technology, and streaming media platforms.

Introduction: Unruly Filmmaker, Fellow Traveller

Alexia L. Bowler and Adele Jones

Jane Campion is commonly thought of as an exceptional talent, winning numerous awards for her work, including some of the most prestigious both in Hollywood and in European film. Campion was only the second woman to be nominated for a best director Academy Award, eventually winning the Oscar for best original screenplay for *The Piano* (1993). In addition, until 2021 Campion was the only woman to win the Palme d'Or (twice), the first time for best short film for *Peel – An Exercise in Discipline* (1982) and latterly in the best film category for *The Piano*, with another nomination for the coveted Cannes prize for *Bright Star* (2009). Campion went on to be the first female director to preside over the jury at the Cannes Film Festival in 2014, while more recently she was awarded the 2021 Prix Lumière as part of the Lumière Festival. Her latest feature, *The Power of the Dog* (2021), received twelve Oscar nominations in 2022, winning her the award for best director, only the third woman to have won in ninety-four years.

With over thirty years standing as a director, Campion is renowned for creating complex female characters and is fêted for exploring the power dynamics of sexual and familial relationships, homing in on the often-troubled dialectic between her female protagonists' internal desires and the external environment in which they operate. It is true to say that Campion's representation of women often focuses on those at the edges of society, from the misunderstood writer Janet Frame (Kerry Fox) in the made-for-television biopic *An Angel at my Table* (1989) to the masochistic Frannie Avery (Meg Ryan) in the erotic thriller *In the Cut* (2003). More recently, in Campion's return to the television format with *Top of the Lake* (2013), Detective Robin Griffin (Elisabeth Moss) undertakes an emotionally and psychologically traumatic return journey to her home to solve a case in which incest, sex-trafficking, and rape form the backdrop to the first season. In the second season, *Top of the Lake: China Girl* (2017), Griffin investigates another series of abuses against women and young girls in the Australian capital, Sydney. As such, Campion's name is synonymous with modern feminist cinema. Indeed, the director's interest in women's lives extends to the workings of the industry itself and Campion has lent her name in support of other Antipodean women, championing and promoting the visibility and vitality of female directors like Julia Leigh, for whom she acted as mentor (and producer) for Leigh's directorial debut *Sleeping Beauty* (2011). Campion has also lent her name, shared her vast knowledge and experience, and given support to initiatives such as 'Females First' (a project set up by *Dazed and Confused* magazine to profile work by women) in service of increasing the diversity of female voices within the industry (indieflurry.com 2014). Julia Erhart (2019) suggests that Campion's work with this wider industry community of female practitioners indicates a connectedness between her films, her professional practice, and her personal values.

Campion has, more recently, also been a voice willing to critique the status quo in which institutional support for female projects is stymied, or to champion work that is, in her view, overlooked. Her comments about director Debra Granik's *Leave No Trace* (2018) is one such critique. Arguing that the absence of women in both 2018's Golden Globes nominations for best director and the AFI's '10 best films of 2018' list was erroneous, Campion suggested that Granik's standing, with a twenty-year history in the industry, and her skills as a director, have gone underappreciated and that, in Campion's view, Granik should have been part of that year's Oscar conversations (Sharf 2019). Similarly, invited to give a speech on the history of women nominated for best director by the Academy before presenting Lina Wertmüller with her honorary Oscar at the Governor Awards in 2019, Campion began by saying 'It's a very short history, more of a haiku' (Keegan 2019, n.p.). She noted that while 350 men had been nominated for best director at the Oscars, only five women had been nominated – 'How do you correct centuries of patriarchal domination?', she quipped (Montpelier 2019, n.p.).

In critiquing the under-representation of women in the film industry more generally, Campion suggests that the historical dearth of women's voices in filmmaking, or at least in visible and key roles, stifles the types of stories and representations that might emerge out of increased commitment to diversity in the film business, and the world is poorer for it. She concludes that, as 'women are going to tell different stories – there would be many more stories in the world if women were making more films' (Pulver 2014, n.p.). Campion highlights the fact that historically, men have been the financiers in the industry and thus 'men control the money, and they decide who they're going to give it to' (Doland 2007, n.p.), something played out in her short film *The Lady Bug* (2007), in which the scenes of a woman in a bug costume getting squashed while performing on a stage are a pressing metaphor for how Campion sees aspects of the film industry.

This issue of under-representation of women in the film industry is something noted not only by Campion and other women film directors, but also by feminist scholars engaged in a recuperation and documentation of women's filmmaking. In addition, campaigners draw attention to the way in which women are treated by the film industry; for example, actress Geena Davis founded 'The Geena Davis Institute on Gender in Media' which tracks statistics regarding roles undertaken by women in the industry (in front of and behind the screen), noting that in 2018 women made up only four per cent of filmmakers working on the top 250 films in the US.[1] The vital research undertaken by the institute also forms part of Tom Donahue's documentary *This Changes Everything* (2018), produced by and starring Davis, along with other luminaries such as Meryl Streep, Cate Blanchett, Shonda Rimes, Mira Nair, and Lena Dunham. The film, about the industry's gender imbalance, highlights what Davis, while promoting the documentary, suggests is a global embarrassment (Reuters 2019, n.p.). While projects like #EverydaySexism and movements such as #MeToo, #TimesUp, and #BlackLivesMatter have given rise to a new emphasis on vocalising women's stories and increased intersectionality, Davis suggests that things have not tangibly improved for women in the industry. She states pessimistically, specifically referring to #MeToo, that the only change brought about by the movement is 'now it is ok to talk' (Agence France-Presse 2019, n.p.).

Davis's comment captures the ambivalence inherent to movements focused on women and their place in male-dominated social, cultural, and political systems. Too often the ideals that characterise collectivism and demand for change cannot trickle down into the everyday experience of individual women, held back by the force of a patriarchy protecting its own interests. As a result, even as women's voices come together, they are also cut off from one another, leading to the kind of exceptionalism that has elevated Campion to 'female auteur'. An example of this was the invitation for Campion to submit *The Lady Bug* to the exclusive, auteur-led film collection *To Each His Own Cinema* (*Chacun Son Cinema*) (various 2007), produced by Gilles Jacob as part of the Cannes Film Festival's sixtieth anniversary celebrations. As Patricia White notes, Campion's was the only short by a female director out of thirty-five films, a fact played out in the press photograph in which Campion strikes a lone female figure amidst a sea of men (2015, 30–4). While considering alternative explanations to the notable absence of other women in the collection (a director's availability being one reason and the issue of who is 'universally famous' being another), White concludes that the discourse of exceptionalism, individualism, and ownership inherent in the notion of auteurism, on which festivals such as Cannes are built, 'presents an uncomfortable fit with women directors' habits and with women's cinema as a collectively imagined formation' (Ibid., 33). White also asserts that while a (re)balanced overview of great directors might be needed, it might also 'be considered fundamentally at odds with feminist work on authorship' (Ibid.), work which pushes at the discursive boundaries that construct the figure of the auteur (Grant 2001).

If Campion's inclusion in the *To Each His Own Cinema* collection forces her to 'embody Woman' (White 2015, 32), then White's assessment of *The Lady Bug* as a short which highlights the notion of authorship as being inherently connected to gendered dynamics is telling (Ibid., 36). Campion embodies (or, at least, has been made to represent) both the collectivism and individualism that informs the scholarly discourse around her work. Her auteur status (the longevity, sense of prestige associated with her work, and the much-vaunted attribution of an uncompromising artistic vision) allows her unusual, individual power in a male-dominated industry. Yet Campion has, as Deb Verhoeven notes, been 'embraced as a figurehead for women's cinema by critics and commentators', linking her inextricably with a sense of collectivism and imbuing her with 'symbolic value' (2009, 3). Her importance to the 'collectively imagined formation' of women's cultural production is reinforced by what Verhoeven dubs the 'Campion comparison' (Ibid.), in which her films are used as a kind of index alongside which many (female) directors appraise their own work, or against which their movies are evaluated by critics and scholars. Thus Campion (willingly or unwillingly) provides a model for female directors who cite her as an influence or inspiration, directors such as fellow Antipodeans like Cate Shortland and Ana Kokkinos, as well as British directors such as Carol Morley.

Campion has, however, been historically and famously cagey about the term 'woman' director and even more so about 'feminist filmmaker', with her commitment to feminism itself tempered by an ambivalence towards the term. In the past, she has stated:

> I no longer know what this [feminism, in the context of her filmmaking] means or expresses [. . .] I am interested in life as a whole. Even if my representation of female characters has a feminist structure, this is nevertheless only one aspect of my approach.
>
> (Fendel 1999, 87)

She has also noted that while working for the government-sponsored Women's Film Unit (WFU) directing *After Hours* (1984), a film about sexual harassment in the workplace, she found the politicised nature of that project problematic. While agreeing that the WFU did much to redress the inequity of the workplace, and that feminist groups, feminist filmmakers, and activists were pivotal in making the government support more women, Campion was also uncomfortable with what she perceived as the didactic nature of the WFU and the film that she was engaged to direct. She explained that she was 'averse to teaching messages – they're a load of rubbish', that she has always been reticent in telling an audience what they should feel, and that her 'orientation isn't political or doesn't come out of modern politics' (Cantwell 1999, 158).[2] That said, as a beneficiary of such collective action, Campion recognises the confidence it gave her to pursue her own creative voice down the line. Indeed, as her career attests, while Campion doesn't always identify with feminism, her works to this point have been about women, how they free themselves from patriarchal structures, and the nature of desire for women and between women and men.

This wish to tell women's stories is not in and of itself 'feminist' in a political sense; rather, it encompasses a range of subject positions. Indeed, the body of scholarship on Campion's work to date is testament not only to the breadth of her filmmaking but to the wide spectrum of interest in that filmmaking. Campion's elevated position within film is confirmed within this scholarship, which has produced an eclectic and wide-ranging mix of responses extending to biography, explorations of nation and identity, adaptation, sex and eroticism, and authorship. While some discussion of feminism appears within these works on Campion, there is no volume that specifically concentrates on Campion's relationship with feminism; as some scholars are keen to attest, this stems from Campion's own protestations against being labelled. Estella Tincknell (2013) perhaps comes closest to a sustained discussion of Campion's feminism in her volume *Jane Campion and Adaptation: Angels, Demons and Unsettling Voices*, where she notes that the issue of auteurism in feminist filmmaking is a complex one, figured as it is in the gendered politics of exceptionalism, notions of hierarchy, and dominance. This is not to say that Campion is not an auteur, but that her auteur status is one that has been conferred upon her by scholars and critics within a particular set of parameters that prize individualism and exceptionalism over collectivity and solidarity (as noted by White).

While it is not our intention here to provide a review of the literature because the work on Campion's oeuvre is both limited (in comparison to other auteurist directors) and widely known, each of the chapters in this collection explicitly draws on the existing body of scholarship. However, it is necessary to point out that each of the major volumes has a similar structure, focusing on the film texts themselves from the thematic perspectives noted above (with the exception of Alistair Fox's biographical reading of Campion's work).[3] Interestingly, though, with Campion's sustained move to television in 2013 – the point which marks, as we argue, a discursive shift in her work and relationship to feminism – the critical focus on her work has also shifted, with a range of articles discussing the feminism(s) of *Top of the Lake*.[4] Both creative and critical shifts can be linked to the wider cultural, social, and political context that has culminated in #MeToo, opening up space for the articulation and analysis of patriarchal violence, symbolic and material.

CAMPION IN THE #METOO AND #TIMESUP FILMMAKING WORLD

So the seeming reluctance (or maybe perceived lack of need) to examine Campion's work from an explicitly feminist perspective has perhaps begun to recede in a (post)#MeToo moment, especially given her own statements about the power of the movement. Indeed, the feminism of #MeToo seems to have been a watershed moment for Campion and in an interview at Cannes in 2018, she stated that the industry was in a key moment akin to the 'Berlin wall coming down, like the end of apartheid' (Muir 2018, n.p.).[5] The strength of this statement stands in almost direct opposition to Geena Davis's rather more pessimistic assessment of the effects of #MeToo, a reflection of the ambivalence inherent within the movement and one which characterises the polarised responses to #MeToo. The (hyper)visibility of the social media hashtag is undeniable: #MeToo was 'used 12 million times in the first 24 hours' after it was posted on Twitter by Alyssa Milano in response to sexual assault and abuse by men in the film industry, and 'the "magnitude of the problem" of sexual violence in women's (and others') lives was all too apparent' (Fileborn and Loney-Howes 2019, 3). However, as Karen Boyle explores in her thoughtful response to the speaking out catalysed by the hashtag, 'speech is not a political end in itself but rather initiates the development of a public-facing, structural, political analysis' (2019, 23). This assessment reflects precisely the point that Davis is making when she states that the only impact of #MeToo is that women can speak out now. So if articulation of the impact of male violence and abuse is only reflected back to us through cultural narratives that examine what happens to the men involved (Boyle specifically considers the media furore around the allegations against Harvey Weinstein), can #MeToo really change the endemic and systemic violence exposed by the act of speaking out? This movement must, as Boyle states, be situated within a history of the feminism(s) that precedes it, informs it, and works alongside it in order to begin to deconstruct that question, though it is our contention that any feminism seeking to undo patriarchal structures is always at least partly characterised by ambivalence, such as that elicited by #MeToo.

Although we do not seek to answer that question here, it is important to acknowledge it because Campion's body of work prefigures the concerns of #MeToo and engages with the notions of women's agency and oppression that inform the movement.[6] Indeed, the strength of Campion's statements about #MeToo demonstrates her level of investment in it and her keen awareness of having made her earliest films in one of the most 'ferocious patriarchal periods' of the twentieth century, as well as her sensitivity to the fact that the world is saturated with male-dominated stories, or what she calls 'hero stories' (Muir 2018, n.p.). This is arguably a rallying (feminist) cry. She states: 'We have lived a male life, we have lived within the patriarchy. It's something else to take ownership of your own story' (Ibid.). Similarly, in an interview with the *European Women's Audiovisual Network* on the topic of #MeToo and her own position as an often-lone female director at the 'top table', Campion proclaims that women cannot 'remain at ease' in a world in which 93 per cent of the films made are by men (LeBris 2018, n.p.). Sensing that post-#MeToo, it will 'no longer be possible to ignore women [. . .] Women are a wealth of the world', Campion suggests the world is now more attuned to hearing what women want and what they think (Ibid.). Her exhilaration at hearing women speaking up at the Golden Globes to demand change is clear: '[it] made me feel like for the first time something was really happening [. . .] a historic turning point' that cannot be undone (Ibid.). She asserts: 'We must work, rush into the now open doors and use this energy to build on' (Ibid.). Campion argues that there is a distinct appetite for this work, citing recent titles in television such as *The Handmaid's Tale* (Hulu, 2017–present), *Big Little Lies* (HBO, 2017–2019), and her own series *Top of the Lake* (BBC, 2013–2017), which all address the complexity of the relationship between the two sexes and women's subjectivities.

And yet, Campion's first film after ten years' absence from cinema is an adaptation of Thomas Savage's *The Power of the Dog* (1967), premiered at the 2021 Venice Film festival and released on Netflix shortly afterwards. The film's premise provides an unusual emphasis for Campion, with a male lead for the first time and a sustained focus on the relationships between men. Several commentators have asked why Campion has shifted gears to concentrate on a distinctly male-centred genre (the Western) and an overwhelmingly homosocial environment, riddled with tropes of so-called toxic masculinity. However, those familiar with Campion's work can recognise a subtle paradox; the male actors and themes so front and centre in *The Power of the Dog* belie the almost constant presence of discourses of masculinity (and its effects on women) in her previous films. In turning to Savage's Western, Campion presents us with the familiar refrain of the family dynamic coming under scrutiny, as well as the psycho-sexual power struggles that perceive female agency as a dangerous subversion of the dominant patriarchal and homosocial landscape. This refrain mirrors the ambivalence at the heart of the #MeToo movement that pits the voices of powerful men in systemically patriarchal structures against women whose only power is the articulation of violence.

Campion captures this dichotomy in her turn to a male-led story; she has said that because the #MeToo movement has 'allowed other women to express themselves', she felt freer to place a male subject at the heart of her next project, stating, 'I can imagine into a male space now' (Canfield 2021, n.p.). Although a film project that focuses on masculinity might seem directly opposed to Boyle's assertion that cultural narratives need to emphasise women's voices in order to effect change, Campion is arguably engaged in a subversive action. She subtly twists the dominant narratives of #MeToo, turning masculinity in on itself in a film that highlights how profoundly destructive masculinity can be for men as well as women. Campion's newfound willingness to engage with discussions around #MeToo, with its distinctly feminist sensibilities, is complicated, then, by her immediate shift to male central characters. Indeed, in an interview with *Vanity Fair* in 2021, in which this notion of making a film with a male centre is raised, Campion opens up about her lifelong commitment to telling women's stories, stating that as these have been ignored, she felt it was her 'mission' to voice them. Prior to the #MeToo movement, Campion felt that to focus on telling male-centred stories would have 'felt like a huge betrayal' (Ibid., n.p.). She explains further, '[e]ven though I see myself as an artist who can go anywhere, I still felt this natural, but also political, necessity to cleave to women' (Ibid.). This is seemingly a direct contradiction of her claims twenty years ago (of being apolitical in her work). However, there is nuance in Campion's statement. Campion sees herself as an artist with a desire to allow her imaginative and creative life and all that entails to remain unconstrained by ideological positions which might not always sit neatly with her own drives. Her anthropological eye also recognises the embedded nature of human life; in a global patriarchal system, as part of an embodied personal, sometimes collective, experience, men too play a role. The work being done by female filmmakers like Campion over the last few decades is coming to fruition with the next generation of female filmmakers such as Sofia Coppola, Ava DuVernay, Greta Gerwig, Cate Shortland, Chloé Zhao, and Patty Jenkins, to name but a few, slowly gaining visibility and confidence, and Campion senses that she can hand the baton on. One might argue that Campion was doing the work of articulation before #MeToo, speaking out and challenging cultural representations of women in order to effect social and political change.

IS CAMPION A FEMINIST NOW?

However, this collection does not intend to 'prove' that Campion is or is not a feminist, or to gauge the extent of her feminist credentials; that would come close to imposing a traditional kind of auteurism on Campion's complex interventions into representations of female subjectivity and agency in film and television. We do want, though, to explore her work from within a specifically feminist conceptual framework which both refocuses critical perspectives on

Campion and takes account of her explicit identification with contemporary feminism, a shift from her earlier disavowals of this subject position. What is very clear is that even where Campion's works have an uncomfortable relationship with specifically feminist considerations, they almost always examine the ambiguities inherent in the relationships between men and women, and the effects of those relationships on female subjectivity and agency. Considered in light of #MeToo – and Campion's commentary on that movement – the connection between these textual ambiguities and the wider landscape in which women's cultural production takes place is highlighted; there is a clear juxtaposition between the ways in which men and women in the film and television industry draw on the cultural value of the auteur and navigate the norms that sustain gendered power hierarchies. While abusive men such as Harvey Weinstein, for example, are able to both employ the tropes of that abuse in their work *and* hide in plain sight (Boyle 2019), women in the industry must either maintain a paradoxical relationship with feminism or disavow it all together.[7] Thus, Campion has almost obsessively worked with those same tropes to highlight the (real and symbolic) abuse to which women are subjected yet has, until recently, consistently problematised the notion that her work can or should be read as feminist cultural production. #MeToo, we argue, has provoked a shift in Campion's willingness to claim a place within feminist discourse.[8]

However, it would be simplistic to suggest that Campion has performed a simple reversal of her ambiguity towards being named as a feminist filmmaker. Although she has long articulated the values and aims of a #MeToo moment through the methods she uses, her resistance to accepting the label 'feminist' embodies wider social and cultural responses to feminism as a political position. Each of the parts that follow explores how the periods of Campion's filmmaking engage with the feminist praxis of the time; her works become, we argue, paradigmatic texts, embodying both her ambiguity towards feminism *and* the dominant, competing discursive practices in which she works. This is not to suggest a crude mapping of Campion's career onto a history of feminist thought nor to see her work, reductively, as a mirror for society. Rather, we suggest, if it is necessary to consider 'gender oppression in the concrete cultural contexts in which it exists' (Butler 1999, 6), then it is also necessary to consider feminism in the same way. Campion's oeuvre represents these considerations in all their complexity.

The first part of this book, then, considers Campion's work from the 1980s, focusing on two early shorts – *Passionless Moments* (1983) and *A Girl's Own Story* (1984) – and her first feature film, *Two Friends* (1986). The two chapters in this part explore Campion's early aesthetic and her overt engagement with notions of familial relationships, 'sisterhood', and friendship. Where Stephen Kuster's chapter provides close readings of these early films through an ethnographic framework considering the power dynamics at work, Zachary Zahos expands the scope of this part by considering the wider production and distribution landscape of *Two Friends*. The two chapters together place Campion's work against a backdrop in which feminist thinking was changing both representations of women on screen and the place and status of female directors within the industry. Although most scholarly and popular work characterises the early films as representative of Campion's coming of age in an industry transformed by feminism,[9] there has been little consideration of how the women's movement itself, as well as the backlash against feminism, affects her representations of gender and women. Thus, the argument in this first part is that Campion's work is necessarily ambivalent as she navigates and explores the social and cultural conflict inherent in naming female agency.

This ambivalence is representative of the thorny, hopeful, often contradictory praxis of any social and political movement, and second wave feminism is no exception. The links between filmmaking, feminist film theory, and political feminist activism are inextricable, exposing, as they do, fundamental questions about images and representations of women and the meanings both expressed and generated by those images. In *Passionate Detachments* (1997), Sue Thornham traces the development of the relationship between the political and theoretical practices that have come to define second wave feminist film theory, broadly charting:

> the difficult triangular relationship between three central figures. First, there is the figure of 'Woman' as image or cinematic representation. Second, there is the figure of the real-life woman, who is always in fact *women* [. . .] Finally, there is the figure of the feminist theorist who – in however complex or theoretical a way – *speaks as* a woman.
>
> (ix–x, emphasis in original)

Perhaps the most striking element of Thornham's comprehensive survey is the consistent recognition that there are necessarily elisions and contradictions in the feminist work of the 1970s and 1980s because, as Annette Kuhn asserts, whereas the links between politics and knowledge are often simply assumed, 'where feminism is concerned [. . .] this is impossible, precisely because knowledge has had to be self-consciously produced alongside political activity' (2013, 2). Even without a detailed history of the development of the theory and practice of second wave feminism (an impossible task in this space), these two articulations provide a useful lens through which to explore Campion's early work.

A major difficulty of the triangular relationship identified by Thornham is that in the desire for knowledge production, the space produced by early feminist theorising necessarily occurred within, and therefore mirrored, a 'totalizing system' of patriarchal discourses in which women themselves are elided (1997, 44).

We are not suggesting that the shorts explored in Kuster's chapter are a direct response to these issues; rather, Campion instinctively creates a representational space in which slippage and ambiguity highlight the difficulty of representation from within the totalising systems themselves. Even taking into account an ethnographic turn in feminist theorising (whether in terms of race or class, for example), the work itself becomes a manifestation of feminist praxis. Kathleen McHugh recognises that *Passionless Moments* 'include[s] the ethnographic' in its representations of class and gender, though she suggests that in its representation of masculinity, 'some of the film's power must certainly be attributed to [Gerald] Lee' (2007, 40). Without doing disservice to Lee's contribution, this implicit link between a male production presence and the representation of masculinity perhaps elides the complexity of Campion's relationship to early feminist discourses, undermining the idea that gendered power dynamics are central to Campion's thinking. It also accounts for the critical tendency to bypass *Two Friends* as somehow marginal in Campion's oeuvre; that is, it is telling that a film with a rich female production context, which focuses on female adolescent experience, is often characterised as 'awkward' and has no sustained presence in the scholarly body of work on Campion (Cheshire 2000, 28–9). Zahos's revaluing of *Two Friends* places this work firmly within a collectivism that – Campion's own ambiguities notwithstanding – speaks directly to the notion of what, in his chapter, he terms a 'healthy culture of feminist politics'. Thus, all three films discussed here engage with the debates of the time.

However, even whilst characterising these early works as interventions into feminist cultural production, it must be recognised that they are uncomfortable in the sense that they do not offer any stable position from which to read women; rather, Campion offers multiple and contradictory subject positions. In fact, these representations prefigure the destabilisation of discrete identity categories leading to the discursive mêlée of the 1990s, which (arguably) asserts the primacy of individualisation, multiplicity, and deconstruction over political analysis of material, hegemonic governing structures. Thornham might also recognise the period as one in which the interrelationship between filmmaking practice and feminist theory was unravelled, pointing out, as she does, the contradiction for a period in which although the loss of 'theoretical and political specificity' is problematic, where identities are 'constantly in flux', the questions we ask about those identities 'remain constantly engaged and in play' (1997, 90–1). Given that this period also represents Campion's shift into the mainstream of the film industry, we question (especially given the involvement of Weinstein's Miramax in distributing her work) whether her work deliberately employs the ambivalence identified in Part One. Thus, the framework through which we read the chapters here concentrates on the tension between Campion's use of overtly feminist tropes and the potential for her representations to feed a growing backlash reinforced by the destabilisation of what it means to be a woman, and therefore increased difficulty in political organising around or representation of that identity.

The four chapters in this second part, then, consider Campion's output since 1989 against this backdrop. It is striking that, despite the shift in attention from 'political' concerns about what it means to be a woman to a more individual focus on embodiment and agency, the thematic engagement with Campion's work remains similar. Catherine Fowler begins by considering Campion's female bodies as unsettling presences in a 'post-visual pleasure' landscape,[10] reflecting the inherent paradoxical relationship between Campion and the feminist praxis with which she engages, drawing on theoretical debates around spectatorship, autonomy, and desire. Leanne Weston uses this bodily framework to examine the expressive and affective functions performed by Michael Nyman's score, inherent, she argues, to understanding female subjectivity in *The Piano*. Both chapters recall Kuster's argument that embodiment is necessarily informed by the political structures through which we recognise ourselves. Alexia L. Bowler's chapter on *Bright Star* (2009) and *The Power of the Dog* traces the line between Campion's past and present representations of men and masculinity, arguing that despite Campion's famed interest in women's psyches, her films have always sought to understand the dynamic between the sexes and often the homosocial landscape within her films. This speaks to the argument outlined by Zahos in which he notes the paradoxical pull for Campion of working in a female collective. This notion of 'women's work' is extended in the last chapter of this part. Rona Murray's exploration of paratexts offers valuable insights into the process of filmmaking and thinking that goes into Campion's work, as well as the collaborative nature of Campion's filmmaking. Murray explores the director-producer commentaries which accompany *The Piano* and *In the Cut*, framing the discussion between Campion and Chapman (in *The Piano*) and Campion and Parker (in *In the Cut*) as examples of Luce Irigaray's *parler femme*. Murray asks what we can imply about women's work from this extra-diegetic collaborative and 'non-market' space.[11]

The third and final part of the collection specifically considers Campion's first television drama since *An Angel at My Table* and brings us back to the arguments that open the collection. Despite the focus on a twenty-first-century politics of gender and race (precipitated by seismic shifts in the discourses that inform cultural production), this part brings together the ideas explored in previous chapters. The move to television is directly linked to Campion's politicised view of the patriarchal values in film and television, but her focus remains on embodiment and agency. Adele Jones writes that *Top of the Lake* engages directly with the concerns and aims of the #MeToo movement through highlighting systemic male violence while also revaluing the role of female communities in reinforcing female subjectivity. This echoes the concern with collectivity and gendered hierarchies, explored by Zahos, Bowler and

Murray. Johanna Schmertz expands on these readings through her exploration of incest in *Top of the Lake: China Girl*, placing the spotlight on the relationship between contemporary feminist concerns and the role played by the family as a patriarchal construct in which women are exchanged; she, therefore, places the family structure firmly within the paradigms of power identified in the preceding chapters. Blythe Worthy, in their examination of *Top of the Lake: China Girl*, characterises Campion's television work as a problematising (and perhaps problematic reflection) of white feminism and generic television conventions. Thus, Worthy's chapter ends where Kuster's began: with a consideration of Campion's (intersectional) politics. All three chapters recognise this phase of Campion's work as directly engaging with feminist responses to the repressive 'postfeminist' paradigm of early twenty-first-century cultural production. It is at this point, then, we argue, that Campion moves from solidly ambivalent – if sometimes paradoxical – representations of female subjectivity to works which more comfortably situate themselves within overtly feminist discourses. Her television work sets the scene for a post-#MeToo landscape in which Campion is happy to acknowledge her feeling that patriarchy has been a driving force in her representations of women. The final three chapters situate Campion, both directly and indirectly, within a history of feminist discourse.

The afterword to this collection considers *The Power of the Dog* as a lens through which to explore the themes developed throughout this volume. Annabel Cooper surveys the uneasy sexual politics in Campion's film, including the filmmaker's preoccupation with power dynamics in human relationships and female embodiment. Cooper picks up the threads in Kuster and Worthy's chapters to consider the uneasiness often engendered by Campion's depictions of Indigenous figures (or lack thereof) thinking through the elisions noted by feminist scholars. It is clear, however, in Cooper's analysis, that there is indeed a nuance in Campion's approach to depicting the (post)colonial. This reflection also demonstrates that the specificities of race cannot be divorced from Campion's portrayals of gendered subjectivity, speaking to the sense of intersectionality inherent in her work. Cooper's afterword weaves together these complexities, all too often elided in contemporary feminist theory and the lived experiences of women in the everyday. This suggests that while Campion's 'feminism' is at times troubling, her approach encourages us to think differently, to explore new ideas and new formulations; to think through our own relationship with ourselves, our feminism, and the dynamic nature of the world around us.

Finally, we want to acknowledge that this collection has taken a broad approach and, therefore, has unavoidable elisions both in terms of the works we have chosen not to discuss at length and in the concepts we could have explored.[12] We would, for example, suggest that a sustained analysis of the trajectory of Campion's television work would be highly welcome, as would further analysis through an Antipodean feminist lens, focusing on the social and political concerns specific to the psychogeographical contexts in which Campion's work is produced (which the chapters in this collection begin to do). The project of this collection, though, is to extend the conversation about the feminism inherent in this oeuvre and to insist that this is a conceptual framework requiring further critical attention. It is never easy to pin down Campion's vision and this is key to the interest she generates. She occupies a central space in film and television making yet operates on the margins; if Campion does indeed 'embody Woman' then she does not do so in any easy way. While exploring what it means to be a woman and being acutely aware of the systemic oppressions faced by women, Campion refuses to be co-opted by any political or intellectual discourse and so creates a liminal space in which her work becomes the site of constant 'negotiation and contestation' (Thornham 1997, 91). It is, perhaps – ironically – her ability to refuse us a fixed point within this ambivalence and ambiguity that makes Campion a voice for our time, a time in which film and television by women can help us represent fragmented female subjectivities 'that have been, at best, subliminally delimited by patriarchy, and, at worst, actively deformed by gendered violence' (Mayer 2016, 2).

NOTES

1. The numbers Davis mentions are only one such set of figures and are specific to the US. See WomenandHollywood.com (2022, n.p.); Lauzen (2018, n.p.); The Geena Davis Institute on Gender in Media (2022, n.p.), and Farrow (2017, n.p.). For findings in a UK context, see Cobb, Williams, and Wreyford (2016, n.p.).
2. It is worth pointing out here that this quotation from Campion is used several times throughout this collection, speaking to the effects of her words on a consideration of her work; there is an ambiguity engendered by the perceived clash between the articulation of her position and the thematic drive of her films.
3. Dana Polan, *Jane Campion* (2001); Ellen Cheshire's *Jane Campion* (2000) and *In the Scene: Jane Campion* (2018); Virginia Wright Wexman's collection of interviews with Campion (1999); Kathleen McHugh's *Jane Campion* (2007); Deb Verhoeven, *Jane Campion* (2009); Harriet Margolis, *Jane Campion: The Piano* (2000); Hilary Radner, Alistair Fox, and Irène Bessière, *Jane Campion: Cinema, Nation, Identity* (2009); Tincknell, *Jane Campion and Adaptation*, and Alistair Fox, *Jane Campion: Authorship and Personal Cinema* (2011).
4. Part Three of this collection engages with this work.
5. Again, reference to Campion's interview with Kate Muir is made in several of the chapters that follow; the ubiquity of this interview speaks to the significance of the shift in Campion's tone and position.
6. Fileborn and Loney-Howes, Boyle, and Sarah Banet-Weiser (in *Empowered: Popular Feminism and Popular Misogyny* [2018]) provide excellent explorations of the issues at the heart of #MeToo as a feminist movement.
7. Here, we mean both disavow feminism and disavow the film industry. Although Campion is on the margins of the industry as a female director, she is one of the only women directors to have won the Palme d'Or and an Oscar for direction. The longevity of her

career both inside and outside the Hollywood system is notable, yet her jump to TV was quicker than everyone else's. It is arguable that Campion does not function entirely comfortably within an industry that she knows to be sexist and oppressive and so she does not embrace it entirely – or, to some extent, disavows it.
8. See, for example, Le Bris (2018) and Muir (2018).
9. This is how Kathleen McHugh (2007) characterises Campion's work.
10. Fowler uses this term to refer to the production of work after Laura Mulvey's famous essay, 'Visual Pleasure and Narrative Cinema' (1975).
11. See Murray's discussion of Luce Irigaray's text (1985) in Chapter 6.
12. For example, *Tissues* (1980) and *Mishaps of Seduction and Conquest* (1984) were produced while Campion was studying and are not readily available. *An Angel at my Table* (1990) and *The Portrait of a Lady* (1996) will be the most obvious omissions for the reader. The thematic concerns of both are, however, mirrored in discussions on masculinity, the female auteur, female subjectivity, and subjugation.

PART ONE

CHAPTER 1

Claiming Campion: The Question of Jane Campion's Politics Revisited

Stephen Kuster

In 2017, the Film Society of Lincoln Center held a Jane Campion retrospective to celebrate the release of *Top of the Lake: China Girl* (2017). To inaugurate the series, they hosted 'An Evening with Jane Campion', at which Campion narrated her life and work. Naturally, the same themes and ideas that have followed Campion throughout her career were discussed. Among the issues explored was the ever-thorny subject of feminism. Programming director Dennis Lim asked Campion, 'As somebody who went to art school in the 70s and 80s, was feminist film theory something that was formative to you?' (Film at Lincoln Center 2017, 1:19:38). Ever the humourist, Campion sidestepped the question by joking about her film school's 'conservative' nature (Campion attended the Australian Film, Television and Radio School [AFTRS]). While Campion followed up the comment with statements on gender parity, this discomforted-turned-facetious response is not out of the ordinary for her when asked about her relationship to feminism. She has long expressed unease around the term's application to her work, and after she directed *After Hours* (1984) she went as far as to claim that she regretted the feminist project, citing feelings of artistic constraint (Ciment 1999a, 35).[1] Yet despite her protests, trade publications, curators and academics have continued to attach the feminist label to Campion and her films.

It's not hard to see why such writers and publications do so. Not only was she the only woman to win the Palme d'Or for almost seventy-five years, an individual win sometimes extrapolated for the collective, but also unlike some other visible women directors, Campion roots her films in the female experience, tracing the lives and histories of women. Patricia White summarises the impulse to claim Campion as feminist: 'If I were to pick one woman filmmaker to stand for the lot, I would much rather it be Jane Campion, whose work speaks to feminist concerns and incites my passion, than, say, Leni Riefenstahl' (2015, 34). With the mention of Riefenstahl, White recognises the particular history and problem of the German director, who attempted a rehabilitation of her image by separating her talent and gender from her Nazi context. This rehabilitation was accepted, in part, in some feminist circles. However, critic Susan Sontag quashed Riefenstahl's aesthetics-politics extrication with the reminder that the aesthetic *is* the politic, meaning *Triumph of the Will* (1935) was not merely fascist because of the temporal context; rather, the film was fascist because of the rhetorical techniques developed by Riefenstahl (Sontag 1975, n.p.).

It is not my aim to equate Campion with Riefenstahl, but I use the latter to foreground a wariness when we forgo history in order to achieve a certain feminist attachment. In an effort to evaluate the meaning behind the often commoditised and simplified label of 'feminist', I explore the question of Jane Campion's politics by asking: what are the politics behind the feminist label, and do they warrant the attachment? This chapter focuses, then, on Campion's final student films, *Passionless Moments* (1983) and *A Girl's Own Story* (1984), and the 1980s as a time period marked by experimentation in efforts to find her own voice, a goal that got her into trouble with the aforementioned 'conservative' AFTRS (Rickey 1999, 52). In particular, I centre my analysis on the intersections of colonialism and feminism, the two most commonly applied and debated discourses in Campion's filmography. For *Passionless Moments*, I examine Campion's interpretation of the ethnographic film, which arises out of a masculinist colonial knowledge and power production and its relationship to filmed subjects and objects. To read *A Girl's Own Story*, I use Adrienne Rich's concept of feminist 're-vision' (1979) to analyse Campion's centring of female subjectivity of the 1960s that otherwise has been marginal in cultural representations of the decade. Despite being a second wave feminist text, Rich's act of looking back remains an important concept within feminist discourse, and this specific concept has found continued use in recent scholarship, including in Stella Bruzzi's *Approximation* (2020). This, in turn, is indicative of a larger reclamation and reconsideration of the second wave in contemporary scholarship.[2] Through close analysis, I foreground the films' contradictory politics in order to demonstrate the slippages and ambivalences that come with politics: simply put, they are beyond a one-word descriptor. It is the contradictions themselves I ultimately argue for as the centring principle when examining these politics in the work of Jane Campion, as it is through contradictions that we can enhance understanding of film history and historiography, particularly in their intersections with feminism and politics.

PASSIONLESS MOMENTS

In Campion's oeuvre, *Passionless Moments* has been relegated to the sidelines. Rochelle Simmons's account of the film epitomises its less-than-satisfactory status, as she claims: '*Passionless Moments* bears the traces of somebody else's work, in that it has a lighter tone than is characteristic of the films we associate with Campion' (2009, 177). In reference to this 'lighter tone', Simmons further explains that *Passionless Moments* purports an 'affirmative' outlook on the Australian suburban milieu, as it celebrates and therefore elevates the banal to cinematic representation, whereas other Campion works critique the geographic and cultural locale (Ibid.). While Hilary Neroni (2012) argues that elevating the mundane makes the film a feminist work, Alistair Fox, similarly to Simmons, claims that the film is 'a less deeply layered work' (2011, 55). Fox references an early interview where Campion says that she 'wanted to show sweet, ordinary people that you rarely see on the screen and who have more charm than better known actors' (Ciment 1999a, 33). Here, Campion's own perspective ostensibly lends itself to such dismissive analyses of the work. *Passionless Moments*, as a short that documents vignettes of suburban life with sweetness, would stand apart from other Campion efforts which deplore the concept of 'niceness' and confront the 'world as it really is' (Preston 1999, 12). However, although *Passionless Moments* is characterised as possessing doses of saccharine suburban life, there is something deeper at work – the debris of colonialism in the Australian suburban utopia.

To expose the colonial undertones of *Passionless Moments*, I would like to adopt and push further Kathleen McHugh's (2007) ethnographic framework. This is an apt lens through which to view the short, bearing in mind Campion's undergraduate degree in anthropology from Victoria University of Wellington. In drawing on discourses in anthropology, I approach the film from a postmodern sensibility that argues anthropological studies themselves are 'performances', and that these narratives are intrinsically tied to imperialist and colonial demands (Clifford 1994, 205). In his landmark study *Orientalism* (1979), Edward Said explains the discursive power of knowledge-production concerning the Other in that it allowed for metropoles to extend their colonial projects and control that Other. Furthermore, if we consider the ethnographies that occur in Campion's Antipodean homes, Fatimah Tobing Rony argues the '"native" is even more Other', thought to be 'trapped in some deep frozen past, inarticulate, not yet evolved' (1996, 5). However, as Brian Hochman contends, sometimes the exotic Other found in the South Seas has provided a less contentious way of thinking about race than the issues of black-and-white, as the native has been seen as closer to white than black (2014, 133). In either case, it is clear that the racial Other – that is, a non-white body is paramount to the construction of ethnographic representation.

Cinema, as an institution, is not separate from ethnography and its colonial discourses; rather, it contributes to them. Visual iconographies aid ethnographic research and contribute to ethnographic spectacle most notably through the ethnographic film, which, as defined by Rony, is a work where 'the viewer is presented with an array of subsistence activities, kinship, religion, myth, ceremonial ritual, music and dance', and these moments are meant to amount to 'a metonym for an entire culture' (1996, 7). However, as Paul Henley contends, a film about 'other cultures' is not necessarily an ethnographic film; instead, an ethnographic film is more about the 'method of research employed' (2020, 9). As a subset of documentary, the seemingly strange moments are portrayed with the utmost belief in 'cinematic realism', assuming that 'the camera records a truthful reality' (Russell 1999, 12). The profilmic events before the camera, no matter how strange they may be, must be perceived as pure in order to maximise their strangeness. Yet the paradox of documentary practice is that documentary 'both proclaim[s itself] as factual – as true to reality – while also asserting the need to reveal (that is, narrate) a truth found not in the simple image of reality but in an understanding of it' (Cowie 2011, 49). Moreover, concerning the history of ethnographic cinema, anthropologists were initially wary of cinema as a discrete tool and, therefore, accompanying early ethnographic films was text, which the motion pictures relied on for meaning (Groo 2019, 162).

For this textual explanation, ethnographic films utilise perhaps the most (in)famous cinematic device: voice-of-God narration. This narration style is the classic device we think of when we are told to imagine voice-over, where presumably (given the ideological framework of ethnographic practice) a white man with a masculine voice makes sense of the sights and wonders before us. It is a well-known device, and its associations with systems of patriarchy and dominance abound (Bruzzi 2006, 49). Stella Bruzzi best summarises its practice when she writes that the 'purpose of the "voice of God" model is to absent personality and any notion of the internal monologue, to generalise, to offer an omniscient and detached judgement, to guide the spectator through events whilst remaining aloof from them' (Ibid., 63). Here, detachment stands as the key operating idea. Detachment lends the filmmakers power in their distance. As someone who is outside of the action and the culture, they are in a privileged position because they observe what happens before them clearly and objectively. Moreover, as an immaterial voice, a bodiless body, the narrator can witness all.[3] He exists on a different and higher plane from the people captured on screen. While the Other, in their corporeality, is dissected in the most microscopic of ways, the narrator, as a function of his whiteness, is allowed to be absent, to be 'without properties' and, thus, is not suited for study (Dyer 2017, 80).[4] With this ethnographic framework set, I turn to Campion's fictional ethnographic film, *Passionless Moments*.

In essence, *Passionless Moments* sets itself up as an ethnographic film that studies the everyday Australian suburb. It is structured around ten self-contained vignettes that run the gamut from two neighbours (Alan Brown and Jim Simpson) who cannot discern if the other is waving at them, to a young man (Yves Stenning) trying to keep two objects in focus. Guiding each moment is the ever-serious voice-of-God narration, and through the juxtaposition of the ethnographic tone and the visual content, *Passionless Moments* skews the ethnographic film's sobriety to produce absurdity, which exposes the discourses of power at work, not only in the filmmaking process but also in wider contemporary society. Here, I select two vignettes, 'No Woodpeckers in Australia' and 'Angela Eats Meat', for close analysis. These two encompass the politics that inform the whole series, where the former interrogates ways of knowing in ethnographic films, and the latter applies common ethnographic rhetoric to its suburban subjects. 'No Woodpeckers in Australia' deals with the verisimilitude of sound in ethnographic films, whereas other vignettes like 'Focal Lengths' question the ability to keep two objects in focus (that is, they question the objectivity of ethnographic film). Meanwhile, 'Angela Eats Meat' employs the common ethnographic trope of the animalistic Other. These problematic tropes also inform other vignettes such as 'Ibrahim Makes Sense of It All', where Campion explores the complicated sexualisation of the exotic Other. A focus on the white characters exposes the absurdity of the ethnographic discourse by using it on itself.

'No Woodpeckers in Australia' begins with Mrs Gilbert (Anne Berriman) kneeling on the hardwood floor of her home, inspecting and arranging her flowers in a vase. While this mundane action occurs, there is the ceaseless sound of something at once familiar and unfamiliar, and this question of the misplaced sound drives the ensuing narrative. The narrator begins: 'Mrs Gwen Gilbert, hearing this sound, at first thinks it's a Japanese woodblock being played in Mrs Vitachek's backyard next door. This seems very unlikely. It's probably just a woodpecker she tells herself.' As the narrator asserts this unlikely possibility, the camera changes abruptly from a medium shot to a tight close-up of Mrs Gilbert's face, illustrating a new level of proximity to the vignette's subject and, in fact, her subjectivity. The narrator does not simply observe her actions; he is omniscient, allowing us to hear her inner thoughts, suggesting that we can know everything about our object of study. As Mrs Gilbert turns her head towards the closest window to investigate the sound, we are confronted with a break of indexicality. Suddenly, a cartoon woodpecker appears. The drawing does not attempt to approximate realism and, as the animated bird pecks at the tree, its pecks are not synchronised to the still misplaced sound. From here, we find Mrs Gilbert in close-up again, this time with her face directly next to the window. We then cut to her point-of-view, which sees Mrs Vitachek hitting her clothesline with a stick. On seeing, and hearing, this image, it becomes clear that Mrs Vitachek is the source of the sound. However, as Kathleen McHugh points out, the sourced sound is noticeably different from the one heard before (2007, 35). It is a fact the narrator acknowledges as he concludes, 'Mrs Gilbert doesn't understand how Mrs Vitachek could be making that sound by beating a clothesline with a stick. She reminds herself that we don't have woodpeckers in

Australia', and we see one final flash of the cartoon woodpecker before moving onto the next vignette.

Here, 'No Woodpeckers in Australia' hinges on the premise of (non-)synchronised sound and the (mis)recognition of such. As a function of documentary, and ethnographic film, synchronised sound is a main strategy through which a work obtains verisimilitude. Trinh T. Minh-ha lists 'sync-sound' as a standard technique that reinforces the common conflation of realism with truth, a world without rupture (1991, 56). But 'No Woodpeckers in Australia' prioritises its ruptures and, therefore, the impossibility of realism. Sync-sound is heavily narrativised to ask the question of what sound tells us. This question arises from the moment the vignette begins. Before the narration begins, we see a black screen accompanied by the odd and unidentifiable sound, sparking our curiosity. At the end of the film, we are left wondering about the true source of the sound; as Hilary Neroni notes, the elusiveness of the sound creates 'a wrinkle within the objective fabric of the filmic narrative' (2012, 295). Whereas other ethnographic works produce worlds as knowable and their representations as scientific, ethnography in 'No Woodpeckers in Australia' fails us and we do not learn any more about the world, except the amusing reminder that woodpeckers do not, in fact, live in Australia.

The intrusion of the woodpecker pushes us to question what past ethnographic representations of the Other and the world have taught us and what we retain from them. Along with studying Indigenous peoples, ethnographic films examine the natural world, often tying both together (Rony 1996, 12). In this sense, the travelogue film, which showcases exotic views from across the world, can be seen as a relative of the ethnographic film, representing the idea of travel as 'penetration and discovery' (Ibid., 82). Metropoles sought to make the world a discrete and knowable world in all of its facets, whether that Other was another culture, landscape, or species, so they could 'control, contain, and master' that 'field of the Other' (Russell 1999, 120). Yet in 'No Woodpeckers in Australia', we arrive at a supposedly postcolonial world where everything should be known; however, the descendants of colonisers know nothing of the natural world. When we first see Mrs Gilbert, her lone connection to the outside is through the flowers that populate her domestic interior, and Australia in its grand natural splendour is nowhere to be seen in the suburb. In fact, out of the ten vignettes in *Passionless Moments*, only two of them transpire in the exterior and they occur in highly constructed spaces of the outside (front yards, back yards, roads). After taming the unruly, the only things allowed to invade the suburb are those that add controlled, innocuous beauty: bouquets of pretty, yet dead, flowers or yards of homogenous grass. They are referents to an outside without danger.

When Mrs Gilbert misplaces the geography of the woodpecker, the moment highlights how little the colonial project has amounted to knowledge transferred to the modern white world. Thus, the moment exposes how representations have influenced and distorted our understanding of the world. For example, the words that appear on screen with the woodpecker – the onomatopoeic 'peck' and 'peckitty' – marry the ideas of sound and false referents. 'Peck' and 'peckitty' are intended to describe what we hear, to capture the woodpecker striking the tree. Yet those words do not approach the reality of the sound we hear, and this misrecognition is embedded in our concept of the woodpecker, as the name for the animal centres around the onomatopoeia as knowledge production. To apply this to ethnography, the eternal problem of the ethnographic film is the slippage of trying to capture the thing in front of us, but never quite doing so. As Katherine Groo explains: 'One writes what one hears. One films what cannot be seen. One takes what one can get and puts it all on-screen' (2019, 207). The ethnographic object as it exists in the world is passed through layers of mediation to arrive as the image on the screen, and with each mediation something from reality is lost. For all its claims to verisimilitude and positioning as a (social) science, the ethnographic film falls short. Given the 'penetrative' ideology of the ethnographic project and its masculinist attempt to colonise the physical and psychical topography of the Other, it is difficult to avoid the conclusion that its failure in this vignette is also highly gendered. While Campion may disavow an explicitly feminist position in *Passionless Moments*, her representation of the intersections between patriarchy and colonialism are clear.

This gendered representation of ethnography also appears in the later vignette 'Angela Eats Meat', where Campion deploys another classic ethnographic trope: the relationship between the object studied and animality. It begins with a wide angle shot of a young woman named Angela (Sue Collie) kneeling on the floor, awaiting a call. By Western standards, Angela embodies the ideal of beauty. Her skin is white, her hair light and curled, and her frame slim yet full. Moreover, in the short's establishing shot, the high angle privileges the modest yet revealing cleavage of her little black dress, paired with fishnets. After her beauty is established, Angela lies down and grabs a slice of ham, and this is where the miniature narrative begins. The narrator explains:

> Seeing this cold slice of ham, which she's about to devour, Angela is suddenly reminded of her uncle's pet pig, Rufus, with whom she'd become acquainted at his farm many years earlier. It occurs to Angela that this is the kind of thinking that turns people vegetarian.

Matched with the narration is a cut from a close-up of Angela's face to a close-up of Rufus. This cut is alarming as it undermines the viewing pleasure maximised by the previous shot. Prior to the cut, Angela exudes an explicit sex appeal: she opens her mouth wide to prepare entry for a slice of ham, which slowly and sensually descends into frame and the 'o' formed by her lips echoes the act of fellatio (Figure 1.1). At the height of the sexualised fantasy, the film cuts, and we see a shot of a pig's head (Figure 1.2). The shot cuts

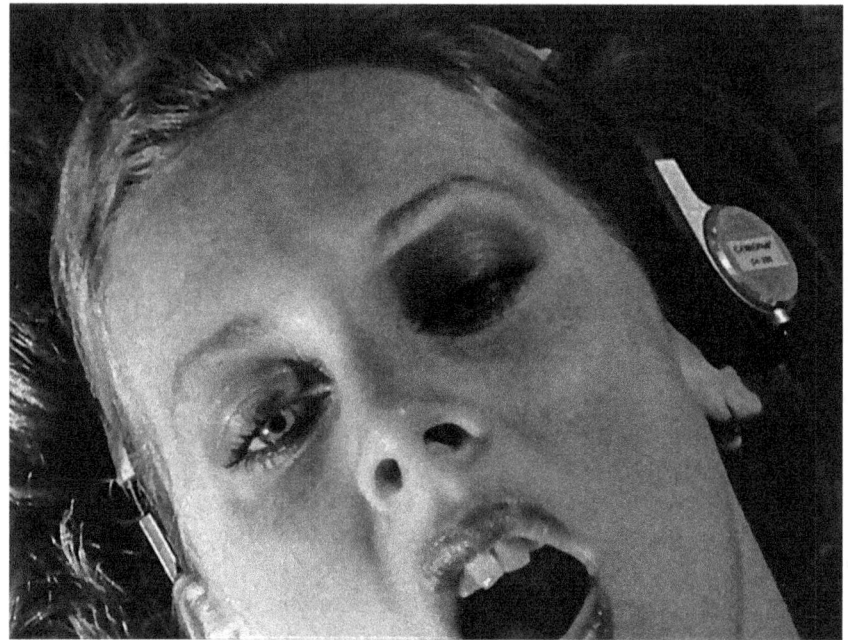

Figure 1.1 Angela, mouth wide open, in 'Angela Eats Meat', *Passionless Moments* (1983)

Figure 1.2 Rufus the pig in 'Angela Eats Meat', *Passionless Moments* (1983)

short whatever pleasure might have been, and while the edit is motivated by Angela's subjectivity (she thought of a pig, so we saw a pig), the cut establishes a connection between Angela and Rufus. This parallel is then solidified by another cut between Angela and a second pig. This time, Angela crawls on the floor to reach a phone, and the film cuts to a pig moving through a field and wearing a dress. The sequence becomes more complicated than the last, since Angela's subjectivity does not lead to the pig's manifestation on screen; instead, the film places the connection onto her.

This connection between objects of ethnographic study and animals dates back to the establishment of ethnographic film. In her analysis of *Nanook of the North* (Robert J. Flaherty 1922), a film that can be seen as a codification in style and rhetoric of prior ethnographic films and of those to come, Fatimah Tobing Rony notes the connection drawn between the Inuit people and the dogs that pull their sleds. Multiple crosscuts conflate Inuit children with puppies, and Inuit adults with dogs (1996, 111). The cuts stress both the supposed animality of the Inuit people and their culture and through the inclusion of babies, makes the connection an inevitability: the children will always grow to be animal-like. Therefore, when Angela becomes the product of the same rhetoric, similar questions arise. Traditional Western ethnographic discourse reserves the trope of animality for the Other. Therefore, Angela, as a white Western woman, cannot be associated with animality, represented here through her control and consumption of the pig. Yet, paradoxically, the film cut from Angela to the pig equates her with the animal, collapsing their distance and implicating her in the bestial discourse. Thus, the absurdity of the ethnographic rhetoric of animality is highlighted. The discomfort created by the application of this trope to a white woman is heightened by the comedy; the viewer is encouraged to laugh at Angela, a now explicit object of misogynistic ridicule. Following this line of thought, the real question of a project like *Passionless Moments*, which uses the rhetoric of past ethnographies, comes into view: by reversing the ethnographic framework onto the descendants of colonisers, and rendering them the Other, is the rhetoric of colonialism destroyed or reified?

For a work like *Passionless Moments*, which operates on a humorous level, there is something to be said about making light of colonial rhetoric. A subversion of the former ideology can come when that ideology is exposed for its absurdity by its own tools, but subversion does not equate to dismantling. When discussing the specifics of documentary, Elizabeth Cowie argues that the reuse of those tools reifies their power, writing, '[t]he fake or "mock" documentary, which puts forward fictional events or acted scenes as documentary, thereby confirms its rules in breaching them' (2011, 51). In *Passionless Moments*, when a moment like Angela being crosscut with a pig occurs, the mockery of that technique 'confirms' it. The moment does not move past the former rhetoric and its systems. Rather, that rhetoric is placed onto a different object, perpetuating a colonial, anthropocentric mindset, which sees the comparison of human to animal as a jest at best and a degradation at worst. In a similar fashion, Trinh T. Minh-ha elaborates on the dangers of using the same techniques to 'correct' the past:

> The question is also not that of merely 'correcting' the images whites have of non-whites, nor of reacting to the colonial territorial mind by simply reversing the situation and setting up an opposition that at best, will hold up a mirror to the Master's activities and preoccupations.
>
> (1991, 72)

The hypothetical situation described by Trinh is almost exactly the technique that Campion uses in *Passionless Moments*, in which colonisers are studied. The difference is that it is not the Other who anthropologises the white Australian colonial in *Passionless Moments*; it is the colonisers examining themselves. This becomes apparent when in 'No Woodpeckers in Australia', the narrator says, 'We don't have woodpeckers in Australia.' The 'we' is fundamental, as the film seeks a transcendence past dichotomies. It is not us studying them; instead, it is us studying ourselves. In this sense, *Passionless Moments* can be seen as a work in line with Richard Dyer's (2017) study of whiteness, in which he asserts that a lack of critical focus on whiteness as a racial category has led to its functioning as the norm against which all other categories are examined.

Therefore, the structure of *Passionless Moments* in repurposing colonial tools is useful in that it does examine naturalised systems and renders them 'strange' (Ibid., 4). However, I do not wish to overstate *Passionless Moments* as a pure work of decolonial cinema. Instead, I contend that the film is, to borrow a phrase from Erika Balsom, 'ideologically inconsistent'; though inconsistency does not preclude use, as Balsom explains: 'Films are often ideologically inconsistent, sometimes in progressive and productive ways' (2020, n.p.). Put in the context of *Passionless Moments*, the slippages produced by its ethnographic framework fall into the traps of colonial objectification. Those slippages are productive for us to understand rhetoric that may not otherwise be dissected and to acknowledge that producing a work of decolonial cinema is an impossibility (no matter how critical it is) when working within a colonial system and rhetoric. Therefore, the politics of *Passionless Moments* ultimately exist in this bind of colonial-decolonial that cannot be reconciled.

A GIRL'S OWN STORY

Whereas *Passionless Moments* sees a complicated investigation into pre-existing representations, Campion's final student film *A Girl's Own Story* feels like an experiment that fulfils the desire for a unique voice. As such, in the Campion canon, *A Girl's Own Story*, unlike *Passionless Moments*, has never been seen as anything but crucial in the formation of her artistry. In particular, as Dana Polan notes, the film received a positive reception from feminists (2001, 71). Often billed as a coming-of-age film, *A Girl's Own Story* follows three adolescent girls who cross the bridge from innocence into adulthood as they interact with the world around them in the 1960s (Senn 2017, n.p.). Through interacting with formal histories and personal memories of the 1960s, Campion accomplishes what critic and poet Adrienne Rich describes as 're-vision', a political move that centres on 'the act of looking back, of seeing with fresh eyes, of entering an old text from a new critical direction' (1979, 35). Put otherwise, Campion shifts focus from the formal, tried-and-true histories of the decade, in which we fixate on decision-makers (that is, the men of the time from politicians to musical stars) to the neglected social actors – in this case, three adolescent girls. Drawing from Rich and the tradition of 're-vision', Stella Bruzzi coins another useful concept in 'approximation', which is an 'area of representation that both transcribes information and factual events and transgresses the frequently crudely delineated boundaries between "fact" and "fiction"' (2020, 9). The key characteristic of 'approximation' is its fluidity in relation to typically hierarchical delineations between fact and fiction. For *A Girl's Own Story*, its 'approximation' of history makes the past 'material, tangible, and *lived*' through the experiences of its women (Ibid., 85, emphasis in original). This project, then, draws parallels to *Bright Star* (2009), in which Campion 'unsettle[s] the canon' of John Keats (White 2015, 36). However, Campion's 're-visions' are not simply about 'a chapter in cultural history', rectifying a flawed account; rather, they are an 'act of survival' that refuses 'the self-destructiveness of male-dominated society' (Rich 1979, 35). Here, Campion interrogates the act of historiography itself and the destruction of its subjects in order to create something all her own.

For a short film that is historically minded, *A Girl's Own Story*, strangely, begins in a void. In a prelude to the narrative, the opening shows three girls in close-up: Stella (Geraldine Haywood), Gloria (Marina Knight) and Pam (Gabrielle Shornegg), whom we will track throughout the film. They sit in pure blackness and hold pointed yet blank stares. In what will become typical Campion fashion, the sequence performs, as Hilary Radner describes, a 'rupture' – that before narrative action, the film draws attention to its own 'createdness' (2009, 7). With the reflexive turn, the girls' action (that is, looking) holds its own power. The second girl, Gloria, gazes directly at the camera, creating an interocular moment between the camera and her, between us and her. Her eyes confront ours through the camera, and, thus, she confronts the apparatus of cinema in its objectification, denying an unchecked scopophilia that is also present in *Passionless Moments*. Despite not looking at the camera, the last girl, Pam, also suggests her own potentiality for confrontation, as she wears glasses. Feminist critic Mary Ann Doane explains:

> Glasses worn by a woman in the cinema do not generally signify a deficiency in seeing but an active looking, or even simply the fact of seeing as opposed to being seen. The intellectual woman looks and analyzes, and in usurping the gaze she poses a threat to an entire system of representation.
>
> (1999, 140)

And a threat she certainly becomes, as the film cuts to a book, which includes a drawing of a fragmented nude with an erect penis, captioned by the sentence: 'This sight might shock young girls.' As Kathleen McHugh details, this sequence with the depicted phallus demonstrates the 'mixed messages' girls faced in the 1960s, concerning sexuality – that they were inundated with 'sentimental tales' but restricted from any sexual information; they are not supposed to look at the image, yet the caption invites their gaze (2007, 41).

To trace the contours of 're-vision' in action, the concept of the ocular in the opening sequence is key. At first, we are lulled into a false sense of security. We start with looking at Stella, who gazes elsewhere, allowing us a brief moment of unchecked visual power. In a similar fashion to *Passionless Moments*, we are privileged with proximity to the protagonist via a close-up, and while we wonder about her subjectivity – what she looks at and what she thinks of – our speculations transform her into an object in our minds. But what Laura Mulvey calls the passive 'to-be-looked-at-ness' of female objects in masculinist cinema is quickly denied by Gloria and Pam, through their own ways of looking at us and the world (1999a, 63). By prioritising their own actions of looking and limiting their being-looked-at in the prelude, Campion reimagines the girls as subjects instead of objects from a certain historical period to be studied and known. Furthermore, the act of gazing upon the phallus could be read as a naïve reversal of the male gaze, where women objectify and fragment their counterparts, enjoying their own share of scopophilia. However, in the prelude's vacuum, we are made aware of the device of looking through the prior interocular gaze and the now-present and uncomfortable sonic counterpoint of an infantile music box score. If there is pleasure to be had in the blunt image before us, it is meant to be minimised or, at least, criticised. Through this interrogation of the cinematic apparatus, Campion's 're-vision' comes into view, where it not only emphasises the subjectivities of the girls but also deconstructs their interactions with the world and, indeed, the camera.

As the film transitions out of the opening rupture, it enters the historical world of 1960s Antipodean life. We see cultural touchpoints that ground us in the temporal milieu: schoolgirls in period-specific uniform and, perhaps most famously, The Beatles, whose images and songs populate the short. In the discernibility of the setting, Campion describes the short as a 'homage' to that time in her life:

> I wanted to talk about the Beatles whose music touched my generation since I was born in 1954. The episode of incest wasn't a personal experience but I remember a very young neighbor who got pregnant by a classmate and the scandal it created.
>
> (Ciment 1999a, 34)

In her description of the short, Campion offers a summary of Bruzzi's 'approximation', in that she follows the well-known cultural marker of The Beatles with an intensely personal and non-formally documented memory of the pregnancy scandal. There is an equivalence of importance from the global to the personal, and given the film's structure, Campion for the most part focuses on the individual – how the three girls interact and move through space and time. However, in the workings of Campion's 're-vision'-come-'approximation', these personal moments are not made to be clear-cut in order to compete with official historical narratives that centre on knowability; rather, the 'loosely' connected 'set pieces' emphasise moments that cannot be fully captured (McHugh 2007, 40). I now turn to the episode of incest to explicate how Campion imagines the lives of these girls.

Despite being one of the central scenes in *A Girl's Own Story*, and one of the central focuses for Campion, the incest plotline is often briefly remarked upon, but is rarely analysed. For a film that is filled with young female sexual energy, from the opening image of the phallus to the girls kissing each other through masks of The Beatles, it is the only scene where one of the girls has sex. But in Campion's re-vised coming-of-age, the well-worn stereotype of losing's one virginity in its associations of love and romance is perverted through incest. The scene begins innocently enough, as Gloria and her brother vacillate in a back-and-forth of whether to play a childlike game of cats. But even from the sequence's beginning, something feels off when, in an early shot, Gloria walks into the room and the camera is at a slanted angle, resulting in Gloria becoming a horizontal line. Maintaining the shot, the camera rotates as it tracks Gloria, ending with her being the 'right' side up. The movement skews the idea of the invisible long-durational shot, as we are made aware of the camera and what we see. In the growing unease produced by the cinematography, the game takes a similarly unexpected turn when Gloria's brother Graeme (John Godden) says that in order to play cats 'properly' they must take off their clothes, a suggestion that Gloria initially rejects. This is the starting proposition that leads into the moment of incest, and since it is not Gloria's idea, the question arises: 'Whose sexuality is it, exactly?' (Mayer 2016, 147).

So far, the easy answer would be not Gloria's, especially as the final proposition to have sex is again from Graeme. But this time, instead of soundly rejecting the request, Gloria enquires about her role, asking 'What do I do?'. 'Just lie there, I suppose', Graeme answers. This response is not untypical in dominant culture's understanding of women's sexual roles, as Laura Mulvey explains: 'All too often, the erotic function of the woman is represented by the passive' (1999b, 125). In Campion's challenge to the passivity of the representation of female sexuality and Mulvey's observation of 'to-be-looked-at-ness', Campion's female protagonist, Gloria, is not wholly passive. Rather, in a thematic echo of *In the Cut* (2003), woman's passivity is traded in for 'transgressive desires [that] exist in painful tension with their social and physical vulnerability' (Park and Dietrich 2005, 39). In response to Graeme's expectation for her to be his passive object, Gloria says, 'Mom and dad will be home soon', followed by, 'Come on'. She then lies down on the floor and places her hands behind her head, becoming stiff, and through this act, she initiates, or at least allows the act to come to fruition. Her actively passive initiation renders judgement of her and the moment difficult. The question of 'whose sexuality is it' becomes ever more complicated when later at the home for pregnant teenagers, Gloria, not Graeme, demands a kiss from her sibling. While the moment may function as a trauma response to soothe over what happened, or act as a way to experience some of the romance she is promised by cultural norms, it does not make the moment, or the entire plotline, any more palatable or readable. Through the discomfort, it is clear that Campion pushes against patriarchal notions of women as passive playthings, while simultaneously not making them overly active or aggressive. Instead, existing in the in-between, Gloria holds a potential agency in her submissiveness and, therefore, Campion does not adhere to the view of women and their sexual expression, which assumes 'that if female sexuality were ever to get free of its patriarchal contaminations it would express no violence, would have no relations of power, and would produce no transgressive sexual fantasies' (Williams 1999, 20). In the end, it becomes hard to delineate where Gloria's subjection ends and where her agency begins. Both co-exist, as women's lives, including their sexual subjectivities, are fragmented. Therefore, in Campion's 're-vision' of female lives, nice, neat narratives with clarity do not exist. For what could be a simple plot point – that Gloria and Graeme engage in incest – Campion, rather, explores the murky underwaters and ambivalences behind the act.

This ambiguity is consolidated by the inclusion of a musical segment in which the three girls, as if in a music video, sit separately in front of heaters as the song 'I Feel the Cold' begins. The song, written by Campion, opens the door to the inner musings of her female characters and the 'film within a film' takes on a highly abstract feel in which all sense of narrative is abandoned, as the music video takes hold and the ending of the short denies any classical resolution; rather, much like the beginning of the film, it becomes another 'rupture'. 'I Feel the Cold' sees the girls back in the black void, sometimes singing alone, sometimes together. At other moments, videos of bodies ice skating are superimposed onto them. We see a pair of hands slowly wave back and forth as if they are swaying to a concert. Edited like a music video montage, this section of the film is substantial in its fragmentation and elusive in its meaning. This strange segment mirrors and reinforces the ways in which the world encloses all girls, so 'I Feel the Cold' seemingly recoups its three leads by bringing them out of the diegetic world that oppressed them into a liminal, undefinable void. Thus, the space created by 'I Feel the Cold' could arguably be characterised by So Mayer's concept of 'girl 'hood', a place in which girls come 'together' to 'inhabit' themselves (2016, 151). However, this 'inhabiting', particularly with regards to female collectivity, is not, in Campion's vision, as clear-cut or as distinctly empowering as Mayer's own formulation. Whereas Mayer suggests 'girl 'hood' as a space to reconceive trauma through 'collaboration', lending agency to disempowered girls, the space of 'I Feel the Cold' does not feel solely like a reclamation of agency or power (Ibid., 137). Instead, the space is sombre. The girls coexist in the void, but they do not interact, let alone commune or collaborate with each other. The film's final shot leaves Pam by herself with a single heater, still feeling the 'cold' of the world and perhaps this space.[5] Moreover, some of the images and experiences to which they were subjected in the diegetic world, such as an older man's hands grazing their skin, resurface, recalling their trauma. However, these images are more fragmented and disjointed than ever, and this is the 'inhabiting' power in 'I Feel the Cold'. If there is any recouperation from trauma in 'I Feel the Cold', it is not through an agency that eliminates or redefines the ways in which the girls experienced the world. Rather, the film stays attuned to those realities and, in the words of Ara Osterweil who critiques Mayer, it then 'render[s]' their experiences as 'queerly and incomprehensibly' as possible (2016, n.p.). It is ambiguity and incomprehensibility in 'I Feel the Cold' that lend the girls the agency to 'inhabit' themselves, being and feeling without dissection from the world or from us.

In this sense, because *A Girl's Own Story* trades coherence for subjective, subconscious exploration, the film becomes emblematic of an early women's cinema ideal. In her famed essay 'Women's Cinema as Counter-Cinema', Claire Johnston writes, 'Any revolutionary strategy must challenge the depiction of reality; it is not enough to discuss the oppression of women within the text of the film; the language of the cinema/the depiction of reality must also be interrogated' (1999, 37). This is what *A Girl's Own Story* accomplishes. It both challenges popular narratives of women within society and, in the end, the very concept of narrative itself, by finding a different language in the spectacle of 'I Feel the Cold', where the film wears its emotions on its sleeve yet makes them unknowable. In its fragmentation, we have limited access to the girls' interiorities, but as Kara Keeling writes, because the emotions are something that 'escape [ ] recognition', or 'meaning and valuation', they are something that cannot be broken down and used by hegemonic culture (2019, 83). Here, Campion's restrictions produce ambiguity, and by rejecting a clear historical account, Campion's 're-vision' allows the girls' subjectivities to stay their own.

A CODA FOR CONTRADICTION

In 2021, the twenty-eight-year-long drought of a female Palme d'Or winner ended. However, this statement would probably make both women who won the award wince. In a strikingly similar fashion to Campion, Julia Ducournau, the director of *Titane* (2021), divulged in one of her first interviews after her win that she did not wish to be defined by her gender:

> For me, as a woman, I don't want my gender to define me at all. When people say I'm a woman director — I mean, that's always a bit annoying, because I'm a person. I'm a director. I make movies because I'm me, not because I'm a woman. I'm me.
>
> (Kohn 2021, n.p.)

The idea of not liking the title of 'woman director' is nothing new. Often the term comes with a perception of ghettoisation, in which the person's work must be prefaced by gender in order to matter. However, Ducournau's insistence on 'I'm me' does not fit the ghettoisation rhetoric; rather, it points to the fact that she does not wish to be defined. The only acceptable definition is a non-definition, an amorphous 'me'. In this sense, definition as limitation is reminiscent of Campion, who finds the application of feminism limiting; unlike Campion, though, Ducournau describes herself as a feminist (Clare 2017, n.p.). Therefore, Ducournau's statements on gender definition are not antithetical to feminist discourse, especially considering the influence of queer theory. Yet this definition-limitation equivalence interests me when thinking about what lies in the title of 'woman director' or 'feminist' that leads to Ducornau's and Campion's rejections.

The idea that woman directors do not feel seen is not necessarily new. As Jane Gaines argues, feminist film theory has long ignored these women in order to retain some of its critical concepts. Writers of the 1970s in their theories of 'no women in the industry' neglected the women who proliferated in the early industry, and despite the now uncovered empirical history, the theoretical principles of absence have remained (Gaines 2016, 12). Genevieve Yue also takes up this issue of privileging immaterial principles over real, physical women through the narrative of Gravida and Zoë, who first appear in Wilhelm Jensen's *Gravida* (1903) and later inspire critical interventions by Freud and Derrida. The story goes that 'a young man is obsessed with a woman [Gravida] he sees in an ancient marble relief, and later as an apparition in his dreams and waking life', only to find out what he sees as Gravida is an actual woman named Zoë, a childhood friend (Yue 2021, 103). Despite the material woman before him, the image of Gravida still looms. By using this story, Yue explicates the 'concealment of the woman's body' in the film archive in order to privilege the 'dematerialized' image (Ibid., 112). To return to the case of Campion (and Ducournau), I argue that scholars have been similarly obsessed with the idea of Campion, the woman director who claims herself to be a feminist rather than the material Campion, who denies such a fixation. In this sense, scholars craft their own Gravidas, ignoring and obscuring parts of the material that do not fit their argument or projection. Of course, accounting for the full existence of an object, whether that is a person or a film, is impossible, similar to the problem of ethnography trying to capture what is before it. However, in my analysis, I have accentuated the unseemly or contradictory that perhaps has been passed over for the more straightforward: the political slippages in *Passionless Moments*; the ambivalences in the episode of incest, the elusive nature of 'I Feel the Cold'. In this way, to allow for the fullness of the 'I'm me' – for Campion as Zoë or, rather, Campion as Campion – to exist, I argue for centring contradiction as the defining principle. Through contradiction, we recognise not only that politics and objects will always exist beyond a simple title, but also that there will always exist that which cannot be quite pinned down or explained.

I end this chapter with one last refutation that is often employed to dismiss contradictions and imperfect politics – the idea of 'another time'. In their introduction to *Doing Women's Film History*, Christine Gledhill and Julia Knight provide the most nuanced account of this commonplace rhetoric: 'Like ourselves, the women we research are formed by their times – while they may push against the grain, they are nevertheless caught within what their times allow to their imaginations and roles' (2015, 5). This rhetoric of another time operates in half admission. It recognises the unseemly parts of the woman studied, but through recognition coupled with the guise of context, the contradiction is explained away. Tinged with grief for the what-could-have-been in the narrative of social progress, the woman examined simply did not know what we know now (about her time). However, Jane Campion is not from 'another time' – she lives in our present. Her statements, which evade feminism (she opts for her own terms like 'ovarian', or others that recognise the significance of #MeToo and #TimesUp but compares them to the end of apartheid), happen in the here and now.[6] Therefore, to suggest Campion is the product of her time is to disregard that her time is ours, and thus, she is even more 'like' us in that her contradictions are our contradictions. Here, I am not suggesting that her specific hang-ups with feminism and politics are our personal ones, but rather, that her ambivalences demonstrate the entanglements of contemporary politics, that contradictions are part of the game, so to speak. Only through investigating and reckoning with the entanglements, slippages, and contradictions of our politics and political movements can we attend to the world.

NOTES

1. This interview with Michel Ciment is used throughout this collection, reinforcing the interest generated by Campion's explicit ambiguity towards political feminism.
2. With regard to the periodicity of feminism, I do not buy into the strict formulations of the waves because they often obscure the intersections and, furthermore, perpetuate an idea of progress with waves. Progress, as a concept and reality, is much more complex than that. For interventions that look to the 'second wave', see: Fraser (2013); Hesford (2013) Fabian (2018); Warren (2019), among many others.
3. For more discussion of the relationship between sound and body, and the possibilities and powers between them, see Michel Chion's 'acousmêtre' (1999).
4. Here, I am using Dyer's idea of whiteness as absence, a result that comes about from defining whiteness solely by negation.
5. There have been several analyses which compare the cold in the song's lyrics to the frigidity of the patriarchal world; see Fox (2011, 59) and McHugh (2015, 45–7).
6. See, for example, Jennifer Vineyard (2017) and Kate Muir (2018).

CHAPTER 2

Two Friends: Circumstances of a Historic Feminist Collaboration

Zachary Zahos

An academic volume on Jane Campion presents the opportunity to reconcile two prevailing, competing approaches in authorship studies and film historiography, both of which revolve around 'the auteur'. On the one hand, some feminist film scholars, beyond simply critiquing the male-dominated canon and its norms of representation, have long appropriated the framework of auteurism to advocate for female directors and to argue for their inclusion within the highest echelons of film art. In the late 1980s, after philosophical broadsides from Roland Barthes (2005) and Michel Foucault (1992), literary theorist Nancy K. Miller defended the 'political potential' of female authorship when she wrote the following:

> The postmodernist decision that the Author is Dead and the subject along with him does not, I will argue, necessarily hold for women, and prematurely forecloses the question of agency for them. Because women have not had the same historical relation of identity to origin, institution, production that men have had.
>
> (1988, 104)

One of the most honoured women in film history, Jane Campion has, as much as anyone, seized this 'question of agency' for female filmmakers, earning the esteem of even the most orthodox auteurist institutions.¹

On the other hand, Campion's vaunted, now-canonical status presents certain perils for the film historian tracking the collaborative and institutional realities of feature film production. While auteurist criticism excels at identifying the formal and ideational qualities of a filmmaker's work, an auteur-centred analysis tends to simplify the context of creation and circulation that ultimately impacts the meanings ascribed to a given work. In other words, one can both argue that Campion has an integral oeuvre, united by idiosyncratic formal strategies and themes of womanhood and transgression, and also challenge the assumption that Campion is the sole or primary creative agent behind all of 'her' films. To zoom out to a wider production context does not obscure the feminist project that is inextricable from Campion's auteurism, but rather sharpens it. Campion's overlooked first feature film *Two Friends* (1986) offers an ideal case study for an expanded, contextual analysis of her films, as the conditions of its production and distribution were directly shaped by feminist political action and female creative talent.

Two Friends occupies a marginalised place in Campion studies only in part due to its ambiguous authorship. In Campion's filmography, *Two Friends* is one of three features without a Campion screenwriting credit. At producer Jan Chapman's request, Australian writer and novelist Helen Garner wrote the script with an innovative reverse chronological structure (Garner 2016, 3–4). This partly explains why, out of all of Campion's features, *Two Friends* has arguably received the least attention from scholars. Three recent books on Campion hardly mention the film, while those that do tend to recuperate it as a prototypical Campion project.[2] Alistair Fox devotes ample attention to Garner's contribution, insofar as it provides thematic and symbolic material akin to Campion's other films and thus can be incorporated into her oeuvre via Campion's personal 'authoring strategy' (Fox 2011, 67). Such an interpretation teases out the film's engaging textual qualities, but it does not depict, in full, the production context behind *Two Friends*, which involved Campion, Garner, Chapman, costume/production designer Janet Patterson, and several Australian feminist initiatives and film institutions.

Other factors, chief among them distribution, could also explain why scholars have overlooked *Two Friends*. After all, the two other films not written by Campion – *An Angel at My Table* (1990) and *The Portrait of a Lady* (1996), both scripted by Laura Jones – do not suffer similar neglect. For one, they both share, more so than *Two Friends*, a proximity to celebrity. In the case of *An Angel at My Table*, the famous life of its subject, Janet Frame, endeared the television production to Australian and New Zealand audiences and popularised Frame abroad (Thompson and Bordwell 2003, 666). In considering *The Portrait of a Lady*, the star status of Nicole Kidman, who starred in *Batman Forever* (Joel Schumacher 1995) the previous year, as well as the canonical reputation of Henry James's source material, further distinguish it from the non-professional leads and original premise of *Two Friends*. *The Portrait of a Lady* furthermore followed the international success of *The Piano* (1993), which elevated Campion to genuine celebrity status. Most importantly, Campion's name recognition, from *Sweetie* (1989) onward, spurred North American and European theatrical distribution for *An Angel at My Table* and *The Portrait of a Lady* within months of their respective premieres at the Sydney Film Festival and Venice Film Festival.[3] While *Two Friends* boasted a respected literary figure as screenwriter, it did not follow its 1986 Cannes Film Festival premiere with prompt international theatrical distribution.[4]

Instead, *Two Friends* premiered on Australasian television via the Australian Broadcasting Corporation (ABC) in 1986 and played eighteen film festivals, from the Cork International Film Festival to the Hawaii International Film Festival, between 1986 and 1987. The theatrical distribution of *Two Friends* arrived ten years later, after US arthouse distributor Milestone Films acquired the film in September 1995 and premiered it at New York's Film Forum on 24 April 1996, where it received positive reviews from American critics (Heller and Doros 1995). Since then, though, *Two Friends* has still reached only a limited audience. Rather than consigning the film to a footnote in Campion's career, however, the impure authorship, televisual mode of production, and belated theatrical distribution of *Two Friends* mark it as an especially pivotal, unheralded turning point for women in Antipodean cinema. More than has been credited, *Two Friends* intervenes in the history of Antipodean feminist cinema and global art cinema narration, and it serves as a telling example of how the vagaries of international film distribution shape critical reputation.

In the context of women-produced Antipodean cinema, *Two Friends* united for the first time four of the most prominent women in the country's industry: director Jane Campion, producer Jan Chapman, writer Helen Garner, and costume/production designer Janet Patterson. The latter three women would again work together on *The Last Days of Chez Nous* (1992), directed by Gillian Armstrong, while Campion, Chapman and Patterson later collaborated on multiple acclaimed productions, including *The Piano* (1993). As an historical object alone, *Two Friends* deserves a place in history for bringing together some of Australia's most influential female filmmakers and shaping their subsequent careers. As a formal object, *Two Friends* innovated both within and beyond the context of Campion's style through its collaborative production. Garner's script employs reverse chronology years before the device re-emerged in Hollywood, while Campion and Patterson developed a distinct approach to *mise-en-scène*, described by Garner as 'oblique and subtle' (Milestone Films 1995, 10). Critics praised these qualities and more upon the 1996 theatrical release of *Two Friends*, though the film's distribution history ultimately offers an object lesson on the challenges of reviving early work from directors who find success years later.

This chapter advances the historical and artistic significance of *Two Friends* across three sections, each with a different methodology. The first section reviews the film institutions and feminist reforms that uniquely enabled the production of a dramatic television film like *Two Friends* and the feminist collaboration between Campion, Chapman, Garner, and Patterson. Adopting more of a bird's eye view than the rest of the chapter, this section synthesises secondary literature, including a 2002 speech by Chapman, to offer a fresh understanding of how *Two Friends*, and Campion's subsequent career, came into being at the right time and place. The second section compares the film's striking narrative structure and visual style against contemporaneous trends in Hollywood and global art cinema and later developments within these filmmakers' careers. Rather than regard its structure as a gimmick as many critics do, this chapter reframes the film's reverse chronological structure as a restrained and humanistic iteration compared to subsequent nonlinear narratives. This section incorporates interviews with the filmmakers, including an original interview with Helen Garner conducted in August 2020. The third section documents the film's staggered distribution history and qualifies its subsequent reputation as a 'minor' or 'early' film in Campion's oeuvre. This section draws evidence from trade press, correspondence and financial documents provided by Milestone Films. Overall, this chapter argues that *Two Friends* should be regarded as a breakthrough film in Antipodean feminist cinema and nonlinear film narration. Because these innovations do not register within a strictly auteurist framework, this contextual analysis of *Two Friends* makes a larger case for the collaborative and institutional forces that determined Campion's career and in turn opened doors for later Antipodean female filmmakers.

INSTITUTIONAL CONTEXT FOR A FEMINIST PRODUCTION

Appreciating the institutional history of feminist organisations and initiatives within Antipodean cinema affords a refreshing angle on Campion's reputation as a feminist auteur. In interviews across her career, Campion herself has been reluctant to identify, first and foremost, as a feminist filmmaker. This particular artistic sensibility has been highlighted by critics and scholars in Campion's dismissal of *After Hours* (1984), a half-hour short film she directed via the Women's Film Unit. The film's story revolves around a young woman harassed and assaulted by her boss. In 1986, Campion assessed the film as follows:

> I don't like *After Hours* a lot because I feel like the reasons for making it were impure. I felt a conflict between the project and my artistic conscience. The film . . . had to be openly feminist since it spoke about the sexual abuse of women at work. I wasn't comfortable because I don't like films that say how one should or shouldn't behave.
>
> (Ciment 1999a, 35)

Whether her assessment is fair or not, the discourse around Campion's feminism tends to focus on the modes of representation and textual meanings of her films. Even within an 'institutional' context, Campion still tends to characterise herself or be characterised as a solitary trailblazer. Yet *Two Friends*, along with *After Hours* and Campion's broader career, exists within a longer history of feminist politics in and around the Australian and New Zealand film industries. Regardless of Campion's own views, the material conditions for the production of *Two Friends* resulted from explicitly feminist political action that reshaped major institutions within the Antipodean film sector in the prior decades.

Beyond an auteurist framework, one should consider *Two Friends* a significant nexus in the longer history of Antipodean feminist cinema. *Two Friends* occasioned the coming together of four women early in their careers before most of them had received wider recognition. The film's domestic success, including its win for Best Telefeature at the 1987 Australian Film Institute Awards, inspired further collaboration between these four artists (Ibid.). In particular, Campion, Chapman, and Patterson formed an enduring partnership across several acclaimed films: *The Piano*, *Holy Smoke* (1999), and *Bright Star* (2009). In addition, Campion and Patterson collaborated on *The Portrait of a Lady*. These subsequent films, and indeed the direction of these women's careers, can be traced back to *Two Friends*.

Naturally, the feminist qualities of *Two Friends*, as a female-led production and female-centred story, did not materialise in a vacuum. Rather, a history of filmmaker cooperatives, government funding, and opportunities in the Australian creative industries set the stage, directly and indirectly, for these female filmmakers to first meet and for their collaboration to materialise. Jan Chapman has testified to these factors, which enabled her career and spurred a sea change of greater female agency in the country's film industry (Chapman 2002). In her 2002 Longford Lyell Lecture, delivered before the Australian Academy of Cinema and Television Arts (AACTA), Chapman cited a number of institutions crucial to the empowerment of female talent: the Sydney Filmmakers Co-operative, the Sydney Women's Film Group (SWFG), the Women's Unit within the ABC, and the Australian Film Commission (AFC).[5] The women-led creation of *Two Friends* only followed collective action by feminist activists and filmmakers who in the years prior had made inroads into the Australian and New Zealand film industries. One should first understand the histories of these organisations to appreciate how *Two Friends* came to be.

Through its connections to funding bodies and cultural gatekeepers, the AFC performed an invaluable service for both *Two Friends* and Campion's career. As an agency of the state, the AFC succeeded the Australian Film Development Corporation in 1975 and performed a similar function as its predecessor, by commissioning production for a wide swathe of Australian films. Eventually, the AFC worked in tandem with the Australian Film Finance Corporation (FFC), a government financing body established in 1988, two years after the premiere of *Two Friends*.[6] As Lisa French has argued, since the 1980s Australia's film industry has exported an unusually large share of female auteurs compared to other comparably-sized national cinemas, credited in part to state production and funding bodies like the AFC and FFC (2014, 655). Even more specific to the case of *Two Friends*, the AFC sponsored the 1986 visit by Cannes Film Festival scout Pierre Rissient (Chapman 2002). This trip proved fortuitous, for Rissient encouraged the selection of *Two Friends* that year along with three early Campion shorts, of which *Peel* (1982) won the Short Film Palme d'Or. Rissient famously championed Campion's work from that point onward and has been credited for lobbying for *The Piano*'s 1993 Palme d'Or win (Goodfellow 2018). Even if exemplary talent like Campion's would inevitably find wide recognition, an agency like the AFC benefitted Campion generally, by virtue of its connection to international film networks, and specifically, by helping establish contact between Campion and one of her most unwavering advocates. The remaining film institutions identified by Chapman practiced a more perspicuous form of feminist politics, which influenced the filmmakers behind *Two Friends* and enabled the conditions for its production. In the case of the SWFG and the Sydney Filmmakers Co-operative, these two must be understood as a special interest group functioning within a larger independent collective. The Sydney Filmmakers Co-operative formed in 1969 upon the merging of Melbourne's Carlton Cinema Group and Sydney's Ubu Films, both of which boasted largely male membership at the time. The Co-Op assembled independent filmmakers to screen each other's work, foster collaboration for future production, and publicise larger concerns (Hughes 2015). The SWFG formed within the cooperative in 1971, and Chapman took part in both SWFG and cooperative activity at this time. In Chapman's words, the SWFG consisted of 'some strongly politically motivated women' with 'the initial emphasis [. . .] on instructing women in production skills' (Chapman 2002, n.p.). SWFG produced original films, including the 24-minute avant-garde feminist work *A Film for Discussion* (1973), and distributed others, such as Jackie McKimmie's debut short *Stations* (1983) and Campion's early short films (Stott 1987, 122).[7] Established during the peak years of Women's Liberation in Australia and New Zealand, the SWFG organised a creative, intellectual space that shaped the early careers of Campion and Chapman.

This feminist political organising also impacted the country's television industry and preeminent film school. At the Australian Broadcasting Commission (retitled the Australian Broadcasting Corporation in 1983), the Women's Unit sought to 'gain access as producers and directors in drama and documentary from the more traditional education and children's departments' (Chapman 2002, n.p.). Chapman would eventually produce for the ABC drama department such projects as *Two Friends* thanks to this initiative. In tandem with the SWFG, the Women's Unit also successfully lobbied the Australian Film and

Television School, or AFTS (renamed the Australian Film Television and Radio School, or AFTRS, in 1986), to implement women's training programmes. The school started admitting women in 1976 (Ibid.).[8] For perspective, Campion joined the programme in 1981. Similarly to the ABC's moves toward gender parity, the AFTS's 1976 affirmative action policy initiated a diversification effort that reshaped the country's film industry downstream, benefitting Campion directly.[9] Following *After Hours*, her first project post-AFTS, Campion directed an episode of the ABC miniseries *Dancing Daze* (1986), which was produced by Jan Chapman, designed by Janet Patterson, and featured a songwriting credit by Helen Garner, preceding their work on *Two Friends* (Ciment 1999a).[10] Before the film's production, Garner recalls meeting Campion at Chapman's house, where they watched some of Campion's student short films.[11] Around this time, the SWFG screened these short films, generating word-of-mouth for Campion's talent before Cannes took notice.

All these feminist organisations and progressive reforms laid the groundwork for *Two Friends*, Campion's career, and an expanded field of women-run Antipodean film production. *Two Friends* materialised at a fortuitous time to benefit from these reforms and anticipate a wave of feminist film production that reached the mainstream in Australia and beyond. Institutions like the AFC, the AFTS, the SWFG, and the ABC Women's Unit all played a role in realising *Two Friends*, and other institutions would soon form to further support a similar kind of female-driven production often deemed risky. According to Chapman (2002), the FFC (founded in 1988) covered the entire budget of *The Last Days of Chez Nous* through a new fund that financed promising projects in exchange for lower box office returns for the filmmakers. Garner's script for *The Last Days of Chez Nous* tells the story of two sisters, Beth (Lisa Harrow) and Vicki (Kerry Fox, star of *An Angel at My Table*), and their complicated, competing affections for a chauvinistic French intellectual played by Bruno Ganz. Similar subject matter, focused on women in original dramatic situations, flourished in Antipodean cinema beginning in the mid-to-late 1980s, as women like Jane Campion, Gillian Armstrong, Jackie McKimmie, Margot Nash, Samantha Lang, and Rachel Perkins directed multiple films. Many other women, like Janet Patterson and cinematographer Mandy Walker, also started careers in other production departments around this time (Simpson 2000). A network of institutions at both state and collective levels enabled this feminist rejuvenation of the country's film industry, which is still ongoing (Henkel 2019). With the benefit of hindsight, it is clear that the creators of *Two Friends* leveraged fresh institutional opportunities at the right time, producing a film that serves as a crucial hinge point in the subsequent history of Antipodean feminist cinema. This history demonstrates that when unpacking the ways feminist theory and practice influenced Campion's work, scholars should first appreciate the spirit of collective action and solidarity that permitted her education and earliest films.

EXPERIMENTS IN REVERSE CHRONOLOGY AND VISUAL STYLE

If Jan Chapman and Jane Campion factor prominently in the institutional context behind *Two Friends*, then Helen Garner and Janet Patterson, in addition to Campion of course, inform the film's ambitious formal project. The film innovates in two respects. Firstly, the script by Garner shares a sense of theme and scale with several later Campion screenplays, but it distinguishes itself with an unorthodox, reverse chronological structure. Garner's work predates, by over a decade, a resurgence of reverse chronology narratives in Hollywood and elsewhere, but it rarely receives mention in critical or scholarly discourse devoted to unusual narrative structures.[12] This absence, I argue, is likely on account of the film's temporal isolation from other similarly structured films, its staggered distribution, and its dramatic focus on young women. In addition, the collaboration between Campion, Patterson, and cinematographer Julian Penney produced a distinct approach to cinematic perspective and *mise-en-scène*, one perched between naturalism and overt stylisation. The strained working relationship Campion reported having with Penney might lead us to think of this liminal style as a compromise and not the signature Campion style that emerged with *Sweetie*, but that perception could be reframed more affirmatively given the specifics of the collaborative process and the ABC's mode of production.

Some Campion scholars have regarded the film's reverse chronology as a gimmick, or at least a feature not worthy of extended analysis.[13] I want to reframe that perception, given the humanistic aim of *Two Friends* and its relative formal restraint compared to other reverse chronological narratives.[14] Campion herself is on record as having said: 'I also liked the script a lot, even if the idea of telling a story by going back in time was not what I would have chosen. What I loved was the freshness of observation and the truth of situations' (Ciment 1999a, 35).[15] Given that Chapman commissioned her for this ABC production after Garner's script was written, Campion did not have the privileges to restructure the film that early in her career. That said, it is interesting to note how Garner has, in an interview, identified the 'emotional way' the structure unfolds, just as Campion praises the fresh, observational 'truth' of Garner's dramatic situations (Hawker 1986, 9). An attention to interior life, experience, and ambiguously motivated character behaviour runs throughout the rest of Garner and Campion's work.

A reconstruction of the film's collaborative production, through filmmaker interviews and an analysis of narrative form and visual style, can vouch for both the development of Campion as an auteur and the natural give-and-take of commercial filmmaking. *Two Friends* was set and filmed in Sydney, which first of all limited Garner, a long-time Melbournian, from visiting the film set most days.[16] This detail clarifies what the 'collaborative' process behind the film actually looked like: not an assembly of all creative personnel under one roof, but a series of steps, each with a different set of agents and constraints. To start, Garner wrote the script with the setting of Melbourne in mind, and she appraises the two cities in distinct terms:

> Melbourne and Sydney are very different cities, they have very different vibes and reputations, their geographical surroundings are totally different – Sydney is the warm city, with a wilder history going way back to convict times, it's got wonderful surf beaches and a crazily beautiful harbour and curving roads and hills, it's an outdoor city of movement and physical freedom and people in colourful clothes; Melbourne's more southern — a colder, greyer, flatter city, laid out very formally in straight lines and grids—it's thought of as a serious place, more intellectual even . . . Sydney's air streams in off the ocean, always slightly damp and salty; Melbourne (though it's on a large bay) breathes the dry air of the great plains and grasslands that lie north of it. Because of this difference in climates, A HOUSE has a different meaning in each of the two cities. Or so I've always thought.[17]
>
> (2020, n.p.)

This comment not only illuminates Garner's intentions and sensibility, but it also corresponds to the film's visual style. According to editor Bill Russo, Campion 'originally wanted to shoot the film in black and white' but encountered 'considerable resistance from the director of photography' Julian Penney (Russo 1995, n.p.). Thus, her preference for a monochromatic palette was initially overruled. At the post-production stage, however, Campion achieved a version of her original desire, with the help of Russo, colourist Caro, and colour grader Arthur Cambridge, who together desaturated the film stock. 'This look is very important to the film', Russo wrote to the film's American distributor, Milestone Films, in 1995 (Ibid.). The 'colder, greyer' look that Garner associated with Melbourne was applied to footage shot in Sydney. For example, the film's opening, set at a wake and then a cold October beach, departs from the warm, popular image of Sydney and Bondi Beach. In essence, Campion shared with Garner a novel visual idea for the film's setting, and they achieved that desaturated look, despite obstacles, with the input of other creative personnel.

Ultimately, reconstructing the reality of collaboration and compromise actually underscores the integrity of Campion's personal vision, as much as it spotlights the creative input of her collaborators. For Campion's first feature production, Chapman teamed her with an experienced crew, which included some who did not intuitively grasp or agree with Campion's directions. Though

Campion tends not to attribute on-set difficulties to disparities in gender, she has stated that negotiating with the all-male electrical and camera departments negatively impacted her first feature film production experience:

> I like to look in the viewfinder because I am very precise about the frame that I want. During the shooting of *Two Friends*, the crew under the director of photography felt some resentment towards me because they weren't used to a director who deals with things like that. My director of photography didn't understand what I wanted very well and I had to be very obstinate to impose my views. On the other hand, with Sally Bongers, a friend who studied with me and who also shot *Peel* and *A Girl's Own Story*, I had a very good relationship. For *Two Friends*, by contrast, I had to use the television crew. They were very competent, but we very simply had different methods of shooting.
>
> (Ciment 1999a, 36)

Campion, Penney, and the camera and electrical department settled on an economical shooting style without traditional expectations of coverage. For this reason, most short scenes elapse in one take. As indicated by her colour grading preference (Figure 2.1), Campion enjoyed more freedom in post-production. For instance, the film features a prominent drawn-on-film animated sequence, an auteurist touch also echoed in *Passionless Moments* (1983) and in *The Piano*.

Figure 2.1 Auteurist touches in *Two Friends* (1986)

That said, *Two Friends* demonstrates well the labour of other female filmmakers, such as that of costume and production designer Janet Patterson, in achieving the 'Campion look'. A distinct, wide-angle shot approximately eight minutes in epitomises Campion's view of the world: it depicts Louise (Emma Coles) sitting on her legs in her room with her mother Janet (Kris McQuade) at the doorway, off-screen save for her right arm (Figure 2.2). This shot matches with Garner's description of the Campion aesthetic:

> The camera seems always to be in an unexpected place. I feel she is gently urging me to look at the world I know in a fresh way, from an angle slightly at odds with the usual one, tilted and tinged by her own idiosyncratic touch. The effect of this is both hilarious and moving.
>
> (Milestone Films 1995, 10)

With its wide focal length and high angle perspective, the camera emphasises depth in Louise's small bedroom, while Janet's outstretched arm in the frame right foreground nestles the viewer uncomfortably close between Louise and Janet mid-conversation. Campion clearly exerted control over this framing, but Patterson's production and costume design naturalises the shot's more distortive effects, in keeping with the story's muted tone. The curve of shoes to Louise's left and the pair of doors to her right function as aperture framing devices, guiding the eye toward Louise. Patterson's use of colour furthermore

Figure 2.2 Campion's unusual framing in *Two Friends* (1986)

balances the composition's key elements with an alternating pattern of red and white: from left to right, a red carpet, Louise's white shirt, a reddish pink wardrobe door, and finally a white bedroom door. Patterson, who worked on four more Campion films before her death in 2016, is just one of the most influential, visible women to inform Campion's personal vision.

To analyse the narrative structure of *Two Friends*, one must first contrast the events of the story with its more elaborate, nonlinear plot structure. As arranged in chronological order, the story can be summarised as follows: in October 1984, working class teenage friends Louise and Kelly (Kris Bidenko) devote their energies to passing an entrance exam to City Girls' High, a respectable school. After Kelly writes Louise a note proclaiming how much she depends on her, the two celebrate the news that they have both passed their exams. Two months later, in December 1984, Louise, Kelly, and each of their divorced parents attend an orientation at City Girls' High, which Kelly's stepfather Malcolm (Peter Hehir) finds elitist. Malcolm prevents Kelly from enrolling in the school. Broken-hearted, Kelly drops off a Christmas present to Louise while her mother and stepfather idle in their car on the street. A month later, in January 1985, the friendship between Kelly and Louise has grown strained. One month later, in February 1985, Louise, now at City Girls' High, interacts with Kelly much more infrequently. After fighting with her stepfather, Kelly visits her father, who leaves her with an older friend, Kevin (Steve Bisley). After Kevin gropes Kelly, she leaves and stays overnight at Louise's house. Five months later, in July 1985, Janet and her ex-husband Jim (Stephen Leeder) attend a wake for a teenage girl who died of a drug overdose. Louise and Kelly have not seen each other for months. Kelly has grown increasingly rebellious but writes to Louise, who is clearly moved after reading the letter. Kelly apologises, recalls her love for Louise, and issues a standing invite to visit. In Garner's non-linear narrative plot structure, the film begins with these final July 1985 episodes. The July 1985 block of story proceeds chronologically forward to Louise reading Kelly's letter, fades out, and announces via title card, 'February / 5 months earlier'. From this point, the block of story covering 'February 1985' ensues, until it jumps again backwards to 'January 1985', and so on, to the end of the film.

Why did Garner tell this story in reverse chronological order? In addition to admiring Harold Pinter's play *Betrayal* (1978), which features a similar reverse chronology, Garner has stated her motives as follows:

> I wanted a structure, a paper bag to fight my way out of [. . .] I really like the sense of it developing; you know what happens right from the start, bits slot into place behind you, you work backwards in an emotional way and the pattern is finally fitted together for you [. . .] It's the first time I have ever planned something, I usually go fumbling into the dark.

(Hawker 1986, 9)

As opposed to writing novels, a process she has described as 'blundering through a trackless forest', Garner wrote the screenplay with a pre-determined, self-imposed constraint (Garner 2016, 4). The constraint of reverse chronology achieves several effects, one of which is to foreground thematic parallels between characters. For instance, in the film's opening scene, given the way Janet and Jim enter a ceremony already underway, the viewer may speculate the deceased is someone they knew but to whom they were not close. Within this depressing space, Jim expresses concern to Janet about their daughter and Louise then asks Janet if Kelly is 'all right'. Janet responds that she does not believe so and that Kelly has 'dropped out of sight'. In the next scene, Kelly, dressed in punk clothes, walks along a beach with an older boy; Garner's script describes the boy as 'fairly horrible looking' (Ibid., 132). The structure establishes a clear thematic connection between the dead girl and Kelly, which the ensuing reverse chronology will render poignant as Kelly 'grows' younger and more optimistic.

While the reverse chronology might on paper seem to abstract the dramatic progression and thus estrange the viewer's emotional involvement with the story, the structure's transparency arguably has the opposite effect. Through the use of title cards, fades, and symmetrical plotting (for example, Kelly's letters at beginning and end), the logic of dramatic irony in *Two Friends* verges on classicism, so transparent is the expectation that the viewer will know increasingly more than the characters do as the film progresses. This excess of knowledge does not produce an adverse effect of information overload, but instead hands the viewer a bifocal lens through which to perceive the action. From a macro perspective, the structure inverts the archetypal bildungsroman arc by ending with innocence rather than maturity. The viewer need not strain to perceive the broad outlines of the story, yet the structure's manipulation introduces a novel degree of difficulty through its inherent de-dramatisation. It tasks the viewer to think consciously about structure, as the film's turning points (for instance, Malcolm barring Kelly from City Girls' High) are first telegraphed through their after-effects, before they are depicted on screen. From another, more local perspective, the de-dramatised structure frees the viewer to focus on the visual and behavioural detail of the drama. Here, Garner's literary talent and Campion's professed disinterest in reverse chronology intersect to pleasing effect. Through naturalistic performances, restrained drama, and wide-angle *mise-en-scène*, the filmmakers direct viewer attention to a wealth of on-screen material. Unlike other reverse chronological narratives, this abundance of material need not be reformulated by the viewer into a larger 'puzzle' structure.

This commitment to realism and humanistic drama furthermore contrasts *Two Friends* with the more masculine, 'cerebral' showmanship of some popular later reverse chronological narratives, like *Memento* (Christopher Nolan 2000) and *Irréversible* (Gaspar Noé 2002). Its relative unobtrusiveness could in part explain why *Two Friends* has not received significant attention for its innovative narrative structure. Unlike *Memento*, for instance, the structure does not add a competing narrative strand that eventually merges with the dominant reverse chronology, nor does it announce its unusual treatment of temporality with an outré gesture such as *Irréversible*'s inverted-then-sideways opening credits. By contrast, the structure of *Two Friends* is modestly indicated and intuitive to follow. Like many successful screenwriters, Garner revived this rare technique, which before Pinter could be found in popular one-offs such as the Czech film *Happy End* (Oldřich Lipský 1967) and the Broadway play *Merrily We Roll Along* (George S. Kaufman 1934) (Bordwell 2006, 90–1). *Two Friends* premiered a few years before a cluster of Hollywood and international festival auteurs (from Quentin Tarantino to Atom Egoyan) achieved popularity for similar, if flashier, nonlinear narratives. Of course, one cannot overlook that Garner, Campion, and the film's protagonists are women, unlike the filmmakers and protagonists of the most popular reverse chronological films. A subtle, 'quiet' drama that stars two young women and experiments with narrative form is rare to the degree that it is a contradiction in terms, by the standards of mainstream film critical discourse. This gendered bias deserves mention as another likely cause for its obscurity, as does the film's circuitous distribution history.

BELATED DISTRIBUTION AND ACCLAIM ABROAD

To claim *Two Friends* has been overlooked implies a non-Antipodean frame of reference. The film won Best Telefeature at the 1987 Australian Film Institute Awards, it received a full-page anticipatory write-up in the Australian film magazine *Cinema Papers*, it screened at a number of film festivals in the country, and it premiered on national television (Anon. 1986). However, by the standards of international exposure established just a few years later with *Sweetie*, *Two Friends* remains under-watched and under-appreciated for a Jane Campion film. More than any other factor, the film's lack of theatrical distribution in the decade following its premiere explains this marginal status. When Milestone Films acquired the film's rights for US and Canada distribution in 1995, *Two Friends* received, in Chapman's words, a 'new lease of life' (Higgins 1995, n.p.). *Two Friends* nevertheless epitomises the challenges of re-releasing early work by filmmakers who later find popular acclaim.

The belated distribution of *Two Friends* faced a number of challenges atypical for a film that, at the time of its acquisition, was less than a decade old. First came the problem of it being an unknown quantity outside of the Oceanic region. Even Amy Heller and Dennis Doros, the co-founders and core personnel of New Jersey-based distributor Milestone Films, had never heard of the film prior to 1995. New Zealand International Film Festival Director Bill Gosden first introduced the film to Doros and Heller, who watched it via a tape supplied by the ABC (Heller and Doros 1995, n.p.). Having loved the film, they contacted Chapman and Garner, who supplied material for the press kit and answered questions from film journalists (Fried 1996). Second, the 16mm print of *Two Friends* used for its initial festival dates had been scrapped, so Milestone, ABC, Bill Russo, restoration company Cinema Arts, and sound mixing company Zounds restored a new print (Thompson 1996). While striking an interpositive print from a negative is a routine task, properly sizing the film's image track for theatrical exhibition proved unusual. As Russo informed Doros and Heller in December 1995, Campion composed shots for the film using a special viewfinder, the dimensions of which did not correspond to standard film exhibition formats. For the original festival dates, Campion applied a black velvet mask to the bottom of the venue screen, but Milestone's release adopted a more symmetrical aspect ratio, with minor pillar boxing for the home video release (Russo 1995, n p ; Doros 1995, n.p.). After news of Milestone's deal circulated, the British Film Institute followed suit by acquiring *Two Friends* for UK distribution (Doros 1995, n.p.). Doros and Heller booked the film's premiere at New York's Film Forum theatre, followed by a series of arthouse theatre screenings and a DVD release in 2002 (Milestone Films 1995, 3).

Since 1996, *Two Friends* has received virtually uniform praise from American critics, though in the years since its proper theatrical release, admiring critics have come to regard the film as something of an overlooked gem. Major newspapers *Los Angeles Times*, *The New York Times*, and *Chicago Tribune* all filed positive notices praising the film's structure, style, and pathos (Thomas 1996; Holden 1996; Wilmington 1996). For *The Village Voice*, Amy Taubin proclaimed *Two Friends* to be Jane Campion's 'most perfectly realized film', superior to the 'overrated *Piano*', 'less forced than *Sweetie*', and 'cinematically richer than *An Angel at My Table*' (Taubin 1996, n.p.). Sporadic reviews of the film since – mostly by online critics – tend to sound similar notes of enthusiastic praise, though they always simultaneously lament the film's status as a marginalised, underseen entry in Campion's oeuvre. In 1999, Nick Davis marvelled at the film's quality, relative to that of 'old student work or television projects' by most other auteurs (Davis 1999, n.p.). In 2009, Tim Brayton concluded: 'Though often relegated to minor status in Campion's filmography, this is a striking and powerful debut feature for a woman who'd already proven herself something of a natural talent for the language of cinema' (n.p.). For *Senses of Cinema* in 2017, Gwendolyn Audry Foster follows a lengthy, insightful analysis of the film with the verdict: '*2 Friends* remains one of Campion's most heartfelt and feminist films – and a real discovery' (2017, n.p.). These latter three critics all observe that *Two Friends*, through its comparative obscurity, has been branded as 'minor', 'early', and ripe for 'discovery'.

The film's belated distribution is the primary cause for this reputation, but not the only one. Scholars who study and write about Campion have also tended to undervalue the film, not just because of its obscure status but also due to its shared authorship and origins in television. The landmark nature of the film's production, featuring a predominantly female creative team at the dawn of their careers in the Australian film industry, tends not to occur to those who write about *Two Friends*.

This chapter has sought to correct the tendency to undervalue *Two Friends* by widening the lens beyond that of a solely auteurist appreciation of Campion. Assessing the timing of the film's production vis-à-vis institutional reforms in the Australian film industry privileges *Two Friends* as a turning point in Antipodean feminist cinema. Furthermore, an analysis of contemporary interviews and the film's form, specifically its visual style and nonlinear plot structure, reveals that *Two Friends* should not be viewed as only a formative text for Campion's style or themes. Like so many great films, *Two Friends* testifies to the countless ways that collaboration, at the production stage and beyond, shapes and contributes to a director's vision. *Two Friends* demonstrates the natural affinities between collaboration, in its formation and in practice, and a healthy culture of feminist political action. That Campion started making films in the climate outlined in this chapter only generates more questions about her particular creative agency.

NOTES

1. Until 2021, Campion was the only female director to have won the Palme d'Or (at the 1993 Cannes Film Festival).
2. *Two Friends* goes unmentioned in Kathleen McHugh's *Jane Campion* (2007). It receives passing mention by Deb Verhoeven (2009, 63), and by Andrin (2009, 29). Ellen Cheshire concludes her perceptive analysis of *Two Friends* by saying Campion's later films 'would explore more fully, more subtly, more sensitively, issues that are touched on here' (2018, 47).
3. Fine Line Features distributed *An Angel at My Table* in the USA, while Artificial Eye handled UK distribution (IMDb 2022). Meanwhile, Gramercy Pictures managed US distribution and PolyGram handled UK/France distribution of *The Portrait of a Lady* (IMDb 2022).
4. Helen Garner's debut novel *Monkey Grip* (1977) attracted controversy and was adapted into a 1982 feature film, which she co-wrote.
5. Chapman's speech cites scholarship on this subject, namely Jennifer Stott (1987, 118–26).
6. See Stratton (1980, 16) and Maddox (1996, 75). The AFC and FFC effectively merged, along with Film Australia Limited, with the creation of Screen Australia in 2008 (Parliament of Australia 2008, n.p.).
7. Stott also mentions the Feminist Film Workers (FFW), a distribution and exhibition outfit formed within the Co-Op in 1978 (1987, 120).
8. In addition, the AFTRS's website details this history in the section on 'Our History', (*AFTRS* 2022, n.p.).
9. Campion said she still found the AFTS of the early 1980s to be too conservative and commercially focused: see McHugh (2007, 13–17) and Chapman (2002, n.p.).

10. In addition, Campion and Chapman cast actor Kris Bidenko from Campion's *After Hours* as co-lead in *Two Friends*.
11. Helen Garner describes her introduction to Campion as follows: 'I was first introduced to Jane at Jan's house, before it was decided that Jane would direct it. I vividly recall that Jane looked dauntingly beautiful and stylish, but then she smiled and she had lipstick on her teeth. This endeared her to me at once' (2020, n.p.).
12. Between Google and library databases, a keyword search of 'Two Friends' and 'reverse chronology' yields few hits outside of isolated reviews of the film. For more general discussions of reverse chronology, *Two Friends* appears not so much in academic studies of film narrative, but in filmmaking manuals and informal 'listicles': see, for example, Rabiger and Hurbis-Cherrier (2013, 66), and Krishnan (2017, n.p.).
13. Ellen Cheshire claims Campion found the structure 'clichéd' (Cheshire 2018, 43–4), whereas Alistair Fox does not directly mention the reverse chronological structure in his analysis of the film (Fox 2011, 64–7).
14. The most popular reverse chronology narratives tend to be genre films that cue the viewer to 'piece together' the events of the story (for example, Christopher Nolan's *Memento* [2000]).
15. In addition, in the decades since the film's release, Garner claims not to recall the inspiration of its nonlinear structure but does vividly remember the character traits of Louise and Kelly (see Fried (1996) and Garner (2020)).
16. Garner recalled: "I have a fleeting memory of being on the set one day – the girl who plays Louise [Emma Coles] had developed a crush on one of the young guys in the crew and every time he glanced in her direction she would lean on 'Kelly' [Kris Bidekno] and go off into fits of muffled shrieking – it was very funny but also brought back painful memories of being very young and very foolish" (2020, n.p.).
17. Also in this interview, when asked if she considers herself as part of a 'team' with Campion, Patterson, Chapman, and/or Armstrong, Garner responded: 'No, I don't, really. As a writer with no experience of film-making, I always felt very much a [. . .] sort of background or preliminary figure in the process. I don't remember ever feeling fully a part of a team. This wasn't because I wasn't welcomed by them – I was, and very warmly. I liked them very much and felt that they liked me. But they are 'film people' and I'm 'a writer' of the non-movie, introverted kind – we belong to two different tribes. I didn't understand their work and I felt awed by their professionalism and deep experience' (2020 n.p.).

PART TWO

CHAPTER 3

Unsettling Presences: Agentic Embodiment in Jane Campion's Films

Catherine Fowler

Elena del Rio has argued that the suspicious attitude of feminist film critics of the 1970s and 1980s towards the female body was limiting their understanding of its 'possibilities of action and meaning in addition to, or in place of, those stipulated by culture' (2003, 11). For del Rio, rather than repressing or omitting the fetishised female body, the solution to this problem lay in 'the construction of a different body' altogether (Ibid.). This chapter will argue that we find del Rio's 'different body' in many of Campion's films, as produced by her elastic audio-visual engagement with female bodies that stretches from understanding them as semiotic and discursive signs to experiencing them as lived, embodied presences. By recognising the multi-dimensional attachment to female bodies that Campion's practice allows, we can add to conceptions of what Kate Ince has called 'agentic embodied action on the part of women' (2017, 41).[1] Conceiving of how Campion's female protagonists move and relate to space as 'agentic' is what helps us to understand the feminist import of their unsettling presences.

The stakes of this chapter are two-fold: first, the chapter shows how methodologies of feminist film criticism construct and – as del Rio's enquiry suggests – de-limit their object of study, in this case the female body; second, by focusing on the embodied nature of the framing of female bodies in Campion's films *Sweetie* (1989), *Holy Smoke* (1999), and *In the Cut* (2003), we find that she complicates our understanding of feminist agency. Ultimately, we are left with a sense of Campion's ambivalence towards feminism. Measured materially on visual and sensual levels and in terms of how they occupy space and move through it, Campion's protagonists present as riddled with complexities and contradictions. The paradox thus produced is insightfully summed up by Kathleen McHugh, who argues: 'If they [Campion's women] are avatars of feminism, it is a feminism that Campion finds impossible to articulate' (2007, 157).

Coming to filmmaking in the mid-1980s, Campion can be situated within what I would call a post-visual pleasure generation, a term which distinguishes women filmmakers who emerged in the 1970s and had their work measured against Laura Mulvey's foundational text (including Chantal Akerman, Sally Potter and Yvonne Rainer)[2] from the generation who began their feature careers in the 1980s (including Catherine Breillat and Claire Denis).[3] Campion's cinema belongs then to a trajectory of women filmmakers tackling both the perils and the pleasures of an audio-visual engagement with the female body on screen in the wake of a feminist consciousness. In the frames of the post-visual pleasure generation, the female body is central to the narrative world as, moving on from del Rio's diagnosed repression and omission of 1970s cine-feminism, all these directors have a shared interest in women who do not behave as one might expect or even prefer. As Pam Cook puts it, these filmmakers 'are influenced by feminist debates without being in the least inhibited by them' (1993, xxii), an observation which partially explains the challenge for feminist film theory when grappling with Campion's framing of female bodies.

Despite the commitment by women directors in the 1970s to – consciously or unconsciously – make visible the gaze of female directors, characters and spectators, the female body remained an ambivalent object, largely because of what Myra Macdonald diagnoses as 'woman's long history of action as a depthless sign, responsive to masculine whim' (1995, 101). Equally, Mulvey's insistence that the over-signification of the female body meant it could only ever be the site of visual pleasure for the male gaze seems to have resulted in its removal from the scrutiny of 1970s women directors. In response to the over-signification of the female body, women filmmakers used it to comment on woman's status as a seductive or castrating presence, or attempted to empty it out to leave it as a blank presence.[4] Consequently, the task of later generations would be to fill in this blank with their own meanings. Whether or not these filmmakers would recognise the visual and post-visual pleasure framework through which I examine their works, the influence and consequences of Mulvey's model have, nevertheless, permeated to the extent that it is possible to trace her conceptual patterns in these works.

The visual pleasure generation's impulse was to develop an anti-pleasure stance, as articulated by Mulvey, in which the female body was a repressed presence, variously embodied in a housewife who kept order in place through a strict routine (witness here Chantal Akerman's *Jeanne Dielman 23 quai du commerce 1080 Bruxelles* [1975]), a melodramatic heroine whose narration and alienating camera and editing stripped her body of any spectacular qualities (Yvonne Rainer's *Film About a Woman Who. . .* [1974]), or a laughing, androgynous medusa, who disrupted narratives and revealed to the heroine her role as sacrificial victim for the male hero's glorious tragic cause (Sally Potter's *Thriller* [1979]). The conundrum of these early feminist classics was how to express an erotics of female desire when the female body had such strong visual connotations. The answer given to this puzzle most frequently was to banish it altogether. Therefore, nude female bodies and fulfilling relationships were sacrificed for films that re-told the story of women's oppression or lobbied for equality.

In contrast to the visual pleasure generation, the filmmakers of the post-visual pleasure era exhibit distinctive relationships to their protagonists' female bodies that unsettle our expectations, influenced by the cultural and political discourses generated by Mulvey's work. Campion's strategies sit alongside those of Breillat and Denis; all three invest bodies with agency in often contradictory ways. For Carrie Tarr and Brigitte Rollet, Breillat's trademark is: '[a] narrative centred on an active controlling female who willingly subjects herself to acts of masochistic sex' (2001, 104). In Breillat's most commercially successful film, *Romance* (1999), 'a woman-centred mediation on sex and sexuality', Tarr and Rollet argue that although it films its main character's naked body, including her sexual organs, in direct close up, it 'avoid[s] being fetishistic because of the lack of a mediating male gaze' (2001, 103). Similarly, Judith Mayne comments that the bodies of her male and female characters form the substance of Denis's cinema: 'Denis' approach to the cinema – wandering through space, curiosity, vagabondage – centre[s], sooner or later, on a fascination with the human body' (2005, 25). For Martine Beugnet, Denis's bodies refuse to reveal themselves in conventional ways: 'the representation of the body shuns voyeuristic and exploitative aims: bodies are not displayed merely to be "consumed" visually by spectators' (2004, 137–8).

Campion's qualifications for inclusion in this post-visual pleasure generation are that her female protagonists are often unusual, unruly and unsettling. This fact has not gone unnoticed, yet the feminist import of being unsettling was initially overlooked in favour of a more gender-neutral quirkiness and, as a result, the full dimensions and consequent reverberations of the ways in which Campion frames female bodies took a while to be recognised. Conceiving of how Campion's female protagonists move through and relate to space as 'agentic' is what helps us to understand the potential feminist impact of being unsettling. Having contextualised Campion's emergence as a filmmaker as part of a turn in the 1980s towards the female body, in what follows I will introduce, analyse and discuss the female body as an unsettling presence in three parts. First I speculate upon why initially Campion's female protagonists were not widely discussed in feminist terms; second I practice reading Campion's earliest female protagonists through models of embodiment, and third, I extend this method via case studies from *Sweetie*, *Holy Smoke* and *In the Cut*, in which differentiations between women rather than between men and women are possible in such a way that we grasp the multi-dimensionality, complexities, and contradictions of agentic embodiment.

BURYING THE FEMALE, FEMININE, FEMINIST BODIES

Surveying interviews, reviews, and academic literature around Campion's work, we can make three observations as to why initially Campion's female protagonists did not evince feminist engagement. First, Campion's own hesitancy in referring to gender – whether her own or within her films – had an impact upon the critical directions taken regarding her work. Early interviews in mainstream press frame her challenging representations as unusual for a woman director, repeating her assertion that she's 'not committed to niceness' (Preston 1999, 12), the implication being that women directors are expected to be nice. The unusual becomes the surreal, as surrealism remains a reference point in the early part of her career up to *Sweetie*, deriving from Campion's reference to Buñuel as an influence (Williamson 1999). Hence Dana Polan identifies 'a systematically arranged "making strange" as part of her 'comical and [. . .] quirky' early films (2001, 57–8), Anneke Smelik points to how 'imagery in *Sweetie* is excessive in its highly artificial construction' (1998, 139), and a reviewer of *Sweetie*'s 'twisted roots' refers to an 'enveloping peculiarity' (Hinson 1990, D1). This reference to surrealism allows for an easy dismissal of any engagement on a feminist level since it suggests that we should not take 'strangeness' seriously. In sum, Campion's fierce style appears to act as a kind of McGuffin for reviewers of her early films, leading them to attribute agency to space rather than to bodies.

The second aspect that obscures feminist engagement is the development of Campion's style into a pronounced treatment of space which sometimes obscures the interdependency of the expressive relations between bodies and space. Consequently, interest in space manifests as an engagement with Campion's use of genre and landscape, blanking out the female bodies. For Eva Reuschmann,

> from her early art-school shorts such as *Peel* (1982) and *A Girl's Own Story* (1983/4) through her first feature *Sweetie* (1989) to *Holy Smoke* (1999), Campion gothesizes both interior and exterior landscapes in order to articulate the essential 'homelessness' and sense of social entrapment of her white Australian and New Zealand heroines.
>
> (2004, 9)

For Reuschmann the gothic has thematic implications, yet if we think of the gothic also as a mood deriving from landscape, we should not forget that it also affects the bodies that are enveloped by the space. Hence, in the case studies that follow it is the relations between figure and ground, bodies and space that will be emphasised.

Characterisations of Campion's early female protagonists as simply part of quirky, surreal, or generic narratives can explain away their unusual, unruly, and unsettling presences as merely adhering to these narrative conventions. Such a position fails to grant agency to these female bodies. This dismissive manner of engagement continues even into her later films in a related though slightly different form, with the insistence that Campion focuses upon 'lunatic' women.[5] Thus my third observation is drawn from a long view of Campion's oeuvre and entails Cook's diagnosis of the influence of, yet accompanying lack of constraint by, feminism. Recognisable feminist characteristics can be applied to the narrative function of all Campion's protagonists: they are unusual and go against the norm (Kay [Karen Colston]; Janet [Kerry Fox]; Isabel [Nicole Kidman]; Ada [Holly Hunter]; Ruth [Kate Winslet], and Fanny [Abbie Cornish]); they can be unruly and cause trouble for those around them (Sweetie [Geneviève Lemon]; Ada; Ruth), and their behaviour unsettles patriarchal structures (all concerned). However, at an audio-visual level there is even more going on that muddles our reading of the films. The embodied nature of Campion's protagonists introduces the messy (relative to agency in narrative terms) terrain of agential 'bodily and emotional experiences' (Ince 2017, 42). Feminist engagement with Campion's phenomenal female bodies is not so much lacking as inhibited. To explore how a fuller engagement is possible I will now turn to Campion's early short films.

UNCOVERING PHENOMENAL FEMALE BODIES: METHODS

To uncover the female, feminine and feminist bodies in Campion's early work we need to pay attention to them as embodied presences following del Rio; such is the intention of Ince, as she attempts to join up tranches of feminist philosophy to supplement feminist film criticism.[6] Ince's inspiration lies with Iris Marion Young's applied feminist phenomenology, which 'takes differences between male and female modes of moving and relating to space as the starting point for its enquiry into differentiated embodiment: body comportment, motility and spatiality are among its chief concerns' (Ince 2017, 42). In her chapter entitled 'Body', Ince's method is to focus upon movement and bodily action such as dance in *Fish Tank* (Andrea Arnold 2009),[7] walking backwards in *The Beaches of Agnès* (Agnès Varda 2008), and giving birth in *Romance* (Catherine Breillat 1999). Borrowing this method from Ince, we can try it out on Campion's early short films as a preface for the three case studies to follow. What import for feminism emerges once we look beyond the quirky, strange, and peculiar designations applied to Campion's early work? And how are the female bodies implicated and oriented in space?

The perspective Campion's early films offer on the world is a questioning, puzzled one. Adolescent narratives of uncertainty in which characters are unsure of themselves are accompanied by a cinematography that films from unexpected angles, and editing that favours disjunction rather than continuity. In *Passionless Moments* (1984) both male and female bodies lounge in the privacy of their bedrooms, contemplating the secrets of life and randomly inquiring about idiosyncratic details that come to mind. The prone position that each adopts suggests an embodied relaxation, the settled stance of the habitual private zone. At the same time, the relation between the act of lounging and the bedroom implies the adolescent fumbling and sexual rites of passage to which these rooms could play host in coming years. Immediately the multi-dimensionality of these bodies is apparent as Campion (and Gerard Lee, her collaborator) frames them as signs, as part of discourse and as lived presences.

The lounging that we encounter in *Passionless Moments* becomes a motif in Campion's other short films. In *A Girl's Own Story* (1984), the main group of school friends stretches out languidly across a playground, as their teachers chase other girls into class. The girls derive agency from this act of occupying institutional space, as well as from refusing motility and remaining settled in their place, which is out of place. Equally, the being-together feels powerful; it offers an amplification of disdain and disorder. Later on, this elongation of limbs can be read in del Rio's terms as 'indivisible from symbolic and discursive structures' (2003, 12) when echoed in a scene in Pam's (Gabrielle Shornegg) home in which her mother (Colleen Fitzpatrick), pounced on by Pam's father (Paul Chubb), battles frustratedly, before stretching out and submitting.[8] The self-possession resonant in the school friends' occupation of the playground is, it is implied, only a temporary release; it will soon be impinged upon by, as Young puts it, 'the woman's social existence as the object of the gaze of another, which is a major source of her bodily self-reference' (1980, 148).

In *After Hours* (1984), lounging and stretching out becomes floating as Lorraine (Danielle Pearse) experiences precisely the impingement diagnosed by Young.[9] Lorraine, a dedicated swimmer and secretary, experiences sexual harassment from her boss. Her body becomes subject to the patriarchal gaze, as it is objectified by the boss and his lawyer, who share the leery observation: 'big girl I suppose, being a swimmer', 'no she's quite a slight build, firm'. As the mistreatment overwhelms Lorraine, so her relinquishment of control takes on physical dimensions, abandoning her regimented routine of diurnal swimming practice to simply float in the amniotic fluid of the pool.[10] The switch from propelling her body with force to allowing the water to carry her through operates on both phenomenal and symbolic levels. Hence, in Campion's short films adolescent female bodies often fill the frame, blocking the horizon with their horizontality and confusing our understanding of figure and ground. The uncertainty of these adolescent bodies is replicated by the ungainliness lent to them by cinematography and editing.

A further aspect of the ungainliness of adolescent bodies is to reinforce their physicality, their weight and volume. Contrary to Macdonald's diagnosis of female bodies as 'depthless signs' (1995, 101), we feel the tight dimensions of the space these girls take up and how they move through it. The adolescent female body's movement and presence becomes the 'problem' in these early narratives because the men, boys, teachers, and parents cannot make it signify in the way that they want it to: as subject to their control. Instead, by filling the frame through lounging, stretching, and floating, these bodies blur boundaries and binaries. They are neither active nor passive, neither sexual nor sexless, and neither in nor out of control. As we will see, the conceptual blurriness of the female bodies in Campion's short films becomes an audio-visual blurriness of focus in her later features, adding haptic, tactile and sensual dimensions to the female bodies' materiality.

ANALYSING AGENTIC EMBODIED ACTION

Sweetie, Holy Smoke and *In the Cut* have been chosen as case studies because embodiment is central to the narratives, as the push and pull of family relations are condensed into the demands and impressions made on the bodies of the main protagonists – Kay, Ruth, and Frannie (Meg Ryan) respectively. The choreography, cinematography, editing, and *mise-en-scène* create these bodies as unsettling presences which we can neither sum up nor easily consume. Instead, we have to get to know them phenomenologically, by watching their gestures and the ways in which they move as well as how they relate to other bodies in space and to the space around them. Therefore, the difference that a post-visual pleasure framework represents for these films can be seen in her female characters' positions off-centre, at the edge of Campion's frames, or competing for attention with a background of light, colour, and pattern. These female bodies remain thick with meaning that spills over frames and across shots.

The opening shots of *Sweetie, Holy Smoke* and *In the Cut* demand adequate ways of accounting for the experiences of the protagonists. *Sweetie* begins with Kay's intimate voice-over confessing her fear of trees. A swirl of green, yellow, and brown flowery carpet fills our view and jutting out from the right bottom corner of the frame we see some body parts, identifiable as a woman's legs. But the legs are awkwardly placed at a dangle from whatever they are lying on and one black shoe also hangs by a thread, as if at a crime scene. Next, the film cuts to a head and shoulders shot of Kay protruding from the left bottom corner of the frame, lying on her bed, her arms bent in a similarly awkward fashion to the legs. The voice-over narration invites us into Kay's head, establishing her neuroses. Together the two shots suggest discomposure in the space she has to occupy, as her body splays gawkily across the bed in a graceless attitude. Despite the introduction to Kay in the intimate setting of a bedroom, she seems far from relaxed, and the camera angles and editing exacerbate a feeling of discomfort. Therefore, Kay's gauche occupation of space is quickly established and we are made very aware of the troubled relation between her body and the space it occupies.

Holy Smoke is similarly brisk and economical in introducing us to Ruth. A hand-held shot of a dirty bus window with hangings swaying jerkily is exchanged for a low-lit shot of what we gradually discern to be hands pressing hard against the roof of the bus. The third shot gives us a close-up on Ruth, as she turns her head from right to left, establishing the first shot as her point of view. She continues to look around herself and we understand that she is squeezed tight among largely male passengers, some of whom we can see staring at her. As the camera bobs up and down with the rhythm of the bus, Ruth glances down and we travel with her to catch sight of her friend asleep, with her head resting on Ruth's thigh. We cut to the window again and then back to Ruth's gaze. Then the camera comes to rest with the passengers behind Ruth, and we see fingers touching her hair and her responding by putting her hand over that area, as if to protect it from invasion. As with Kay in *Sweetie*, Ruth's point of view is swiftly established, along with both a sense of discomfort and of her strength in this situation, as she stands tall and rejects the unwanted fingers – and by association, gazes – that reach for her.

At the start of *In the Cut* we meet the sisters, Frannie and Pauline (Jennifer Jason Leigh), in varying states of reverie. It is Pauline, however, whose presence is most firmly established. Again, a hand-held camera introduces us to a protagonist in movement, though in this instance Pauline is propelling herself, tottering dreamily upon the uneven cobblestones underfoot. Her shoes and legs are blurrily out of focus at the bottom of the frame, while sharp focus attends to her black skirt. The camera angle and lighting draw attention to the see-through lace at the bottom of her skirt, which caresses her bare legs as she moves. As we cut to her face, Pauline turns wistfully in a circle, before her gaze settles upon her neighbour practising his morning tai chi. The camera pans back to settle on her face and then we cut away to blossom falling, blown by the wind. We then cut back to Pauline as she stretches out her hand to be touched by the blossom. If Kay appears awkward and Ruth strong, then the prevailing adjective for Pauline would be transcendent. In the case of all three women, we are given their points of view while also experiencing their situations through the actresses' bodily movements and the camera's reaction and framing.

These introductions to Kay, Ruth and Pauline map uncannily on to Iris Marion Young's three modalities of female bodily comportment: an ambiguous transcendence (Pauline), an inhibited intentionality (Ruth), and a discontinuous unity with its surroundings (Kay) (Young 1980, 145). For Young, the three categories sit within de Beauvoir's oppositional poles of transcendence, where the typical situation and definition of women is overcome, and immanence, where the woman lives her body as a thing and 'retains a distance from her body as transcending movement and from engagement in the world's possibilities' (1980, 148). Oriented by de Beauvoir's notion that 'every human existence is defined by its *situation*' (Ibid., 138, emphasis in original), Young argues for a combination of understanding the lived differences in the behaviour and experiences of men and women with 'the situation of women within a given socio-historical set of circumstances' (1980, 139). Young's use of the words 'ambiguous', 'inhibited', and 'discontinuous' to modify transcendence, intentionality, and unity enact an increasingly strong withdrawal of the agentic from embodiment. Transposing these three categories into the audio-visual realm we find these modifiers enacted through framing, camera movement, and *mise-en-scène*.

In Young's first category, transcendence is ambiguous because only a part of the body moves out towards a task. Pauline's dreamy early morning walk through the garden below Frannie's flat is laden with hapticality, from the evocative hem of Pauline's skirt brushing her bare legs, through the blurring of edges caused by the shifting focus of the lens, which adds an impression of enveloping materiality to Pauline's body, to the elemental touch of the wind, whose effect we hear, see – moving her hair and clothes – and feel, as the blossom drops upon her skin. Ambiguity enters into this reverie in the combination of the cobblestones and sandals, which together create a 'tottering' that is unsteady, as well as Pauline's gaze at her neighbour, following which she appears to modify her movements slightly, turning away from him in order to reach out for the falling blossoms. The camera supports Pauline's adjustments by panning and cutting the neighbour from the frame.

Akin to the opening of *In the Cut*, the modification of Ruth's intentionality in *Holy Smoke* can also be explained as a reaction to others in a public space. Ruth's roving gaze in the claustrophobic bus is significant in establishing the strong stance that she will carry through the narrative; in this foreign context, to take up space as a woman who is also white is to put oneself in danger. Yet Ruth is far from a physically timid female, with eyes lowered. Her upright stature, in contrast to that of her friend who sits, and is out of view, is indicative of intentionality, or a purposeful reaching out. Inhibition, Young argues, takes the form of a withholding of 'motile energy' (1980, 147) and just as we sense that Pauline would reach out even further if she were on her own, so we glean from Ruth's restless gaze, upright stature, and reaction to the unwanted touch of her hair that such inhibition does not come naturally to her.

Despite her separation of them, Young admits that her three categories are interdependent and cross fertilised. It is the extent of the interruption to body motility that gradually shifts as we travel from categories one to three; hence ambiguous transcendence brings on inhibited intentionality. Accordingly, Kay's situation is less obviously transcendent and exhibits less intentionality than those of Pauline and Ruth. We are not permitted to approach Kay as we are

Pauline. Instead, the framing of either end of her body (feet and legs, then head and shoulder) confined to the corners means she remains self-contained and withdrawn. Through this framing, the exhibitionist patterned carpet becomes a kind of mind-screen onto which we may project the fear of trees to which she refers in her narration. For Young, unity is fulfilled '[b]y projecting an aim toward which [the body] moves [. . .it] unites itself with its surroundings' (1980, 147). With Kay's narration and the dominant carpet in mind we are subject to competing discourses: the narration is intimate, the framing of the shot means that the carpet threatens to invade Kay's body space, while Kay's limbs enact an uneasy withdrawal into a guarded state of anxiety and discomfort quite opposite to the lounging, stretching adolescent bodies of Campion's short films.

Having explored our initial introductions to the female protagonists in *Sweetie*, *Holy Smoke* and *In the Cut*, we can extend our analysis in order to deepen the differentiations of embodiment between women. This comparative dimension builds upon del Rio's and Ince's scholarship. Del Rio's focus is upon one film – Sally Potter's *Thriller* – while Ince's enquiry, despite being more extensive, does not significantly employ comparison across and between her chapters. By encapsulating the variety of ways in which Campion portrays agentic embodiment, so her position amongst filmmakers of the post-visual pleasure era is elucidated.

Kay's body is construed as problematic at the level of both narrative and image, with her lack of confidence manifesting in a body that is unassuming; this is evident in the way it hangs back from the front of the frame or is filmed off-centre on the edges. Looking to Young, we could suggest that Kay's perception of her place in the world is such that: '[t]he space [. . .] that is *physically* available to [her. . .] is frequently of greater radius than the space that she uses and inhabits' (1980, 149, emphasis in original). However, whilst Young reads this inadequacy as an example of the 'confinement of feminine lived space' (1980, 150), in Kay's case it is less that she feels confined and more that her own sense of self has to do with retaining personal and private space on her own terms. It is more accurate, then, to say that Kay intentionally withdraws from view. Withdrawal is revealed as a historical strategy on Kay's part as soon as we are introduced to her sister, the excessive Sweetie. Hence the film offers us two different examples of agentic embodiment that to some extent respond to and are the effect of each other: Kay's withdrawal from it and Sweetie's excess.

In the opening of *Sweetie* the placement of bodies draws our attention, and no doubt contributes to one reviewer's reference to 'enveloping peculiarity' (Hinson 1990, n.p.). However, with the benefit of a phenomenological lens the unusual relation between figures and background can suggest the toppling of the male gaze as a defining presence; the scenes in which first, Kay acquires Louis (Tom Lycos) as her boyfriend, second, he moves into the family home, and third, Sweetie arrives, provide further evidence for this interpretation.

The opening of the film establishes Kay's different attitude to romantic love in contrast to that of her workmates. As Doreen D'Cruz maintains, in the pivotal scene when Kay acquires Louis' attention: '[w]hat is notable in this mise-en-scène is Kay's refusal to rely on the methods and paraphernalia of siren or seductress who, in a similar situation would have turned her body into an alluring fetish for the male gaze' (2006, 14). Importantly then, and forwarding the notion that the empty space establishes a different kind of presence in the frame, the attraction between Kay and Louis is one that cannot be seen, and therefore has nothing to do with the visual pleasure of the male or female body, but must instead be felt. The felt nature of Kay's and Louis' attraction is evident when Kay's workmates come down to the car park where Kay and Louis have just got together. Interrupted in their first kiss, the couple slide under a nearby truck. The workmates wander towards where they are hiding and then stop when they see the coins that Kay had used to convince Louis that they were destined to be together. As if sensing the remnant of attraction left over in this space, one of the workmates suddenly says, 'oh I feel all sexy', then abruptly stands up and returns to work.

When Louis moves in with Kay their need to be together takes on spatial expression as they share the same small spaces in the family home. However, the equilibrium that sustains Kay's existence is shattered when Louis plants a tree in the concrete of the backyard. The tree should represent a visible manifestation of the felt bond between Louis and Kay. Yet Kay sees it as a being to be cared for much like her sister Sweetie, and one which will invade the space she shares with Louis; hence the tree portends the actual invasion of Sweetie soon after. From the first moment we meet Sweetie it is evident that her material reality differs greatly from that of Kay. Unlike the initial shot of Kay confined to the edges of the frame, we literally bump into Sweetie as she swerves down Kay's hallway. She has entered Kay's house not through the door – furniture is not treated well by her – but by breaking the glass because the door 'wouldn't open' (Kay's retort is that it was locked). She has then made herself and boyfriend Bob (Michael Lake) at home in Louis's bedroom, where they lounge around. It is worth recalling the lounging and stretching out bodies of Campion's short films here, as Sweetie possesses a similar sense of adolescent disinhibition and disorder. Yet unlike those adolescents, who we can forgive their embodied attitudes because of their in-between states as girl/woman and consequent blurring of binaries, Sweetie's attitude is practised and calculated to challenge Kay's attempted agency.

Rather than remaining as background or theme, space in *Sweetie* is the site for agential embodiment, thus becoming the battleground between the sisters. It is clear from our first glimpse of Sweetie that she portrays 'the unruly woman', whose bodily and verbal excesses transgress the bounds of conventional femininity. This woman is analysed at length by Kathleen Rowe (1995), who likens her to Miss Piggy, Mrs Noah, and Medusa, figures then whose bodies, tongues, and looks set them outside of the bounds of hetero-seductive feminine behaviour. As we have seen, Kay also shuns normal feminine behaviour. Sweetie's disturbance of those around her appears to explain Kay's contrasting reluctance to seduce and her craving for control over her private life and space. Kay's withdrawal of her body is in contrast (and perhaps response) to Sweetie's overabundance, because the unruly body of Sweetie is seen as an invading presence that strikes a further blow between Kay and her fiancée Louis. This invasion of space is literalised in Sweetie's behaviour, such as when she refuses to be moved from the kitchen, or de-camps to the car so that the rest of the family cannot leave to pick up their mother.

The psychological impact of the infringement on Kay's space is evoked effectively when the family members return from their journey and their euphoria turns sour on being greeted by a pugnacious, growling Sweetie. As the camera adopts a thrusting close-up, Kay urges her sister to 'pull' herself 'together' – at which point, in what seems to be an all too familiar routine, Sweetie grabs hold of Kay's dangling hair, pulling it into two adolescent bunches, while Kay attempts to pull away. From the way that Sweetie expertly turns Kay's regurgitated complaint at her behaviour into an attack on Kay's hair, it is evident that past fights must have featured similar tactics. Thus, one of the key characteristics of the unruly woman, that she 'is unwilling or unable to confine herself to her proper place' is enacted here (Rowe 1995, 31). The indication that Sweetie's behaviour is familiar to Kay suggests that if left unchecked, Sweetie will gain an excessive, almost liquid presence that might spill over if she lets it, much like the tree that Kay imagines 'crawling right under the house'. Ultimately then, Kay's agential embodied action consists of the withdrawal of her body from view. Hence, she does not use it to attract Louis and we often find her at the edge of the frame. Whilst it might appear that this withdrawal follows Young's characterisation of feminine motility as involving bodily timidity (1980, 150), a comparative analysis sensitive to relations between the sisters reveals that once Sweetie arrives it seems more likely that Kay is strategically differentiating herself from her sister in order to protect her own subjectivity.

If in *Sweetie*, family dynamics involve very different ways of occupying space and moving through it, in *Holy Smoke* Ruth's body becomes the entire focus for the family drama. For her mother, and by extension her family, Ruth's body is a site to be saved; this 'golden girl' must be returned to the role of chaste daughter at any cost. Hence it is primarily the absence of Ruth's body from her family's and especially her mother's sight, and the suggestion that it might have been captured by another, that sparks the battle to return Ruth to their care. What soon becomes apparent through the *mise-en-scène* is that it is Ruth's control over her own sexuality that is really at stake here, distracting us from familial relations that are, in actuality, dysfunctional and dishonest.

Ruth is cast in a favourable light, as an authentic (if somewhat capricious) self, thanks to both the cunning plan by her family and the much more conventional behaviour of her sister-in-law, Yvonne (Sophie Lee), towards PJ (Harvey Keitel). The centrality of Ruth's body and, by extension, her sexuality, to the family's concerns is figured in the sequence in which Ruth is taken from her father and given to PJ. Thus, Ruth visits her supposedly ailing father only to discover that she has been deceived and that this was all a ploy to get her home to Australia. The moment that she discovers her family's deception and threatens to walk away, she is prevented from doing so by her brothers and their friends, who surround her. The circle of alleged mutual support and control that these men make contains Ruth's body within it in a double gesture of pseudo protection and control: from 'he won't hurt you sis' to 'not so lively are you now?'. This key moment initiates the writing of Ruth's body as a space to be given (to religion and India; to PJ) or taken (by the same and by her family) as long as Ruth remains 'unkind'. The state of unkindness – an accusation levelled at her by PJ – seems to stand in for a being-in-the-world that goes beyond the body to include the mind. Just as her family seem worried only about Ruth's body (and who she gives it to), so Ruth also seems unable to connect on the kind of mental level which would require recognition that, again as PJ asserts, 'not all touch is desire'.

In *Sweetie*, Kay's refusal to seduce Louis was respected by the camera, which also refused to objectify her, and instead allowed Kay her own space. By contrast, in *Holy Smoke* Ruth is a conventionally attractive presence in ways that Kay is not. Therefore, some of Ruth and by extension Kate Winslet's 'presence' is suggestively sexual. Akin to *Sweetie*, a comparison between women again yields a multi-dimensional view of agential embodiment. Ruth's attractiveness takes nothing away from her agency because it is contrasted with Yvonne's over-the-top hetero-seductive persona. The different ways in which Yvonne and Ruth react to PJ signify their differences in terms of the feminine. Yvonne constantly seeks attention and is immediately flirtatious with PJ. She incessantly moves her head and hair, bats her eyelashes and displays her whole body, for example, when she wears a bikini in his company. As Young would put it, Yvonne experiences her body more as a thing than as a capacity, due to her enslavement to the male gaze (1980, 144).

Yvonne arranges her body in a manner that she considers pleasing to those she hopes to seduce, while Ruth exhibits intentionality, or the 'engagement with the world's possibilities' (Ibid., 148). The striking contrast between Ruth and Yvonne is revealed by considering Yvonne's tendency to sit, kneel, or fall at the feet of the men. Unlike the upright stance of Ruth, from the moment we first meet her in India, Yvonne cannot remain upright and bows down in order to please. In sitting, Yvonne also takes up less space, whereas, in the outback in particular, Ruth is an unavoidable and dominant presence in the frame. Ruth's stance, her movement, and gestures refuse to please anyone but herself, and as the film proceeds both we and Ruth have to get beyond these to her substance. Unkindness has to make way for compassion and being touched physically has to make way for touching mentally. At stake, in Young's terms, is the continuity between the intention – the goal – and the performance – the body's accomplishment of that goal. Hence whilst Ruth's upright stance suggests she possesses agential embodiment, the push and pull of influences can be said to confuse her goals, introducing inhibition.

Turning to *In the Cut*, we find similar contrasting traits between Pauline's and Frannie's agential embodiment, yet in addition there is also less of an opposition and more of a transference between the two, as if together they create a continuum that flits back and forth across the thing-ness and the capacity of the lived body. As discussed, the opening shots of the film involve the half-sisters in different states of reverie. While Pauline swirls in the garden, Frannie sleeps, stirs and then returns to her dream. The contrasts we are offered between Kay and Sweetie, and Ruth and Yvonne, return with Frannie and Pauline. Like Yvonne, Pauline moves, looks, and lives as if always in response to the 'determining male gaze' (Mulvey 2000, 39), yet she also appears less inhibited than Yvonne. She flirts verbally and physically with the men she encounters and her sexual availability is suggested through the contrast between her red/orange dress and the dark drab clothes worn by Frannie. Frannie is close to Kay in the way she inhabits space, with the suitcase she awkwardly drags behind her when travelling to and from work, suggesting her discomfort in the city space. If Pauline's habitual stance is transcendent then Frannie's is more withdrawn, but in a dreamy way, because of her status as a scholar, which is slightly different from Kay's anxious self-containment.

Following the opening sequence, we gradually re-adjust our assessment of a dichotomy between the sisters via scenes in which they dwell together, and then – following her murder – Pauline's presence appears to infect how Frannie is able to move through the world. Frannie is not well-schooled in the lived body of femininity, whereas Pauline is. Mostly, the half-sisters' relationship seems sincere and loving, as they share each other's apartments and call on each other in times of crisis. However, there are times in which a strangeness sets in at the level of the image due to the excessive spectacle of Pauline's body when the two sisters are alone together. Ultimately the reason for this seems to come back to Frannie and her growing obsession with the pleasures and dangers of Malloy and his murder investigation. Thus, Pauline's sexualised body would seem to represent different agentic possibilities for Frannie to explore, from the adoption of the more active role of being the one who does rather than thinks (as referred to in lines of dialogue) to being someone more certain of her desires and able to make decisions.[11] At other times, Pauline's flirtatious stance and out-going engagement with the world haunts Frannie's interactions after her death. When Pauline meets Cornelius (Sharrieff Pugh), Frannie's student, she coquettishly poses for him with her hand raised as if for him to kiss. At the time Cornelius appears to be thrown by this gesture, yet later in the film, as if in sublimated exchange, he in turn takes Frannie's hand to kiss, much to her surprise. It is as if Cornelius is merging the half-sisters and responding to Frannie as if she were Pauline – as if, after her death, Pauline's stance lingers as a possibility in Frannie's life.

UNSETTLING PRESENCES

I began this chapter by observing that what Campion's work offers to feminist film theory is the construction of a different body. By using the phenomenological methodology advocated by del Rio, Young and Ince, the fuller dimensions of Campion's female bodies come into the light. The feminist import of Campion's strategy is indicated by Elizabeth Grosz, who argues that 'without some acknowledgment of the formative role of experience in the establishment of knowledges, feminism has no grounds from which to dispute patriarchal norms' (Grosz 1994, 94). While the visual pleasure generation of filmmakers largely adopted a strategy of 'anti-seduction' in which the female body was a deconstructed presence, viewing Campion as part of the post-visual pleasure generation restores to the female body its full dimensions. Those dimensions include a messy imprecision, evident in the ways in which, once attended to, the agentic embodiment of Kay, Ruth and Frannie is hard to ignore. Accordingly, we can see in Campion's framing of the female body a keen awareness of the dangers described by Mulvey, a strong need to allow the female body to be seen as a desiring presence and a resolute determination to both engage and unsettle.

NOTES

1. There is a growing body of work on Campion interested in the haptic, sensory, sensual, and embodied nature of her films. See, for example: Bainbridge (2008), Dolton (2011); Richard (2018) and Watkins (2013).
2. Other names to be included in this generation include Helma Sanders-Brahms, Ulrike Ottinger, Lizzie Borden, Marleen Gorris, Margarethe Von Trotta, Agnieszkia Holland, Gillian Armstrong, Vera Chytilova, Kira Mouratova and Coline Serreau, all of whom made their first films in the 1970s or before.
3. Regarding the post-70s generation, alongside Campion, we find Patricia Rozema, Beeban Kidron, Suzanne Osten, Julie Dash, Susan Seidelman, Antonia Bird and Gurinder Chadha, all of whom made their first films in the late 1980s.
4. See Chantal Akerman's *Jeanne Dielman 23 Quai du Commerce 1080 Bruxelles* (1975), Sally Potter's *Thriller* (1979) and Yvonne Rainer's *Film About a Woman Who...* (1974).

5. References to Campion's penchant for lunatic women typically point to *Sweetie* (1989), *An Angel at my Table* (1990) and *The Piano* (1993) as evidence. Cantwell cites a friend's impression that Campion's women are mad before rebuffing this: 'Lunatic women? Except for the simultaneously hilarious and tragic Sweetie, no. But powerful women, which in some minds may add up to the same thing? Yes.' See Cantwell (1993, 40). Other critics also dwell on the preponderance of craziness in these three films: see Fendel (1999, 86–90). This topic is taken more seriously by Michel Chion (2009, 49–51).
6. Regarding the turn to phenomenology for feminist film analysis, see also Lindner (2017).
7. It is interesting that Ince focuses upon dance since Young describes dance as 'structured body movement which does not have a particular aim' (1980, 140). All further quotes from Young are taken from this publication.
8. In *A Girl's Own Story* one of the central troubling plot lines is that of the brother and sister who play sexual games, with the sister ending up pregnant, sent away to a home for 'bad girls', and forced to have her baby adopted. Although we do not see the sex act, we do see the siblings crawling around on the carpet 'playing cats'. The impact of this story is such that every time female bodies lay down, the sad transgression of the siblings and fear of what might be done to the female body in such a position is recalled.
9. *After Hours* was unusual in being commissioned by the Women's Film Unit. Campion comments that it 'had to be openly feminist since it spoke about the sexual abuse of women at work' (Ciment 1999a, 35). Through this comment she betrays her dislike for straightforwardly positive feminist politics. She clarifies: 'I wasn't comfortable because I don't like films that say how one should or shouldn't behave. I think the world is more complicated than that' (Ibid.). It is this kind of point-of-view that I am thinking of when I refer to Campion presenting a challenge to feminist film theory.
10. The final 'floating' shot of Lorraine follows her accusations and the subsequent stigma of being the one to call out sexist abuse. Her body is guilty of making itself noticed by her boss who comments on her lateness due to her swimming practice and calls her in to the cramped space of his office to 'assist' him.
11. For a different reading of the relationship between the sisters see Bowler (2018, 93–112).

CHAPTER 4

'The mood that passes through you': Reverberations of Music and Meaning in *The Piano*

Leanne Weston

INTRODUCTION

The cultural memory of *The Piano* (1993) is characterised by numerous visual and aural cues that remain fixed in the mind, shaping how it has been remembered. For some, it is the memory of Michael Nyman's score, and the now-familiar melody of 'The Heart Asks Pleasure First'. For others, it is the passion of Ada McGrath (Holly Hunter) and George Baines's (Harvey Keitel) illicit love affair. Or, conversely, the life-changing violence enacted by Ada's vengeful husband Alisdair Stewart (Sam Neill), when he severs his wife's finger with an axe. Maybe it is the ending of the film, where Ada imagines her piano in 'its ocean grave',[1] and then herself, tied to it by a rope, floating in the deep, engulfed by silence (Figure 4.1). The film's 25th anniversary re-release in 2018 offered the opportunity to return to *The Piano*, and its final moments have lost none of their resonance, forming the basis of the analysis in this chapter. The rope creates a physical connection between Ada's mind, body, spirit, and her piano. The rope confirms what Ada and the audience who identify with her already know; something which they feel throughout the film but, until the moment of Ada's imagining, they cannot see. The significance of this image is not limited to its affective power, nor its endurance in the memory; it also offers a way into considering the film's relationship to the body, the phenomenological, and the haptic.

Drawing on Laura Marks's (1998) concept of haptic visuality, I examine *The Piano*'s haptic potential, first as a framework through which to read the film, and second, as a textually located quality within Campion's signature style.[2] This quality intersects at aesthetic and thematic levels, strengthening the audience's identification with Ada while amplifying the emotive, affective,

Figure 4.1 Ada enters the sea

and expressive functions of Michael Nyman's score, allowing it to transcend traditional cultural spaces typically occupied by soundtracks. This analysis contributes to ongoing scholarly discussions of the haptic which extend beyond vision and into sound, engaging with work by Vivian Sobchack (2004) and Sue Gillett (1995) on gender and embodied spectatorship, and music theory by Michel Chion (1999, 2007, 2009), Claudia Gorbman (2000), and Kathryn Kalinak (1992), to consider the expressive and affective functions performed by the score. I argue these functions are inherent to understanding how the film explores Ada's subjectivity and why the film continues to resonate with audiences.

THE PIANO AND SCHOLARSHIP: RESONANCES, FEMINISMS, CONTROVERSIES

Numerous articles, reviews, and booklet essays dedicated to *The Piano* consider its significance and the personal, emotive, and affective impact of returning to a film text. Barbara Klinger argues that 'multiple returns to a favourite text can also enhance its original effects, enabling spectators to meditate further on its allure, as well as their own responses' (2006, 19). She suggests these returns are often driven by the 'desire to recapture and to understand the emotions the film initially elicited' (Ibid.). Klinger's reasoning illustrates the affective resonances behind returning to *The Piano* and the potential value of doing so, as the substantive body of literature surrounding Campion's work attests. It remains her most discussed and theorised work, becoming a focal point of

Campion studies.[3] The film's significance is such that it continues to attract a range of readings and approaches, applied in various wider contexts, including auteurism and national identity.[4]

This chapter reflects upon this body of work and seeks to complicate it by offering a detailed close reading of *The Piano* that focuses on the role of music, silence, and sound. In returning to the film, I take an interdisciplinary approach to consider the contribution these elements make to our understanding of Ada, her actions, and treatment. The analysis foregrounds the haptic potential of music, and its capacity to generate an affective, embodied response in the audience. As Margaret Jolly observes in her own 'looking back' on the film, a central facet of *The Piano*'s consolidation as a site of continued scholarly interest is its combination of 'extraordinary critical acclaim, popular success and subsequent controversy' (2009, 99). It has attracted such interest that its reception and subsequent interpretations are themselves a source of debate. Ruth Barcan and Madeleine Fogarty reflect upon the discourses surrounding the film as 'particular and striking' and outline a series of interpretative frameworks that circulated following its release, which 'overlap and overlay each other', informing how the film is read and understood (1999, 3). Through this, they consider what an academic performance of the film constitutes, noting patterns in the readings of Ada's agency, the importance of sound and silence, the complexities of the film's relationship to eroticism and sexual violence, and readings of its narrative as myth. The exploration of Campion's aesthetic, narrative, and thematic preoccupations has led to the film becoming a significant touchstone for scholars of feminist cinema, either when explicitly positioned as a feminist text, or as a focal point to engage with women's filmmaking.[5] Numerous Campion scholars have argued that her films and the issues they typically engage with can be described as feminist, whether through their feminist resonances or the expression of feminist concerns. Campion herself defines her work more broadly, describing it as opposing patriarchal norms, noting the significance of women taking ownership of their stories and by extension, their lives (Muir 2018, n.p.). This takes on importance in relation to *The Piano*; the representation of Ada's wilfulness and reluctance to conform, and her position as a site of identification for women, remain potent elements of the film's affective and emotive power.

By speaking for and about women, Campion's films speak to and are loved by women in return, as Kennedy Fraser (1999), amongst others, has remarked. *The Piano* occupies an elevated position in such discussions, holding a particular resonance for women who identify with Ada or are inspired by her strength. Dana Polan outlines how the 'profound, intense bonding with *The Piano*' (2001, 22) felt by many women has led to the film, as Klinger describes, 'taking up sustained residence in their imaginations and emotions' (2006, 19). Polan and Klinger's comments are similarly reflected in Stephen Crofts's study of the film's global reception, where he notes that there 'was a significant gender dimension to the film's audience' (2000, 139) making a correlation between the 'strong identifications' displayed in response to *The Piano*'s feminist subject-matter and female subjectivity, and comparable behaviour exhibited by the readership of romantic literature (Ibid., 153). This is evident in ongoing scholarly fascination with the film and the impassioned, often intensely personal responses it inspires (such as those by Klinger, Sobchack, and Gillett) which give voice to the feelings shared by the women Polan describes.

THE PIANO AND SPECTATORSHIP: EMOTIONALITY, PHENOMENOLOGY, MUSICALITY

The Piano's critical reception is characterised by the willingness (or unwillingness) of these critics to express and explore feelings invoked by the film. For instance, Lizzie Francke's review for *Sight and Sound* considers her experience of the film, its impact, and what it asks of its audience. She writes: 'For a while I could not think, let alone write, about *The Piano* without shaking. Precipitating a flood of feelings, *The Piano* demands as much a physical and emotional response as an intellectual one' (Francke 2000, 170). Francke's reaction is both typical of the intense, embodied responses to the film, and atypical, in that it makes an early argument for the need to approach it with both mind and body, with an openness towards its emotive and affective capacities. This contrasts to Stuart Klawans's succinct and damning reaction for *The Nation*, in which he states, 'the film gives reason nothing to do', illustrating a lack of openness to emotion (2000, 189). Indeed, Ada's behaviours and the world she inhabits are driven by passion and emotion rather than logic and reason. It is fair to suggest that while *The Piano* 'speaks to' Francke, it does not 'speak to' Klawans. These two examples are extreme in their opposition but their inclusion here is purposeful: to highlight the oppositional readings the film generates, how structures of feeling and gender norms impact them, and thus, how the film is understood. However, I do not wish to suggest that this binary of emotion/reason exists solely across gendered lines.[6] Campion's work attracts critics and scholars with certain sensibilities. Moreover, her films operate within particular aesthetic, narrative and thematic confines, explore feeling, and through characters like Stewart, critique the reluctance to express emotion. Many of Campion's other male characters are jealous and repressed, defined by their emotional stiltedness, including *The Portrait of a Lady*'s (1996) Gilbert Osmond (John Malkovich). However, the depiction of John Keats (Ben Whishaw) in *Bright Star* (2009) is a notable exception, with Keats living in a time where his openness to feeling was inherently linked to creativity and writing as a Romantic poet.

The Piano's continued significance and endurance is contingent on its own encouragement of expressions of feeling, evident in the psychoanalytical, phenomenological, and feminist analyses dedicated to it. Within the field of film phenomenology, both *The Piano* and *In the Cut* (2003) are considered significant texts, naturally suited to phenomenological readings and discussions of embodied spectatorship (Richard 2018). Seminal writings by Sue Gillett and Vivian Sobchack on *The Piano* attest to the film's affective power and its impact on the body, complicating models of cinematic spectatorship. Privileging discussion of the senses, personal reflection forms the basis of many phenomenological readings of the film. Gillett observes, '*The Piano* affected me very deeply. I was entranced, moved, dazed' (1995, 286). Sobchack reflects similarly, declaring, 'Campion's film moved me deeply, stirring my bodily senses and my sense of my body' (2004, 61). Notable here is the depth of their shared embodied reaction, and their desire to make connections between mind and body. Sobchack (2004) developed this into discussion of cinema as a sensorium, where the viewer becomes a cinesthetic subject confounded by their synaesthetic experience – feeling by seeing – also demonstrated in Gillett's description of her dazed state. Gail Jones is one of the few to connect this scholarship to *The Piano*'s haptic potential. Drawing on Marks, Jones notes the reaction of Sobchack and others as being indicative of both 'the sensuous power of the movie', and 'its capacity to implicate the viewer's body' (2007, 14). However, this discussion is limited to the film's narrative and thematic preoccupations with touch and being touched, rather than considering how this operates at a textual-aural level, which I will now examine in more detail.

The film's score offers a natural entry point to build a textually located reading of the haptic qualities of Campion's aesthetic and how this is expressed in *The Piano*. Nyman's score performs several functions that demonstrate the film's haptic potential and its affective resonances. Key to understanding this element of Nyman's score is to consider how it functions both within diegetic space and beyond it, articulating the relationship between mind, body, and the senses. Nyman's work on *The Piano* is itself a source of interest and debate, maintaining cultural value distinct from the film, extending into various avenues, including live performance, and licensing for classical compilation albums. In an interview for the film's Special Edition DVD, Nyman reflected upon the creative process of scoring the film, and its cultural impact, saying 'the soundtrack went beyond a soundtrack', taking on its own life (2006, n.p.).

Just as Nyman's score is not only music, Ada's piano is not just an instrument. Her piano, and the music produced by it, offer her an outlet for expression, becoming her voice and literal extension of her body in the absence of her own speech. As Nyman describes, 'she formulates an emotional world by composing music' (Tims 2012, n.p.). The significance of music to Ada's character required a new approach, following Campion's desire for something different from the modernist style of Nyman's score for Peter Greenaway's *The Draughtsman's Contract* (1982). Nyman envisaged Ada as a 'radical composer' (Nyman 2006, n.p.), building a composite soundscape drawing upon nineteenth-century influences including salon music and popular Scottish folk songs combined with the twentieth-century minimalism with which he is typically associated.[7] This 'process of cultural layering and sedimentation' creates a musical voice for Ada with clear historical referents while maintaining its own identity (Tincknell 2011, 280). Claudia Gorbman summarises that, in musical terms, the results were considered 'simplistic, anachronistic, and relentless' (2000, 43). She offers a more complex reading that considers the emotional and affective value of the score, distinct from its function as music by arguing that the film 'disregards the paradigm of music as illustration' (Ibid., 53).[8] Drawing attention to its expressive qualities, Gorbman asserts that Nyman's score contributes to the collapse, or blurring of diegetic, non-diegetic, and metadiegetic spaces (Ibid., 54). This distinction acknowledges that music in *The Piano* is allied to feeling and the expression of emotion, while also functioning differently to other films where pianos and piano playing are significant, including *Letter From An Unknown Woman* (Max Ophüls 1948), *Shine* (Scott Hicks 1998) and *The Pianist* (Roman Polanski 2002). This difference even extends to music within Campion's own work, such as the sequence in *Holy Smoke* (1999) where Ruth (Kate Winslet) sings along to Alanis Morissette's 'You Oughta Know' (1995) while driving in the outback. While this moment tells us something about Ruth's rebellious spirit, and Morissette's music can be said to 'speak for' her when she sings, Ada's music is her own, something that emanates from and is produced by her.[9] The natural, practised ease with which she plays reinforces the depth of connection between Ada and her piano, 'so that the relationship between body, performance, self and object is thoroughly entwined' (Tincknell 2011, 282).

How are the intricacies of this relationship represented? The narrative of *The Piano* is structured around two interlinked journeys, one geographical and one emotional. Ada's arrival in New Zealand to enter an arranged marriage with Stewart leaves her unmoored and isolated. Until reunited with her piano, she is a stranger in a strange land. Beyond daughter Flora (Anna Paquin) and the belongings that survived the crossing, the piano is the only familiar thing in her new surroundings, her only link to her old life in Scotland. As the opening sequence at the McGrath family estate illustrates, it is the only way she can express herself unaided and unfiltered, without the written notes or sign language she and Flora share. It is the emotional journey that I am most interested in, and in the analysis that follows, I map out significant moments of that journey through Ada's piano playing, examining how these scenes function to express different facets of her character. Discussion of possession and agency, expression and exchange, and resistance and endurance will illustrate how the film's affective register reveals its emotional potential, and how the haptic response is constructed and invoked through it.

'THE PIANO IS MINE. IT'S MINE!': POSSESSION AND AGENCY

Ada's written declaration to Stewart – 'The Piano is mine. It's mine!' – provokes not understanding but disdain. He dismisses her passion, and later, her anger. To Stewart, her plea to keep the instrument is selfish, and her refusal to teach Baines is obstinate. To Ada, this is not, as her husband suggests, a sacrifice for the good of the family, but rather a violation, the severity of which Stewart never comprehends and from which Ada never recovers. These opposing reactions set up a tension that exists from the moment that Ada and Flora land on the beach; no one else understands the significance of the piano as they do. Through the film's *mise-en-scène*, the viewer gains intimate knowledge of Ada, coming to understand the piano's centrality in her life as an object of self-expression that gives voice to her feelings. The intensity of the connection between Ada and the piano is shown through overt patterns of editing, particularly when Ada is initially forced to leave the piano behind on the beach. In a shot-reverse-shot pattern, Ada looks down on the silent and solitary piano from the cliff's edge (Figure 4.2). Felicity Coombs observes that this 'provides a strange opening of our *knowing* of the piano' existing neither in its expected

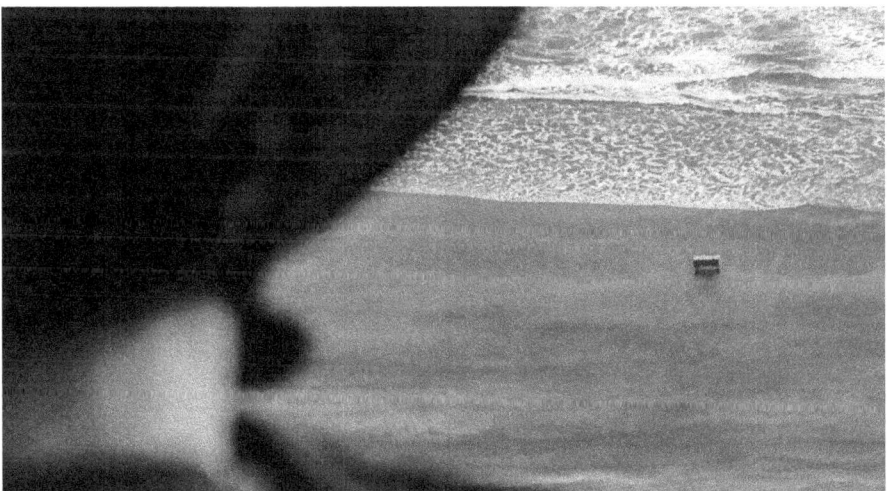

Figure 4.2 Ada watches over her piano on the beach

place nor performing its usual function (1999, 89, emphasis in original). Central to the 'strange' qualities Coombs identifies is the framing and composition of this sequence. The over-the-shoulder shot, in which Ada's bonnet rim frames the piano, allows both Ada and the piano to appear simultaneously. A medium close-up of a forlorn Ada looking towards the piano closes the sequence. From this moment on, she is leaving more than a prized possession behind; she is leaving part of herself.

Narratively and thematically, the treatment of Ada's musical ability within the film is distinct from that outside it. Rather than be impressed by her playing, those around her are intimidated and unnerved. Aunt Morag (Kerry Walker) memorably defines Ada's playing as strange, altogether different from Nessie's (Geneviève Lemon) 'plain and true' style. Instead, Morag characterises it as something that cannot be taught, 'like a mood that passes into you'. She continues, 'to have a sound creep inside you is not at all pleasant'. Of course, that sound comes from Ada as an emotional conduit. While Morag's description of Ada's playing is negative, she is nonetheless affected by it, her embodied reaction implicit. Her statements simultaneously deny and acknowledge Ada's agency, and mirror the intense extra-diegetic reactions felt by audiences and critics, extending beyond the emotional into the physical. For instance, Laleen Jayamanne has described experiencing sympathetic finger pain in response to witnessing Stewart severing Ada's own finger (2001, 48). Jayamanne's reaction illustrates that the film's relationship to materiality, texture, and touch are central to our understanding of its affective and emotive potential. As suggested earlier, these form part of the film's narrative and thematic concerns, but they are also expressed at an aesthetic level. Calling attention to the material and the tactile, they exemplify Marks's concept of haptic visuality. Building upon the philosophies of Deleuze and Riegl, Marks argues that film can be 'impressionable and conductive, like skin' (2000, xi). Emphasising cinema's tactile qualities, she describes cinema as being 'something we viewers brush up against like another body' (Ibid.).

The Piano is exemplary of haptic cinema, narratively, thematically, and aesthetically facilitating the haptic look by focusing upon touch, and by encouraging the embracement of the senses. This results in an embodied, affective response in the audience, which Marks considers central to the appeal of haptic cinema. This haptic relationship and its affective meaning are constructed through our connection with Ada and her piano. It is intensified by an increasing sense of intimacy created through Campion's aesthetic, which is naturally allied to the haptic and the phenomenological. For Hilary Neroni, Campion's style allows her to 'put into practice her female characters' ways of seeing and desiring' (2012, 290), which reinforces Marks's assertion that haptics is a 'feminist visual *strategy*' (1998, 337, emphasis in original). However, Marks's reasoning stems from feminist visual traditions as opposed to any obvious feminine qualities, existing outside of phallocentric models and modes of vision, which resonates with Campion's own statements regarding her work. Repeatedly eschewing the feminist label, deeming it too limiting, she describes her filmic mode of representation as having a 'feminist structure', noting that it remains one facet of her approach (Fendel 1999, 87). Her films may be better described as a space that has, as Kathleen McHugh puts it, 'explored and cultivated female voices, their silences, their delusions, their insights, and their passions' (2001, 197). This exploration and cultivation is characterised by an attention to detail, to texture, and to materiality that is expressed through the use of close-ups, which re-centre the filmic gaze away from the male towards the female (Figure 4.3). Campion's women are passionate, actively desiring, and obsessively engage in their respective passions as an expressive outlet; whether writing for Janet Frame (Kerry Fox) in *An Angel at my Table* (1990), dressmaking for Fanny Brawne (Abbie Cornlish) in *Bright Star*, or Frannie Avery's (Meg Ryan) love of poetry in *In the Cut*, artistic expression and the appreciation of it is a recurring thematic thread in Campion's work, traceable back to Ada and her piano. Through Campion's aesthetic, the detail of these women's lives is rendered in ways that are embodied and relatable – ink, fabric and thread, tears and blood.

In *The Piano*, these aesthetic choices draw attention not only to the texture and detail within Ada's world, but also her piano and those who interact with it. The instrument becomes an object of fetishisation with value and weight – it is a site of bargain, of expression, of resistance – that extends beyond its cultural significance and elevated position within Victorian domestic space.[10]

Figure 4.3 Texture

The piano's presentation within the film complicates Marks's idea that haptic cinema 'does not invite identification with a figure so much as it encourages a bodily relationship between the viewer and the video image' (1998, 332). We identify almost solely with Ada, but that relationship may be better classified in terms of the 'dynamic subjectivity between looker and image' (Ibid.). While the film's haptic capacities are defined in terms of reciprocity, the piano itself is the film's central haptic object – the natural extension of Ada – around which everything else is organised, and its music is the focus of the film's emotive and affective resonances. Its every interaction with the world is motivated and activated by touch. In close-up, we see those who embrace this and those who resist it. To reinforce this structuring, whenever Ada plays her piano, the camera lingers upon its wood and ivory surfaces. This attention remains even when the piano itself is physically absent. Home alone with Flora, and longing to play, Ada carves out the pattern of the keys on Stewart's kitchen table, using it as a substitute to accompany Flora's singing. Her connection to the instrument is such that it does not need to be present, nor does she need to really hear its sounds. Her music is learned, familiar, part of her memory (and Flora's). Upon Stewart's return, Ada backs away from the table, and he lifts the tablecloth, tracing the newly revealed keys, clearly lacking the understanding and familiarity Ada displays.

Over the course of the film, both Ada and the blind piano tuner (Bruce Allpress) Baines recruits are shown to have their own distinct intimate relationships with the instrument that are defined by touch. Ada's fingertips travel deftly across its keys, her feet depress the pedals to change its tone and sustain sound. The piano tuner, meanwhile, offers a different perspective on the instrument, and is a significant exception to the otherwise gendered lack of feeling in response to the piano itself. Through him, we see how Ada's voice is constructed, expressed in the extended close-ups of its hammers and strings as he meticulously tunes it. This sequence draws attention to the relationship between both sound and image and sound and the body, and is the first indicator of sound's haptic potential. The tuner's knowledge of the instrument is like Ada's, built upon sound and touch, but expressed differently. Their care and understanding of the piano stands in stark contrast to Aunt Morag, Nessie, and Stewart's reactions to it. Within these regimes of touch, Stewart begins the film with the least understanding of its value and ends with the knowledge of why the piano was worth more to Ada than anything (and perhaps anyone) else. His choice to damage its top with an axe prefigures the violence he later enacts upon Ada's fleshly body, motivated by jealousy and rage. The piano brings Ada joy in ways he cannot replicate. It is the symbol of what he cannot achieve and the woman he cannot possess. Rendering both the piano and Ada silent is an active refusal of the desire to touch, and to embrace feeling.

The piano's significance within the narrative is defined by people's reactions to its presence, in all their extremes. Campion's aesthetic choices in her representation of the piano as an object – both cultural and haptic – adheres to Marks's notion that 'haptic images draw viewers close and open their senses, making them feel connected and vulnerable to the beheld' (2015, 277). For Ada and the audience, the piano is the 'beheld' Marks references, made object and tangible. We learn to love the piano as Ada does, which is why Stewart's purposeful destruction of it feels so brutal. However, this reaction only occurs because of the emotive, affective, and haptic resonance that has accumulated over the course of the film, stemming from, in Coombs's terms, our 'knowing' of the piano, and its connection both with and to Ada. To Stewart, Ada and her piano are distinct entities, but to the audience, they are one and the same.

'I DON'T THINK OF MYSELF AS SILENT': EXPRESSION AND EXCHANGE

The intimacy of Campion's aesthetic reveals and reinforces its relationship to the haptic, creating its own meta-reflexive narrative regarding the value and meaning of touch. These visual cues, reminders of the body and embodiment, encourage the embracement of the narrative's emotionality, considered as lines of feeling, rather than structures. Lines of feeling are not only connective, but are also conductors of affect, with Ada and the rope being an example of their potency. The privileging of the senses and the openness to feeling allows Michael Nyman's score and, thus, Ada's voice, to 'pass into' the audience, just as it does for characters within the diegesis. However, the film's affective dimension – its haptic qualities and the position of these within the film's overall affective register – are not limited to the visual. As argued earlier, *The Piano* opens up the opportunity to examine the haptic potential of sound. Marks argues sound exists as part of a wider kinaesthetic response – the resonance of bass notes in the chest, hairs standing on end – but also 'operates along a dialectic similar to that of haptic and optical visuality' (2000, 183–4). Like the eye, the ear cannot touch images, but, as with haptic visuality, the perception of what we hear changes our experience of sounds: 'We *listen* for specific things, while we *hear* ambient sound as an undifferentiated whole' (Ibid., 183, emphasis in original). Marks's distinction between hearing and listening is small, but significant. Ada's playing, while framed as natural, operates differently from dialogue; it is akin to how a song performed in musicals functions as a mode of expression for inner thoughts and feelings. Though the narrative rupture they represent is not as defined, Ada's performances offer moments of emotional spectacle, changing the mode of viewing and its affective intensity. Following Marks, we go from hearing to listening and in doing so, our connection to Ada intensifies.

Central to this intensity is Ada's disembodied voice. Only speaking directly to the audience in her 'mind's voice' twice, Campion uses the device sparingly, and never at the expense of the musical line of expression. The bookend narration functions on an affective and emotive level, aligned to moments of narrative and emotional significance, but they also occupy a conventional position where we enter and exit Ada's world. Beyond this, her voice largely exists in the body of her piano. Whether in gestures of signing and writing, or in the melodies Ada composes, Feona Attwood argues these disembodiments are also displacements that 'disrupt synchronicity and make a kind of gap in her positioning as insufficient, known, lacking' (1998, 88). This extends beyond the lack of understanding Ada experiences from others to a lack of understanding toward herself. As such, *The Piano* is a journey of self-discovery, facilitated through an exploration of identity and expression that exists outside or beyond language, where speech is supplanted by music.[11] The notion of Ada's voice as either embodied or disembodied requires further qualification when considered in terms of her relationship with her piano. Richard Leppert's notion of music as an 'embodied abstraction', which takes account of a musician's physicality when playing, offers useful insight (1995, 22). For Leppert, music is an embodied, phenomenological practice, like theatre or dance. Its relationship to the body is integral to how music signifies and generates meaning:

> The body, simultaneously site, sight, and possessing sight, is an object of tactile sensation and an aural phenomenon. The body *sounds*: it is audible; it hears. Sound constitutes the atmosphere supporting and confirming life on and in the terrain of the body.
>
> (Ibid., xix, emphasis in original)

This dynamic and symbiotic relationship is heard and felt in *The Piano*. Music is the film's expressive language and Ada's language of expression. Its notes are her lexicon, and its melodies her rhythm of speech. McHugh argues that its usage changes what would traditionally 'be perceived as non-diegetic background music [into an] ethereal diegetic narrational voice' (2001, 250). This voice is central to how we understand Ada and the value of her piano. The material site of her self-expression, it ultimately becomes a commodity – and thus a site of exchange – for Stewart and Baines because Ada assigns value to it (Zarzosa 2010, 401–2).

Ada's melodies and moods become familiar and, therefore, easily read. While this attentiveness is largely due to the figurative repetition within Nyman's compositions, created to mimic Ada's lifetime of practice, her voice carries qualities that change through her playing style. The dynamic deviations within Ada's playing – tempo, mood, volume, force – are narratively and emotionally significant. Kathryn Kalinak's model of music's expressive function also extends into the realm of the affective, whereby music is 'both articulator of screen expressions and initiator of spectator response [which] binds the spectator to the screen by resonating affect between them' (1992, 87). In this affective feedback loop, predicated upon openness towards feeling, music in *The Piano* creates an acute awareness of changes in Ada's emotions. The primary feeling she expresses when playing is joy, demonstrated in the beach scene where she is first reunited with her piano. Close-ups capture her smiling face, and then her eyes closed in rapture as she plays; she is at ease in her new environment for the first time.

There is a single yet significant instance where she does not play her own composition. During a lesson with Baines, to express her anger at the escalation of his touching, Ada plays a 'clunky Chopin waltz' (Jones 2007, 37). Its loudness and lack of fluidity is purposeful; Ada does not play her own music differently, but instead borrows the music of another, whose style is distinct from her own. This is the musical equivalent of a shout or yell, while also signalling her refusal to engage with Baines. Its distinctiveness grabs Baines's attention, making him aware that she is not comfortable with the increased intimacy and, moreover, she will not be used or abused. This scene makes clear the expressive function of music within the film and Ada's connection to her piano. Here, Ada's voice is not displaced, it is an extension of Ada's mind and body, always clearly and resolutely articulating her feelings, a quality reflected in Ada's opening voiceover narration. Michel Chion observes that Ada's language choices describe her negotiation of her muteness not through music, but through her piano: 'Ada does not say "because of the music", or "because I'm playing music", nor does she say, "because of *the* piano"' (2007, 93, emphasis in original). Instead, Ada declares that she doesn't think herself silent because of her piano. Her ultimate choice emphasises possession, underlining that the piano belongs to her, while also being part of her.

'MY WILL HAS CHOSEN LIFE!?': RESISTANCE AND ENDURANCE

From the opening of the film, Ada's will is as defining a characteristic as her muteness and intriguingly, the two traits become intertwined. She is arguably, as McHugh suggests, '[m]ute by will if not by choice' (2007, 79), and her choice of silence is as significant as the choice to live. Ada's choices, their effects, and subsequent affects are fundamental to recognising how the film endures, and why Ada remains such a potent source of identification. The power of these choices lies in her making any at all. She did not select Stewart for herself, nor did she wish to leave Scotland, but silence and survival are things she chooses to take control of. These choices become wilful acts of resistance that characterise how she is perceived and treated by others. Always defined by her difference, Ada tells us that her father calls her silence a 'dark talent', one that makes her, in Aunt Morag's words, 'a strange creature'. By Ada's own admission, the image of herself and her piano in the deep is her 'weird lullaby'. In Nelson, both her muteness and the mutilation she suffers lead her to being called 'the town freak'. However, this otherness, this contrariness, is something she embraces and even enjoys, something 'which satisfies'. This ownership holds its own power and is empowering. Ada is unlike many filmic heroines, much less those found in period narratives; she is, however, the archetypal Campion heroine – the blueprint for all who follow her.

Central to *The Piano*'s endurance are the mysteries surrounding Ada's backstory, particularly the origin of her muteness and the identity of Flora's father. The latter is comically and dramatically explained by Flora herself, but the truthfulness of this account is neither validated nor refuted, while the former remains the film's central mystery. For Agustín Zarzosa, the 'mystery lies not in the meaning of what she would wish to say, but in her wish to say nothing at all' (2010, 405). Once more couched in terms of resistance and defiance, these multiple forms of ambiguity are inextricably bound with Ada's identity, reflected in Attwood's description of her as 'an unsolved riddle, which refuses to be reduced to logic or to complementarity' (1998, 100). The refusal that Attwood identifies contributes to wider understandings of the film's relationship to trauma. Jones argues that *The Piano* is '[c]haracterised by wounding, forms of forgetting and loss', whereby Ada's resistance can be read as a coping mechanism (2007, 54).[12] Her greatest act of resistance is to survive following the severing of her fingertip. Stewart's choice too is significant, which Gillett acknowledges in her description of the scene. She writes:

> It is her finger which he chooses, her means of connection with language. It is no accident. The axe is brought down upon her index finger, index of her speech, sign of her tenderness. He has meant to clip her wing, to keep her on the ground.
>
> (1995, 279)

It is also a means of breaking her will and taking back control. For Jones, the 'painful and visceral power' of the violence is derived from making 'the severing of a single finger into an utter catastrophe' (2007, 58). The gravity of the incident stems from the audience's knowledge of the piano and Ada. This is not just severing a finger, it is severing the link between Ada's body and that of her piano. With one strike of his axe, Stewart cuts off her method of communication and emotional expression.

The intensity of this moment and its power to shock does not diminish and is testament to the film's emotional, affective, and haptic qualities, which are themselves amplified by Campion's use of slow-motion, making the violence as surreal as it is horrendous.[13] We feel the axe's strike and Ada's pain. The extreme nature of the moment is, one would imagine, enough to break Ada's silence and yet, it does not. Ada resists and endures, and so does the piano, despite damage. On the soundtrack, as Neil Robinson describes, 'the piano asserts itself' (1999, 27). As Ada rises, unsteady, the score – Ada's music, Ada's words – fill the silence, the only time it 'exists beyond the moment of its writing and continues to articulate for its silent author', illustrating how the film constructs Ada's emotional world and the transcendent quality of her music (Ibid.). It also raises the question of how Ada will survive beyond the immediate aftermath of her mutilation.

The ultimate answer comes in what is perhaps the most divisive sequence of *The Piano*, when the narrative shifts to Nelson. These scenes are notably different from the rest of the film. In stark contrast to the dark, naturalistic tones that otherwise dominate the film's colour palette, their comparative brightness is at once dream-like and artificial, echoing the hallucinatory sequences that feature in Campion's later work, including *The Portrait of a Lady* and *Holy Smoke*. Ada's move to Nelson introduces a much-changed version of her, with her 'mind's voice' employed to give context to her new surroundings. Her voiceover tells us she is now employed as a piano teacher and learning to speak. She plays a different piano with the aid of a prosthetic metal fingertip, made for her by Baines, displayed in almost fetishised close-ups (Figure 4.4). The piano is new. It is not Ada's piano, but just a piano, and the instrument has changed as

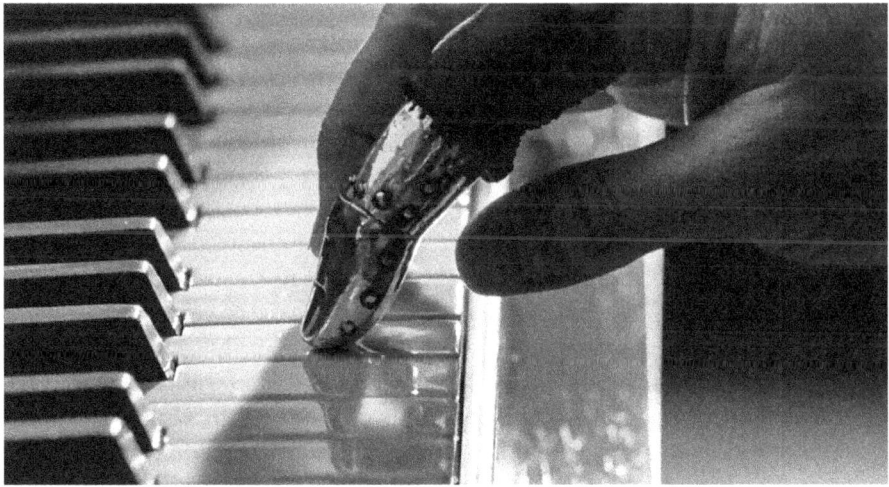

Figure 4.4 Ada's prosthetic finger

much as its player. A disconnect, a gap, as Attwood would have it, has opened between them. Unlike the dull tapping produced by her earlier playing on Stewart's table, the prosthetic's metallic tap produces a different, unnatural sound. This time, the change is a permanent one that immediately registers, due to our familiarity with Ada's music. The intrusion of the prosthetic indicates that her connection to and with the instrument is no longer there, and the character of her voice is altered, signifying a changed relationship with herself and the world. In line with Elizabeth Grosz's concept of prosthetic augmentation, both Ada's identity and creative capabilities have been redefined through accommodation (Baines making the fingertip) and incorporation (Ada re-learning to play using the prosthetic) (2005, 152). Baines's choice of metal also carries additional symbolism within the wider context of the film. Ada's every strike upon the keys now brings with it an additional note, generated by the contact between the metal prosthetic and the ivory keys. This in turn recalls – albeit in a softer tone – the cleaving of Stewart's axe and with it, the memory of Ada's trauma and all she has endured.

CONCLUSION

By way of conclusion, I wish to return to the image of Ada tied to her piano – my primary reason for revisiting the film. Barbara Klinger aptly describes it as an 'arresting image', defined in terms of its expressive, mystifying qualities, which are 'deeply related to its affective dimension' (2006, 24). The relationship Klinger draws out provides a catalyst to explore the intersections between music and film, affect and haptics, to examine the spectatorial experience of *The Piano*, how it is remembered and continues to be discussed. As this chapter demonstrates, the film invites such returns. Discursively rich, *The Piano* prompts deeply personal, often gendered, and embodied responses. These discussions are typified by their author's relationship to the film's narrative and the degree to which they identify with its protagonist, Ada. The strength of this relationship and the degree of identification is determined through the intimacy of Campion's aesthetic, its expressive use of music, and the centrality of touch. *The Piano* is intrinsically allied to the phenomenological and, as this chapter has illustrated, it withstands sustained analysis of its emotive, affective, and haptic capacities, encouraging consideration of the affective and embodied dimensions of cinema and their impact upon how and why *The Piano*, its soundtrack, and imagery continue to endure. Moreover, it establishes the value of expanding haptic readings in feminist film scholarship in order to examine our spectatorial relationship with sound as well as vision, decentring the primacy of the image in close textual analysis.

Why, then, is the image of Ada and the rope so central to my own experience of *The Piano*? It symbolises a multiplicity of meanings, forming part of a series of potential endings, including Ada's near drowning and her new life in Nelson. It draws attention to the affective link between mind and body that characterises both the film's diegetic world and the audience's embodied haptic response to it. A relationship once defined wholly through sound is now marked by its absence. For Ada, the connection she shares with her piano, although physically severed, never truly breaks. It exists beyond language, beyond sound. It transcends all, even the trauma of a severed fingertip. Her survival is her greatest show of will, and the clearest indication of why the film remains such an important touchstone for audiences and scholars alike. The emotional and affective resonances of the film lie in Ada's resilience, and her desire to keep playing in spite of those who wish to silence her.

NOTES

1. All dialogue references from Campion (1993).
2. For the origin of this work, see Marks (1998, 331–48). The theory emphasises embodied reading, focused upon materiality and tactility of film through the contact made between it and the viewer. The term haptic as Marks and I use it originates from art historian Alois Riegl's writing regarding the loss of tactility within art and the figurative sense of space: see Iversen (2003, 78–9).
3. See, for example, Jones (2007) and Margolis (2000).
4. For auteurist studies of Campion see Polan (2001); Verhoeven (2007), and Fox (2011). In relation to national cinemas and national identity Campion is discussed in Radner, Fox, and Bessière (2009).
5. The literature is too numerous to detail here, but for an indication of its feminist positioning see Bruzzi (1995, 257–66). For discussion in relation to women's filmmaking see Cook (2007, 468–72).
6. Critiques of the film in relation to sexism and sexual violence transcend this binary. For example, Sue Gillet quotes a letter from Lisa Sarmas to *Arena Magazine* entitled 'What Rape is?' (1995, 286). Sarmas explicitly defines Ada and Baines's relationship as rape, contributing to broader discussion that viewed their bargain at best as sexual harassment, and at worst, prostitution.
7. The similarities between 'The Heart Asks Pleasure First' and the traditional Scottish hymn, 'Gloomy Winter's Noo Awa', was a source of debate. Pwyll ap Siôn describes its use as a 'melodic and periodic reconstruction' (2007, 193) rather than a copy, with the harmonic changes made reflective of Nyman's compositional intertextuality. This interpretation is in line with Nyman's comments, citing it as part of the numerous influences Ada herself would draw upon while composing.
8. However, there is a notable exception to this in the moments following Stewart's axe attack, wherein the music can be read as illustrative of the mood within the scene.
9. Nyman's attention to detail as a composer is a significant factor in generating this feeling, but Holly Hunter's accomplishments as a pianist must also be acknowledged. Nyman consciously adapted the score to reflect her natural aptitude for what he, Campion, and producer Jan Chapman describe as 'emotional' and 'powerful' pieces. Campion and Chapman discuss this in "*The Piano* at 25" (Studiocanal 2018), reiterating points made on the commentary track for the *Special Edition* DVD in 2006.

10. For work on this in relation to *The Piano*, see Knight (2006, 23–34). The sociohistorical and cultural significance of pianos in this period are explored in Leppert (1995, 119–51).
11. Many scholars and critics have considered the significance of language and the film's relationship to it. Richard Allen's work focusing on the pre-linguistic is indicative of this (1999, 44–63]).
12. Jones, like many other scholars, questions the nature of Ada's past, associating Ada's father with possible acts of trauma within that past.
13. The impact of watching in 2018 amidst increased discussions around violence against women and the #MeToo movement are significant factors in its continued capacity to shock, and its endurance in the memory.

CHAPTER 5

'Only another man': Homosociality in Jane Campion's *Bright Star* and *The Power of the Dog*

Alexia L. Bowler

While it is true to say that Campion's work has been 'predominantly focused on forensic investigations of the female psyche' (Rooney 2021, n.p.), the director's films have arguably always been as much about men as they have been about women. Indeed, undercurrents of homosocial tendencies can often be found in Campion's works, which have a nuanced approach to the subtle power dynamics that exist between men, often upheld by the culture and institutions of the societies in which they live and love. Much has been written about female agency and subjectivity in Campion scholarship.[1] My chapter, however, engages with the central male figures in Campion's *Bright Star* (2009) and *The Power of the Dog* (2021). The Oscar-winning *The Power of the Dog*, Campion's first film released post-#MeToo, provides an opportune moment to consider those aspects of Campion's work that address men and masculinity, in light of her perceived role as feminist auteur intent on championing women's stories. Campion's work provides a rich tapestry of male figures and contentious masculinities alongside her female protagonists. The portraits Campion paints of these male figures often reveal the networks through which hegemonic masculinity operates and how it underpins the delimitation of women's self-exploration, their articulation as speaking subjects, and their creativity (via institutions of family, society, and heterosexual romance). Therefore, Campion's works often speak not only to the past but also to the present, not least in her latest film, which addresses post-#MeToo discourse around so-called 'toxic masculinity'.[2]

Campion's sustained address to the problem of men's masculinity can be seen in early works like *A Girl's Own Story* (1984), in which burgeoning female sexuality is placed side-by-side with ambiguous and threatening sexual attention from adult males, or in Osmond's (John Malkovich) gaslighting of Isabel

Archer (Nicole Kidman) in *The Portrait of a Lady* (1996), and in *In the Cut* (2003) which involves the brutal murder of women by a man whose modus operandi ironically includes courtship rituals. In Campion's television series, *Top of the Lake* (2013) and *Top of the Lake: China Girl* (2017), the director explores similar configurations of problematic masculinities which involve racially inflected femicide, sex-trafficking, and incest, in a world controlled by the narratives' various male authority figures. Alongside these figures, the nature of heteronormative masculinity also comes under scrutiny in films such as *The Piano* (1993), with Stewart's (Sam Neill) restrictive marital regimen, or PJ's (Harvey Keitel) attempted remedial (sexual) schooling of Ruth (Kate Winslet) in *Holy Smoke* (1999).

Accordingly, it is important to recognise that through the often misogynistic, homophobic and habitually heterosexist film worlds in which her female characters exist, Campion pays close attention to her male characters. In addressing Campion's adaptation of Thomas Savage's novel, *The Power of the Dog* (1967), and her exploration of the love-letters and ephemera of Fanny Brawne (Abbie Cornish) and John Keats (Ben Wishaw) in *Bright Star*, this chapter examines Campion's engagement with the power dynamics inherent in the hetero-patriarchal worlds in which her characters' lives are set. Charting the homosocial dynamic between Keats and his friend and fellow poet Charles Armitage Brown (Paul Schneider), I suggest that the exclusion of women from the creative space is countered by Campion's more inclusive vision of creative collaboration. Here, both sexes have equal claim to the marketplace of ideas (including women's re-inscription into our creative histories) and the productivity of men is enriched and enhanced by inclusion within the sphere of feminine influence. While *Bright Star* focuses on the tensions between the spaces accorded to men and women in a patriarchal world, I argue that in *The Power of the Dog* Campion poses questions about the effect of competing masculinities in a fiercely heteronormative and brutalising environment in which the hegemonic masculinity of the film's period admits no variation in its structural organisation. This, then, denies any validation to alternative masculinities and sexualities, or indeed any inclusion of 'the feminine' within men's lives. The oppositional, binaristic and essentialist structural patterns of the past, in Campion's latest work, suggest a life without fulfilment.

PROBLEMS OF RECEPTION: CHALLENGING THE FEMALE AUTEUR

In addressing Campion's treatment of men and masculinity, it is important to take account of the reception of her work as a filmmaker and her status as auteur. As a post-#MeToo movie, *The Power of the Dog* has been critically acclaimed for its portrayal of 'toxic masculinity'. However, the reception of Campion's films has often been inconsistent, specifically when it comes to representations of gender and sexuality; even at the start of Campion's career *Sweetie* (1989) was booed out of Cannes for its unflinching gaze at eccentric female characters, yet it is now a cult classic (Marshall 1996, n.p.). While *Bright Star* was generally hailed as Campion's return to form after two critically panned adaptations, *The Portrait of a Lady* and *In the Cut*, the film did not escape criticism of its apparent subsummation of Keats as the rightful focus of Campion's biopic. *The Power of the Dog*, too, did not escape censure in its unusual treatment of the cowboy.

Much of the criticism levelled at Campion has been highly gendered and strangely proprietorial. The nature of this criticism seemingly rests on her authority to tackle specific subjects or challenge material perceived to be canonical, or inappropriately risqué. A visceral response to *The Power of the Dog* came from actor Sam Elliott, who called the film a 'piece of shit' (Kirkland 2022, n.p.). As a star with a strong association with the Western in film and television, Elliott clearly felt able to denounce Campion (a New Zealander, who shot the film in New Zealand rather than Montana) as having no authority to understand what the myth of the West entails and he railed against the film's homosexual subtext, which he implied was ahistorical, saying:

> They made it look like – what are all those dancers that those guys in New York who wear bowties and not much else. [. . .] That's what all these fucking cowboys in that movie look like. They're all running around in chaps and no shirts. There's all these allusions to homosexuality throughout the fucking movie.
>
> (Ibid.)

Campion's response exposed the sexist and homophobic nature of Elliott's remarks, citing Italian director Sergio Leone's own filmmaking practice as proof positive of Elliott's regressive mindset:

> The West is a myth exposed. There's a lot of room on the range. I think it's a little bit sexist, because, you think about the number of amazing westerns that were made in Spain by Sergio Leone. I consider myself a creator and I think he sees me a woman or something lesser first, and I don't appreciate that.
>
> (Ibid.)

Embedded in her statement is a challenge to the habitual double standards applied to female directors which pit them unfavourably and unnecessarily against their male colleagues. Indeed, in 1996, *Variety* columnist Todd McCarthy negatively compared Campion's *The Portrait of a Lady* with period dramas directed by fellow auteurs Francis Ford Coppola (*Bram Stoker's Dracula*, 1992) and Martin Scorsese (*The Age of Innocence*, 1993). Today, Campion confirms she could not have produced a film like *The Power of the Dog* ten years ago: 'Knowing that it would be carried out by a woman, the financiers would have declined. There was this tenacious idea that women had neither the competence nor the authority to carry out a collective project, especially of this magnitude' – an idea that runs throughout criticism of Campion's work (Juarez 2022, n.p.).

Equally, while *Bright Star* was nominated for Cannes's highest honour, the Palme d'Or, the film didn't completely escape criticism. Campion was taken to task for diminishing the figure of Keats that, for some, was portrayed as overly effeminate: 'a man who cannot stand on his feet' (Alleva 2009, n.p.), who 'at times gets lost in the skirmishes between his companions' and 'seems always to be disappearing into a paneled wall or sofa or under a hedge' (Scott 2010, 511). Accusations of an injustice to Keats's poetry also abound, with complaints that Campion undermined the nature of the poet's sensuous, imagistic writing: Christopher Ricks suggested Campion's film did not 'respect [Keats's] writing' (2009, n.p.), merely providing illustrations of Keats's poems which undermined his literary and creative greatness. Other accusations included Campion's 'chronic tendency' towards underdeveloped characters and an apparent slackening in the narrative in the last half hour of the film (Alleva 2009, n.p.), which in one reviewer's mind was nothing more than 'a visual postmortem' of Keats and his work (Scott 2010, 512).

What is striking about these complaints is that they seek to challenge Campion's vision and creativity within the paradigms of what Tincknell, who questions the useability of the concept of auteur in women's film,[3] calls 'the authoritarian artist' and auteurist critical tradition, contingent as it is on a 'highly masculinist discourse of artistic creativity' (2013, 118). And yet media discourse has framed Campion as an auteur from *The Piano* (1993) onwards. Verhoeven discusses Campion's own ambivalence around the notion of auteur, noting Campion's recognition that there is an 'unpredictable relationship of constant reinvention between filmmaker and film' (2009, 60). This suggests that Campion herself sees the directorial role as 'someone engaged in a constant process of "becoming-author", each film a new opportunity to think through or enact her agency', pointing to 'the idea of filmmaking as a form of self-renewal' (Ibid., 61).

Thus, many of the critiques fail to recognise Campion's sense of her directorial self as an engaged, playful interpreter of the text at hand when adapting material. Indeed, in the process of adapting Henry James's novel, Campion and screenwriter Laura Jones considered it almost unfilmable until they realised that they were making 'the story of *Portrait of a Lady* interpreted by me, with some of the original dialogue' (Ciment 1999b, 178). We could suggest the same method at play in Campion's appropriative or 'interpretive' lens for *Bright Star*, which takes the letters, poems, and biographies of Keats as sources for her portrait of the Romantic poet and Fanny Brawne, promoting Brawne to equal status among her fellow creatives and in her relationship with Keats. Moreover, Campion's response to Elliott, regarding his comments about *The Power of the Dog* and the Western, similarly apprehends that cultural imaginaries like the West (and notions of masculinity) can be contested, reworked, and reshaped, or re-interpreted. Knowingly or not, Campion's own discourse of filmmaking echoes a feminist poststructuralist evaluation of both male and female subject as always already multiple, discontinuous, and in the process of becoming, and of an open exploration of sex and sexuality; in this way, Campion is in tune with the changing nature of gender politics, making it part of her praxis.

CAMPION'S HOMOSOCIAL LANDSCAPES

These gender politics are often embedded in the landscapes of Campion's works. Her films are often set in environments from which women are barred, are bystanders, or in which they are objects in a transaction of some kind. In *Bright Star*, while Campion's dialogue may be tempered to fit the nineteenth century, we see a familiar scenario, and in *The Power of the Dog*, Campion not only brings us into the world of one of the most mythologised heroes in American culture – the cowboy – but also situates us in yet another homosocial and hypermasculine environment. Often used to define a social connection, 'the homosocial' is popularly applied to close, typically non-sexual relationships between men. The term homosocial has also been used to suggest ways in which men seek to defend the patriarchal status quo of male privilege and so-called dominance over women. Frequently characterised as virulently homophobic and enacted through competition and exclusion, the construct of the homosocial is what Eve Kosofsky Sedgwick (2015) calls a discontinuity in the continuum of desire (that is, an affective and social bond) from homosocial to the homosexual, that isn't present in women's relations. According to Sedgwick, discontinuities between homosocial and homosexual are reinforced in patriarchal structures, both prohibited by an '"obligatory heterosexuality" [that is] built into male-dominated kinship systems, or [a] homophobia [that] is a *necessary* consequence of such patriarchal institutions as heterosexual marriage' (Ibid., 3, emphasis in original). Sedgwick uses the idea of the homosocial to discuss the multiplicity of men's intimate relationships and various types of desire legitimated through what she calls the 'male traffic in women' to validate homosocial relations while avoiding allegations of homosexual desire (at the other end of the spectrum) (Ibid., 26). This 'male traffic in women' addresses Western sex/gender and kinship systems in which the exchange of women within patriarchy (through marriage, for example) reify biological sex as a socially imposed divide between men and women. As a system, this division has been used to oppress women and maintain strict prohibitive structures in sexual relations, as well as to strengthen bonds between men.

This male traffic in women is demonstrable in both *Bright Star* and *The Power of the Dog*. In *Bright Star*, Campion provides her audience with a view of the homosocial creative world of Romantic poet John Keats and his circle of friends. It is a world disrupted by the 'very well stitched Little Miss Brawne in all her detail' according to Brown, who competes with Fanny for Keats's attention. In *The Power of the Dog*, too, the homophobic banter between Phil Burbank (Benedict Cumberbatch) and his cowherds at the Red Mill Hotel comes at the expense of the perceptibly effeminate Peter (Kodi Smit-McPhee) and the refined nature of the hotel with its linen and paper flowers, associated as it is with the domestic and therefore the feminine. These comments are exclusionary tactics designed to augment the homosocial nature of the Burbank gathering (of a group of all-male, unmarried cowherders) without endangering the obligatory heterosexuality to which Sedgwick refers.

In *Bright Star*, for Keats's friend and fellow poet, Brown, Fanny Brawne is a distraction to Keats's work and a disruption to the distinctly homosocial environment cultivated by Brown who, in a similar vein to Sedgwick's notion, clearly desires connection between himself and Keats, as fellow poet and male companion. The beginning of the film leaves no doubt as to the lively discourse of 'separate spheres' – a phenomenon of the nineteenth century that distinguished the public and social world of men (with access to knowledge, power, and money) from the domestic (pertaining to women). Fanny's intrusion into Keats and Brown's domain signifies a breach of this discrete world of men, and her attempts to penetrate these male spaces are thwarted by Brown at every opportunity. Holed up in his study with Keats, Brown can be seen shooing Fanny out of the room declaring: 'Men's room, men's room. Out, thank you: poets writing.' Later on, when Fanny and Keats's friendship is more established, Brown continues to bar Fanny's access to Keats by shutting windows, doors, and curtains before barking at her to get out. This hostile and exclusionary environment runs throughout the film as Brown acts as self-appointed gatekeeper to Keats, keeping the would-be lovers apart. Such gatekeeping can be seen in the male-only literary salons held at Brown's home; not only is this a place in which poetry is read, but ideas in the public domain are put to the test here. In later scenes too, fellow poets, friends, and patrons (all male) seek to direct Keats's recuperation from tuberculosis by moving him to Rome without consulting Fanny, to whom he is now betrothed. Denying agency to both Keats and Fanny – Keats feels unable to reject his friends' generosity, while Fanny's voice is ignored – these men claim the authority to decide the poet's fate.

Akin to Sedgwick's discussion of the 'two men, one woman' configuration in British literature, *Bright Star* grounds its rivalry as an erotic triangle including two men and one woman. However, Campion queers Sedgwick's 'erotic triangle': the 'prize' in this situation is the attention of Keats, rather than the conquest of Fanny. As Tincknell rightly notes, Fanny is not the 'object of exchange' (2013, 113). She is not,

> a passive and deferential figure readily satisfied by her inclusion in the charmed circle of Keats's literary-bohemian friends and associates, but [. . .] a defiantly resistant young woman whose pleasure in fashion is presented as a wholly legitimate articulation of selfhood.
>
> (Ibid.)

Fanny's resistance, her independence of mind and creative skill, challenges Brown's own artistry, as well as the homosocial bond between the two men. Quick to remark to Brown and Keats that her 'stitching has more merit and admirers than your two scribblings put together. And I can make money for it', Fanny moves into that perceived male space of creativity and commerce, her 'female masculinity' threatening the patriarchal homosocial order. Fanny's comment is subversive because it serves to expose Brown's contrived investment in a masculinity that values intellect, creativity, and productivity as exclusively male. It is a moment that challenges the homosocial bond between Keats and Brown in a way that Brown's later impregnation of his maid, Abigail (Antonia Campbell-Hughes), does not because Fanny's refusal to don the 'disguise' of appropriate femininity (as object of exchange) contests the validity of Brown's investment in patriarchal social norms. As Sedgwick contends: 'in any male-dominated society, there is a special relationship between male homosocial (*including* homosexual) desire and the structures for maintaining and transmitting patriarchal power: a relationship founded on an inherent and potentially active structural congruence' (2015, 25, emphasis in original). Fanny's female masculinity defies, or does not appropriately recognise, Brown's sentiment that exchange (intellectual, creative or economic) is for men and between men. Fanny's masculinisation queers the relationship between Brown, Keats, and herself because instead of neutralising the erotic charge (as 'object of exchange'), her female masculinity allows that erotic charge to circulate between all three. This, then, threatens Brown's status in Sedgwick's 'erotic triangle', as well as the homosociality of the relationship with Keats.

In addition, Fanny's creativity and productivity is something that Campion's film continually foregrounds in answer to Brown's accusations of indolence in the female sex (contradicting his own seeming lack of productivity within the films' narrative). Indeed, Fanny is constantly on the move and rarely seen prone, in contrast to both Brown and Keats. From the film's beginning, her status as creator and productive figure is foregrounded: in the opening credits Fanny is seen stitching a pillow slip in the early morning light (she is gifted at millinery and dressmaking), while also generously baking gifts for Keats's sick brother. Although it is well-understood that feminine creativity is something typically carried out in the private sphere, Fanny's earlier comments to Brown and Keats contest the consignment of those activities and their creative and economic value to the margins – an observation that bears up in light of Campion's continued statements about female productivity, marginalisation of female creatives and the limiting nature of a world in which only men's stories are put forward for view. As feminist scholars such as Gilbert and Gubar, Showalter, and Spender have all noted, women have previously been excluded or written out of history and denied their place in the history of production of cultural forms and meaning making.[4] In this way, women have been cut off from one another, creating a discontinuity and necessitating a re-inscription into public discourse, a project with which Campion's *Bright Star* is engaged.[5]

The latent queerness of *Bright Star* surfaces in *The Power of the Dog*, which is, according to the critics, an 'exquisitely crafted' drama signalling Campion's 'assured thematic shift to corrosive masculinity and repressed sexuality' (Rooney 2021, n.p.). Nonetheless, although this is Campion's most notably queer film to date, Campion's work has often engaged with the complicated nature of sexuality with undertones of homosocial relations between men, queered relationships and repressed sexuality. However, in *The Power of the Dog* Campion engages more obviously and directly with homosexuality and a range of competing masculinities by delivering a detailed study of one of the most traditional, stereotyped, and hypermasculinised figures in Western culture. Her brave, skilled, and wilderness-taming – if sometimes violent and aggressive – cowboy harks back to other modern Westerns; Ang Lee's *Brokeback Mountain* (2005) comes to mind as an equally lyrical Western from Annie Proulx's 1997 short story of the same name, with its emotionally complex male characters, homosocial landscape, and angst-ridden queer desire.

As a quintessential figure of the homosocial environment of the West promoted by Hollywood, the cowboy, according to Michael S. Kimmel, is an image that continues to be seen as the 'embodiment of the American spirit', and an ideal that the US has 'been trying to live up [to] ever since he appeared on the mythical historical stage' (2005, 94). Ironically, the emergence of the cowboy in literature and popular culture – predominantly in dime novels and Wild West shows of the travelling circuses in the late nineteenth century – came at the point of the figure's disappearance in the real world; that is, with the end of actual cattle drives, the lowly 'cow herder' becomes marketised as a glamorous and mythical Western frontiersman, consolidating a version of masculinity that promoted a figure willing to test and prove his worth in this regard. However, Kimmel argues that this frontiersman was nothing more than a 'masculinist fantasy' (Ibid., 32), a reaction against the increasing feminisation and domestication of nineteenth-century life. He further notes that men who continue to seek a 'grounding for gender identity' in 'the homosocial solace of the wilderness, the frontier, the West' (Ibid., 35), popularised in the 1980s mythopoetic men's movement, will find nothing but a hollowed-out mythical space.

But it is into this masculinist fantasy and mythical homosocial space of the West that Phil Burbank rides. Much like Brown in *Bright Star*, who prefers the company of men, Phil has little truck with women or domestic trappings and psychologically brutalises others he views as displaying femininity, which he sees as weakness. The antipathy towards the feminine is highlighted early on by Phil's treatment of Peter at the Red Mill Hotel, in which the cowboys dine during their cattle drive. Observing paper flowers on their table, Phil derides them as feminine, stating 'I wonder what little lady made these'. When Peter claims responsibility, Phil murmurs a mock apology, adding insult to injury by deriding Peter's waitering skills – a sign of refinement but perhaps also servility – ergo Peter's effeminacy. Peter's lisp, too, offers Phil another opportunity to mock, making the table erupt into laughter at what is seen as a further display of effeminacy. Rarely seen inside the house, which is itself a symbol of the civilising East with its panelled walls, carpets, and imported goods left by their parents, Phil's determination to avoid failure in mastering the frontier is informed by what he sees as a feminine weakness or softness displayed by his family, including his parents (Peter Carroll and Frances Conroy), Rose (Kirsten Dunst), George (Jessie Plemons), and (somewhat mistakenly) Peter. Ironically, Phil's investment in the image of the hypermasculine cowboy, as an antidote to his queer identity, condemns him to live amongst his men but be excluded from the pleasures of bathing and frolicking naked in companionship with the male cowhands. Therefore, Phil's homosexual identity is hidden, causing him pain, but that pain still has, as Kaufman states, 'a dynamic aspect' (1994, 150):

> We might displace it or make [pain] invisible, but in doing so we give it even more urgency [. . .] men learn to wear a suit of armour, that is, to maintain an emotional barrier from those around us to keep fighting and winning.
>
> (Ibid., 148)

This displacement, and acquisition of acquiescence to hegemonic masculinity, impels Phil to cruelty and a competitive masculinity in order for him to maintain his position within the homosocial but patriarchal and hegemonic hierarchy.

COMPETING MASCULINITIES

In men's masculinity studies, strong links are often made between homosociality and masculinity, but also with competitive tensions that substantiate any social grouping, leading to a hegemonic masculinity. According to R. W. Connell (1995) hegemonic masculinity provides a large-scale structural underpinning of gender relations, rather than something located in individual traits. As such, certain masculinities are 'more socially central, or more associated with authority and social power, than others [and presume] the subordination of nonhegemonic masculinities' (Connell and Messerschmidt 2005, 846).[6] Connell and Messerschmidt suggest that hegemonic masculinity works through production of exemplars of masculinity and their symbolic power, while also being careful to stress that hegemonic masculinity is characterised by a combination of 'the plurality of masculinities and the hierarchy of masculinities', which circulate and are legitimised through 'cultural consent, discursive centrality, institutionalization and marginalization or delegitimization' (Ibid.) of alternative masculinities.[7]

This circulation of legitimised masculinities, Flood suggests, is the result of 'highly organised [] relations *between men*' (2008, 34, emphasis in original). As such, in Kimmel's estimation, men are under the 'careful scrutiny of other men' who 'rank us, grant our acceptance into the realm of manhood' (1994, 128). In essence, the markers of manhood, and performances of masculinity, can be seen as approval-seeking activities carried out by men for the attention of men, as they attempt to 'improve their position in masculine social hierarchies' (Flood 2008, 341). Competing masculinities, or the desire to prove one's manliness and status within the group, are something that can be seen in Campion's films time and again: from the scheming and class-conscious Osmond, who sees Isabel Archer's wealth as an opportunity for his own social advancement among the other men in *The Portrait of a Lady*, to *The Power of the Dog*, in which the enmity between Phil and Rose conceals Phil's concern for validation of his masculinity as it comes increasingly under threat from new social arrangements within the household, which includes not only Rose but her effeminate 'sissy' son Peter.

In both *Bright Star* and *The Power of the Dog*, Campion foregrounds this competitive social hierarchy between men, which also harbours a desire to eliminate the feminine from within their ranks. In *Bright Star*, Brown's pseudo-intellectual posturing to Keats regarding Fanny's interest in poetry is such a performance of (a cerebral) masculinity. Brown and Fanny's adversarial relationship reaches its height when Brown challenges her intellect. Brown is suspicious when Fanny claims to have read not only Keats (twice) but also Chaucer, Spencer, Milton, and Homer in one week, and belligerently interrogates her about her thoughts on Homer and Milton's epics. When Fanny answers plainly that she liked them, Brown asks, 'You didn't find Milton's rhymes a little pouncing?' Fanny's answer confirms his suspicion that she has not in fact read the volumes she is returning to Keats, as Milton's tome is written entirely in blank verse.

While Fanny's claim is disingenuous, what is more remarkable is that Brown does not immediately confront the naïve Fanny. Instead, he waits to perform the unveiling of her lie to Keats. Brown's histrionic performance comes just as Keats discovers Fanny has been sent a valentine by his friend, unsettling Keats's faith in their romance, as he demands to know whether Brown and Fanny are lovers. Interestingly, it is Brown who speaks for Fanny – 'She can't speak because she only knows how to flirt and sew'– eager to promote his own position to Keats, whose creative talents he seems to idolise but of which he is arguably also jealous. The prevention of Fanny's articulation by Brown is an example of the historic delimitation of women's access to moments of articulation by men, as well as an exclusion of women's creative authority and production of cultural forms that Campion's film seeks to upend. Brown's exhortation directly looks to Keats's agreement to what is a quintessentially patriarchal position – that of a gendered division in which men and women are placed in binary opposition – to validate Brown's outlook, performance, and ultimately his position in a male hierarchy alongside Keats. Brown goes on to mock Fanny's seeming lack of literacy, revealing her literary mistake. Brown further humiliates Fanny, suggesting there 'are one or two of [Fanny's] kind in every fashionable drawing room of this city "aheming" over skirt lengths'. In Brown's eyes, Fanny's lack of knowledge is typical of the 'fairer sex' and thus serves as Fanny's disqualification as suitable companion. Brown's denial is self-serving and operates as a reinforcement of a patriarchal and exclusively homosocial economy of exchange by silencing Fanny.

In a similar vein to the homosocial and competitive masculine hierarchies seen in *Bright Star*, Campion immediately establishes Phil, George, and Peter's positionality within the male/masculine hierarchy, alerting us to the potential for competing masculinities within the family ranch. At the film's beginning, Peter's voice-over narrates the central question of the film. He asks: 'What kind of man would I be if I did not help my mother, if I did not save her?'. While Rose sees Phil as 'only another man', Campion's film asks us to consider Peter's question regarding the nature of each of these men and their varying masculinities. Campion sets up a dichotomy between George and Phil as two extremes of masculinity, immediately apparent through costuming. Phil's sweaty, leather-clad and lean physique contrasts with George's gentlemanly, business-like apparel. Pushing this incongruity between the two further, while bathing, George asks Phil if he himself ever used the house bath, to which Phil defiantly replies that he hasn't, indicating his disdain for the domestic (by implication the feminine). If any question remains over

Phil's masculine superiority over George (and all the other men on the ranch), we also bear witness to a scene in which we see Phil's gloveless hand castrating livestock watched by his admiring cowherds, while George drives away from the dirt and mess on a business trip. Furthermore, Rose's purchase of the soft, decorative gloves made by an Indigenous American father and son travelling through the ranch, and Phil's refusal to sell his cowhides to the same family, links indigenous masculinity with Rose's femininity and extends the discourse surrounding hegemonic masculinities which subordinate and marginalise others. This is why Rose's later sale of the hides to the father and son undermines that hegemony and so enrages Phil. The waspish Phil is nothing like the sturdy, quiet, and polite George who is perceptibly uncomfortable with his brother, especially regarding Phil's idolisation of the hypermasculine cowboy, Bronco Henry, Phil's long dead mentor. This discomfort is further underscored by George's lateness to a toast in Bronco Henry's honour at the start of their annual cattle drive. Taken as an insult to Bronco Henry's name and a challenge to Phil's authority, it seems that the cattle drive is more than just a chore for Phil; rather, it is a celebratory ritual replete with a toast to the dead cowboy before a 'banquet' at Rose's Red Mill Hotel. George's rejection of this ritual arguably delegitimises Phil's standing in the male hierarchy in Phil's eyes, an act which riles him and later leads him to take his frustrations out on a 'subordinate' male, Peter.

According to Kaufman, hegemonic masculinity and power depend on the internalisation of the ideas of control and domination. He states that power is 'seen as power over something or someone else' (1994, 145). George's rejection of Phil's authority – through his lateness to Bronco Henry's toasting and his secret marriage to Rose, with whom he is able to speak of his feelings of loneliness – destabilises the Burbanks' formerly homosocial and hypermasculine space, as well as Phil's equilibrium. Thus, unable to challenge his brother directly, Phil seeks domination over those on whom he feels he can exact his brutal masculinity, namely Rose and her 'sissy' son, Peter, because of the connection he makes with George's feminine weakness. This revulsion towards feminine weakness, and the challenge to Phil's ranking in the masculine hierarchy seen in his treatment of Peter, is similarly captured in the antagonism between himself and Rose. Phil's antipathy is clearly seen when Rose is asked to play the piano for an upcoming dinner party. As she practises Strauss's 'Radetzky March', her imperfect performance is met with the sound of Phil's banjo from upstairs, which echoes the same tune perfectly after her every pause, amplifying Rose's nervousness.[8] This gaslighting of Rose is fully realised on the night of the dinner party. Crumbling under the weight of George's expectations, Rose is unable to perform, while the unkempt Phil saunters into the room at the end of the evening, whistling the same song with ease. It is a tune which becomes a sinister refrain, signifying Phil's consummate ability at mastering everything including the frail Rose; like Rodriguez's calling card in *In the Cut* (the engagement ring), Phil's whistling signals a perversion of the song's jaunty sound.

As has been noted, Phil's target is not (only) Rose and her son but (also) his brother, or rather the refined (feminised) society he perceives his brother is cultivating, and that Rose and her son represent. Asked by George to wash up for dinner with their guests, Phil's absence at the dinner table underscores this refusal to abide by social norms of polite society. Unlike George, Phil is a college-educated man, able to quote Cicero. He converses easily with the guests as they leave. His refusal to acquiesce to George's request to clean up (and turn up) for dinner signals a repudiation of his brother's standing in the male social hierarchy. Phil maintains his hardened cowboy aesthetic and demeanour as a working man, equal (if not superior) to the other more senior men in the room, and positions himself securely at the head of the male social hierarchy of the Burbank family.

However, the contestation of masculinities in Campion's film is complicated by further, more intricate, triangulations than can also be seen in *Bright Star*. Given the hypermasculinity of the archetypal figure of the cowboy, Campion audaciously extends Phil's queerness, allowing it to seep into the other male relationships within the family. *The Power of the Dog* sees Sedgwick's triangulation, in which the flow of homosocial and homosexual desire attempts to freely circulate, appear in several complex iterations: between Phil, Bronco Henry, and George (who refuses the connection); Phil, Rose, and George, with Rose disrupting Phil and George's forty-year routine of sharing a room and taking Phil's place as George's bedfellow; and between Phil, Rose, and Peter, in which both Rose and Phil struggle for Peter's affection. Like the triangulations of *Bright Star*, domination over Rose is, however, only a means to an end: the elimination of the female/the feminine in the exclusively homosocial relations desired by Phil.

The most significant and liminal triangulation is that of Phil, (the memory of) Bronco Henry, and Peter. The relationship between Bronco Henry and Phil haunts the film and underlies Phil's troubled existence and indeed his brother's discomfort, although by bringing Rose into the house, George circumvents the original triangulation. The closest the audience gets to realising this last queer triangulation is towards the end of the film, as Phil identifies the strong-minded Peter as a kindred spirit, because he has withstood Phil's taunts of effeminacy and is able to see the figure of the dog on the mountain. Keen to mentor Peter, Phil allows himself to be emotionally seduced by the shrewd teen. In a dimly lit scene, Phil and Peter seemingly bond over a shared cigarette and discuss Bronco Henry while Phil polishes the dead cowboy's saddle; the monogrammed neckerchief used by Phil to polish the saddle, we note, is the one gifted to him by Bronco Henry and used earlier in Phil's erotic reverie by the river. The scene amplifies the repressed sexual and emotional pressure Phil experiences through the accumulation of signs of seduction, driven by Peter's self-possession, his knowing gaze and confident actions, as well as those symbols connected to Bronco Henry that allow erotic energy to flow between them. However, the latent sexual tension between Phil and Peter (and the memory of the Bronco Henry), while palpable, is again complicated not least because of the tension that has built up between the men over Phil's cruel psychological violence towards Rose, producing an ambivalence in the erotic charge circulating within the scene. This uncertainty is sustained until the film's end, and perhaps beyond it. Phil's death by anthrax poisoning at the hands of Rose's 'effeminate' and queer son, suggests, on the surface, a more definitive answer to Phil's brutal masculinity and a rejection of the triangulations set up by the film. Indeed, Phil's death is surely a response to Peter's opening question, 'What kind of man would I be if I did not help my mother, if I did not save her?'. As a question that asks us to consider the future of masculinity – its position in relation not only to men but also to women – Peter's avenging answer rejects Phil's hegemonic masculinity, misogyny, and homophobia. George and Rose, too, seemingly recover by the close of the film.

However, while Peter's original question aligns the audience with Peter and Rose's plight from the start, Campion's narrative complicates our response to Phil by affording us a more sympathetic reading of the troubled cowboy. Through the same haptic visuality seen in *Bright Star*, Campion turns the camera's gaze onto Phil in scenes in which he demonstrates the capacity for emotion and erotic pleasure. As the sun beats down on Phil stripped to his waist, he removes the monogrammed neckerchief from inside his trousers and begins to slowly stroke his body. And yet, the scene moves from Phil's body presented as spectacle to a more private and intimate moment of seclusion in which handheld low angles are used and Phil is observed from behind and at a distance (as if observed from the long grass that frames the shot). The arguably feminised scene is highly charged as the haptic transfers itself to the homoerotic. Similarly, while riding with Peter in the wilderness, Phil's caution in asking Peter to kill a rabbit demonstrates unexpected sensitivity from the rancher; the fact that Peter quickly and unemotionally breaks the wounded animal's neck is unnerving both for Phil and the audience and produces a sense of unease regarding the unnervingly quiet confidence of the boy. This charge contributes to the uncertainty in the film. Aside from the fact that the audience doesn't witness Peter's murderous actions, there is a disquiet that is a corollary of the film's denouement; that is, an unanswered question about the habitual reification of bodily violence (as a justifiable response to psychical violence) in hegemonic, patriarchal masculinity. In showing what kind of 'man' he is, Peter's murderous actions are dangerously reminiscent of Bourdieu's claim in *Masculine Domination* that cultural demonstrations of manliness – beyond sexual reproduction – can be comprehended as 'the capacity to fight and to exercise violence (especially in acts of revenge)', which is 'first and foremost a *duty*' that sustains cultural constructions of masculinity (2001, 51, emphasis in original). In this way, Campion's film poses the question as to whether the next generation of men (symbolised by Peter) has learned all too well the lessons and social practices of hegemonic masculinity. Peter's retention of the poisoned rope (placing it carefully under his bed) leads us to consider again the bond between Peter and Phil, in the same way we have wondered about the particulars of the historical relationship between Bronco Henry and Phil: Peter's is a violent inheritance. Typically, Campion's queer family is left at a juncture for which there are no clear answers.

CONCLUSION

In both films discussed here, it is clear to see that while Campion is a filmmaker with concerns about women's stories and trajectories, she has always been engaged with the nuances of relationships between men. Her work continually investigates the complex nature of human sexuality, masculinity, and femininity in a dynamic and open fashion within the self, if not entirely reconciling them. Indeed, her recent comments about *The Power of the Dog* indicate an ongoing interest in men's stories, raising as they do questions about the dialectic between masculinity and femininity. She states: 'I believe that there is no reason why directors should refrain from telling stories of men, especially when they also have an influence on women' (Juarez 2022, n.p.). Campion's attitude to notions of masculinity and femininity can also be seen in a Netflix roundtable discussion about *The Power of the Dog* and its women creatives. In thinking about her directorial style, Campion asks Kirsten Dunst whether she is a 'guyey kind of girl' (Berger 2022, n.p.). Campion's manner of asking the question suggests the director finds the possibility of excluding either masculinity or femininity from her personality as bemusing. Dunst confirms that Campion embodies both aspects. She says: 'You have a very soft, child-like part about you that I love so much, but then you can be really hardcore too, so to have both is very important. You have the balance of both, Jane' (Ibid.). Campion's subsequent self-reflection indicates a commitment to openness and playfulness in her day-to-day creativity, something validated by director of photography, Ari Wegner. Wegner notes that 'playfulness and the curiosity, and even that childlike spirit is actually key to the whole [creative] thing and allows you to think and have ideas' (Ibid.), to which Campion responds in the affirmative: 'If things get too serious, I get a bit depressed, I find I shut down a little bit and start worrying about achieving' (Ibid.). This playfulness and commitment to open-ended, intellectual curiosity can be seen in her films, including those discussed here, which denies the boundaries imposed by normative, hegemonic structures.

Indeed, Campion's films often leave us with a challenge and lack of closure. *Bright Star* does not allow Fanny to fade as soon as Keats passes, but extends Fanny's legacy and the time-image[9] usually given to masculine subjectivities by ending the film with Fanny walking Hampstead Heath reciting 'Bright Star', the poem Keats wrote for her. What is noteworthy here is the fact that Fanny is mobile: enouncing Keats's poem with authority in her own voice as she strides across the Heath. As such, Fanny claims her creative place alongside the famous Romantic poet. Campion's 'little Miss Brawne' becomes an image of So Mayer's mobile female protagonist (2016, 49), moving across the screen with agency, forward and onward through the world. It is, however, a mobility that takes the memory of Keats's own poetic voice with her as equals in a shared creative energy, as the final black screen records Fanny's lifelong, faithful pilgrimage to Hampstead Heath in memory of him. Here Campion's own stamp of creative authority comes to bear on a film that is concerned with reinscribing women's authorship and creativity into a public space that has heretofore consigned Fanny (and perhaps women filmmakers) to the side-lines, but which is not content to sacrifice her male creatives to do so. Campion's authorial and creative praxis recovers the hereditary line in the genealogy of female creativity while intuitively continuing to consider ongoing debates around the asymmetries of gender and sexuality in our socio-cultural discourse. In *The Power of the Dog*, too, Campion questions and breaches the boundaries of hegemonic masculinity, suggesting no easy answers. Phil's subscription to a hardened, macho masculinity of the cowboy is challenged by George's stoicism and perceived feminine passivity and Peter's own self-assuredness. As previously noted, the social practice of hegemony only works through providing paradigms which provide symbolic power. By the film's conclusion, and to Phil's cost, he finds his power has been delegitimised – he is no exemplar of masculinity to either his brother, or to Peter – but the questions still resonate in our minds, long after the film's end, about the future of masculinity and men, as well as our unusual sympathies for Phil. In this way Campion obscures our vision, leaving us to contemplate the answers for ourselves.

In these ways, Campion's films resist easy categorisation, embracing openness, uncertainty, and a resistance to parameters set by others to forge new meanings and new ways of seeing the world. In this way, Campion reveals herself as a liminal figure, existing in an 'in-between', constantly moving forward, questioning. Campion's explorations of her characters' psyches tap into inconsistencies and discontinuities experienced by ourselves, as well as the social constraints within which we live. The contested spaces of her films are thus ripe for her viewers to write their own narrative trajectories, to write themselves into that space through her films' indeterminacy, fluidity, and 'incomplete' endings. In this, Campion's work constantly queers the moment and cements her place as part of the genealogy of female (feminist) filmmakers.

NOTES

1. The list of works is too numerous to note here, but many examples can be found in this book's bibliography. However, noteworthy are Bainbridge (2008) and Bolton (2011).
2. The term 'toxic masculinity', so prevalent in today's popular discourse around masculinity, has a complicated history and will thus be used sparingly here. Scholars such as Carol Harrington and Andrea Waling note that the term has its roots in the mythopoetic men's movement of the 1980s and is a medicalised term, often suggesting there is a 'healthy' masculinity that can be its antidote. Rather than creating any agency for men, Harrington and Waling argue that the term is often used in 'individualising discourses' to target marginalised masculinities, further shoring up gender hierarchies, blocking alternative choices to masculinity. See Harrington (2021, 345–52) and Waling (2019, 362–75) for discussions of the term and its history.
3. So Mayer addresses the auteur and women directors in *Political Animals: The New Feminist Cinema*. She states: 'Authorship, like box office success, is at once crucial to coverage and circulation for feminist cinema, and deeply problematic, invoking Default Man models of the solitary genius' (2016, 16). See also Patricia White (2015); Thornham (2019), and Cobb (2012).
4. See Gilbert and Gubar (1979); Showalter (1984), and Spender (1980).
5. Although limited by space in this chapter, it is worth noting that a further queering of Sedgwick's triangulation might occur if Campion's Keats is read through Laura U. Marks's notion of haptic visuality (2000). In her work, Marks challenges the orthodoxy of traditional filmmaking, which has continually privileged optic visuality and the male gaze, as outlined by feminist film scholars such as Laura Mulvey (Mulvey in Kaplan 2000, 34–47). In such a reading, we might argue that Campion redirects our senses towards touch, taste, and smell within the film. Her focusing of the gaze on Keats as embodied and embedded within those sensory experiences might be seen to blur the boundaries between the space-image (usually associated with women) and the time-image (usually associated with the male perspective). See Sue Thornham (2019, 6–10) for a discussion of space-time images. This reading would enhance the suggestion of a commitment to tactility in Campion's work, and might well offer a different reading in which Keats's masculinity is queered even further.
6. See also *Masculinities* (Connell 1995).
7. Scholarship on masculinity has expanded since the 1990s with the inception of journals like *Men and Masculinities* and foundational texts like Connell's, extending as far as to include feminist critiques of mediated and postfeminist masculinities in light of a boom in Hollywood film about men and paternity (troubled or otherwise). See Hannah Hamad (2013).
8. The piano of this film is not an instrument of Rose's voice in the same way it was for Ada in *The Piano* (1993). Rose's abilities as a cinema-pit piano player, lauded by George, are a weight dragging her down. Rose's refusal of the instrument, and the struggle to get the piano across the rugged terrain of the American West, is arguably a playful nod to a loosening of Campion's bonds with a film that made her famous (but also pigeon-holed her). This reading is supported by Campion's own comments (see Appler 2021). The same implication can be seen in conversation with Katherine Hahn at the AFI's film festival (2021).
9. Again, see Thornham (2019, 6–10).

CHAPTER 6

'I don't think so, Jan, that's just another fantasy': Practice, Paratext and the Power of Women's Talk in Jane Campion's Filmmaking

Rona Murray

The power of the paratext, the extra textual space surrounding film, has been extensively explored by film academics as an addition to film text analysis, evaluating how the persona of the filmmaker can enhance scholarly interpretations of their films via DVD commentaries. This chapter shifts the focus, concerned less with the paratext as a hermeneutic tool and more as another form of public space, one in which a woman filmmaker can mobilise the power of 'women's talk'. This chapter argues that a woman filmmaker can further utilise the paratextual space to reimagine and fantasise: for example, about women's relationships to men, to each other, and most innovatively, about the labour of filmmaking. Campion's talk in paratext is key since it mimics and reinforces themes from her films and, equally as importantly, provides a space to develop an exchange between Campion and her collaborators who join her for these discussions. Previous scholarship regarding the paratext provides a useful starting point to consider this kind of 'women's talk' in a social context.[1] Applying Luce Irigaray's idea of *parler femme* further extends this feminist investigation, uncovering the political potential of Campion's talk and her expressed notions of fantasy for women (1985, 222). Therefore, my analysis will focus on Campion's digital paratexts, produced for *The Piano* (1993) and *In the Cut* (2003), using an Irigarayan framework centred around the exchanges taking place in the paratext, because these reveal new possibilities both in their content and form. These commentaries demonstrate a particular quality of dynamic exchange between Campion and her female collaborators. As such, Irigaray's concept of *parler femme* is crucial since it provides an interpretative framework for the verbal exchanges in the paratext; in particular, how Campion and her collaborators disturb the established patriarchal economy of discourse that exists within conventional film criticism and journalism.

THE FILMMAKER – AUTEUR – IN PARATEXT

By focusing on the paratext, this analysis builds on familiar scholarship relating to authorial agency, originating from the French New Wave critics' invention of the auteur, a persona which gave each considered film a guiding consciousness and an explanation for consistencies within the text itself. Emphasising authorial agency supports the work of both film scholarship and journalism, but it arguably functions differently for women filmmakers than for men. Geneviève Sellier stated that this polemical reconception of film authorship into the idea of the auteur ensured that film direction became 'no longer the apprenticeship of technique, but the expression of solitary genius' (2008, 40). It has demonstrably evolved further through modern film journalism into a technocratic discourse dominated by white, cis-gendered male proponents. The auteur, therefore, is a site more occupied by men than by women, for example, through the interaction of institutional exclusion upheld by public, popular discourses.[2] In other words, as Catherine Grant surmised, authorial agency exists at a 'complex conjunction of text, institution and author' (2001, 122), indicating that it is always a dynamic interaction of authorial intent with institutional pressures and behaviour.[3]

The paratext is where author, institution and text temporarily co-exist and is, therefore, an ideal space to consider these questions of agency. Gérard Genette's conception of the literary paratext has become influential in film scholarship because he introduced a notion of a fluid, dynamic space at the edge of the text, an idea that fits the digital paratext well. Genette's original concept described a space that acted as a 'threshold' to written texts that was: 'itself without rigorous limits, either towards the interior (the text) or towards the exterior (the discourse of the world on the text)' (1991, 261).[4] Applied to film, this 'threshold' is a public space that women filmmakers such as Campion, who have achieved the status of auteur in film analysis, can mobilise and utilise their authorial agency quite consciously; as Genette described it, the paratext can be a 'zone not just of transition, but of transaction' (Ibid.). As suggested above, questions of agency in the paratext may be very different for the female auteur than for the male auteur. There is a political urgency to these questions since women who are considered cinematic auteurs are still rare. As noted in many institutional analyses, the lack of women working in mainstream cinema prevails.[5] Less the lone, Romantic visionary or 'solitary genius', she has a quality of 'aloneness', of being one of the few women literally enabled to speak in public in this particular discursive space.

Specific scholarship regarding DVD commentaries was built out of an idea of the filmmaker and auteur as a communicable brand image. Timothy Corrigan (1990) wrote about how filmmakers could exploit the cultural and commercial possibilities of a space where new relationships with film audiences could be formulated. Catherine Grant argued the DVD commentary was a place where the auteur could present both hermeneutic interpretation and marketable facts as if imparting secrets to interested film fans; it could 'potentially' engender 'different, more comprehensive forms of auteurism than were previously possible' (2008, 103). Quoting Barbara Klinger's wider work on intertexual material, Grant suggests its power lay in a combination of a 'rhetoric of intimacy (i.e. "secrets" of the cinema)' alongside a 'performance of mastery (i.e. technological expertise and media knowledge)' that could be constructed, enhancing a 'sense of owning a personalized product' (Ibid., 111). In Grant's view, this was something consciously produced, recharacterising the film material into documentary form as the film text was '"re-directed" or literally reperformed' (Ibid.). As a performance, therefore, the paratext's possibilities have been anticipated by previous scholarship.[6] Treating the role of authorship as a space for performative agency by the woman filmmaker enables the political, feminist possibilities of this role to become apparent; women filmmakers can utilise their agency in this public space to create a feminist intervention.

An initial exploration of Campion's commentaries readily demonstrates her auteurist 'mastery' through her discussions of aspects of technique and theme. In this, she conforms to expected discourses surrounding a film, which focus on the technical and narrational elements of its construction. However, weaved into and around this, she includes more intimate revelations from her biography and, apparently, from her own beliefs in respect of fantasy and of women's social place in the world. Talking in this dynamic, threshold public space, Campion's intimate revelations are a way to position herself culturally and institutionally, and are also a 'redirection' and 'reperforming' of the film text, with strong feminist potential. Her work has always been engaged with representations of women's experience, aspects of biography and of their own fantasy lives. From her early short films, such as *A Girl's Own Story* (1984), and her first feature, *Sweetie* (1989), Campion has placed women's relationships with each other as central to the narrative. Her performance in paratext complements these representations since she speaks freely and intimately about desire and fantasy. This is reflected in the DVD commentaries available for *The Piano* and *In the Cut*, and is complemented by documentaries and featurettes accompanying *The Portrait of a Lady* (1996), *Bright Star* (2009), *In the Cut* and *Top of the Lake* (2013). This is a greater body of material in moving image paratext compared to most modern women filmmakers. Focusing exclusively on the DVD commentaries, Campion and her female producers engage in a speaking exchange between two women: Campion with Jan Chapman (*The Piano*) and then with Laurie Parker (*In the Cut*). As important as the content is the creation of an intimate space of discussion, confession, and a shared exploration of the struggles of creative labour. Therefore, these commentaries offer unique possibilities in the 'rhetoric of intimacy', distinguished as a speaking exchange created between two women in this space and not just by the woman auteur alone, speaking with auteurist 'mastery'.

CAMPION IN PARATEXT: DISCUSSING ROMANCE INTIMATELY

To hear Jane Campion discuss questions of desire in paratext seems entirely consonant with her films, not only in relation to their content but also to their experience as a piece of cinema. Campion speaks about desire exactly as one would expect of the author of *The Piano*, which made Vivian Sobchack 'achingly aware' of her own body within the cinema (2004, 62). Campion is a rare subject for analysis because of her willingness to talk intimately, to mine directly questions of desire and fantasy from her biography and her experience of film labour. An original screenplay by Campion, *The Piano*, was immediately heralded as an important expression of a woman's viewpoint on love, desire, and the power structures in heterosexual relationships. It is a narrative that works symbolically through women's social repression using the central character, Ada's (Holly Hunter) muteness to represent her resistance and her social silencing. The story begins as she is exchanged into marriage with a man she does not know on the other side of the world. Her symbiotically intense relationship with her daughter, Flora (Anna Paquin), excludes her new husband, Stewart (Sam Neill), but is disturbed finally by her growing attraction to Baines (Harvey Keitel). Through the trading of her precious piano keys, a mutually respectful, sensitive sexual relationship is built between Ada and Baines. Implicitly, a more functional family is formed by the end of the film, after Ada has rejected a watery grave attached to the piano, escaping from its seductive silence at the ocean base.

Throughout the DVD conversations, Campion in her discussion with Chapman moves easily between discussion of the film's detail with more general statements about her belief system concerning desire and sexuality. For example, she sees sexuality as:

> [S]uch a strong part of being human [which] guides you and drives you so much. When you think about the human condition, it's all about sex or power or both, you know. It's hardly anything that's not motivated from one of those two desires. It's very rare but very beautiful when people are really behaving in a disinterested way. And I think that is really what love is.
>
> (Campion and Chapman 2000, n.p.)

Campion's conversation about the film sees her considering her own relationship to desire and to fantasy in a way that mirrors Ada's attempt to negotiate her own subjectivity inside a patriarchal, romantic economy. Campion's willingness to take up a speaking position that supports the readability of those representations within her texts is important. She describes how the character of Baines, for example, is an 'ideal of masculinity' because he represents 'masculine strength combined with incredible sensitivity'; Chapman agrees that Baines's 'understanding' of Ada is a 'means of being herself' (Ibid.). Campion agrees that this ability to be herself is 'liberating' and suggests that:

> [O]ne of the dreams of women is that men are actually interested in them. And it's also, I guess, my theory about sex [. . .] what is really essentially sexy is attention. And the sort of attention that Harvey's character, Baines, gives Ada, is in the end very winning. I think it's not only about sex, it's also about love. Attention [. . .] more or less equals love.
>
> (Ibid.)

In answer to Chapman's enquiry later on, as to whether Ada and Baines found love, Campion affirms her belief that love can be found through 'drives like sex' that could function as way to move towards 'real compassion' (Ibid.). These same questions and preoccupations resurface for Campion in the DVD commentary accompanying *In the Cut* with another producer, Laurie Parker.

For Campion, the social world is avowedly patriarchal and women negotiate through tentative moves, finding only tenuous positions to occupy. Her films overtly engage with what Laura Mulvey described as melodrama's capacity to lay bare the 'ideological contradiction' of women's lives, not as 'a hidden, unconscious thread to be picked up only by special critical processes' but rather as stories dealing overtly with that negotiation women experience in relation to their own desire (1987, 75). Thus, Campion's heterosexual romances often become a mechanism to examine issues of repression and the difficulties for women in negotiating the social expectations placed upon them in these conventional sexual relationships. *The Piano*, metaphorically, expresses repression through the symbolism of Ada's muteness as a response to the patriarchal society she lives in. Yet, whilst her film and television work dramatises this conflict, it makes the relationships of women (including mothers and daughters and female siblings) central to the narrative. This notion of social space dominated by men, in which women construct tenuous relationships with each other and to their own desires, persists into her modern dramas *In the Cut*, *Top of the Lake* and *Top of the Lake: China Girl* (2017).

As her films consistently explore these contradictions, it is powerful when Campion mimics in her conversation a feeling for that contradiction in her own life. When addressing the central thematic device of *The Piano* – Ada's silence – she states:

> Campion: [I]t was a really instinctive idea [. . .]. How silenced women really are in our society and culture. And, in a way, Ada somehow made a

choice that I admired in her, it was a poetic choice, really, that she would act out what she felt inside, that she was unheard and would be unheard. There wasn't anyway, there was, in a way, no point in speaking because the whole world was not interested in what women really think and feel. But even we grew up in the time [. . .] I don't think it's really changed [Both laugh]

Chapman: Changed on the surface.

(Campion and Chapman 2000, n.p.)

The way in which Campion expresses her ideas here is very powerful both in content and form. It reinforces a potential shared history between women, through a shared experience of being silenced in various ways. In addition, the listener experiences Campion's own hesitancy in the halting, incomplete sentences: '[T]here wasn't anyway, there was, in a way, no point' (Ibid.). This hesitancy represents the filmmaker developing her own thoughts, spontaneously, with the spectator contained in the same aural space. It enhances the intimacy of the revelation and its power. This same feeling of intimacy and revelation is also present in the commentary prepared for *In the Cut*. Whilst this film is a crime thriller in a modern setting, it covers much of the same territory of the negotiation of desire and fantasy present in *The Piano*.

Based on Susannah Moore's 1995 erotic crime novella, *In the Cut* follows the story of Frannie (Meg Ryan), an English teacher in New York City and her affair with a detective, Malloy (Mark Ruffalo), who is investigating a serial killer. As in *The Piano*, the protagonist has an intense relationship with another female; in this case, with her half-sister, Pauline (Jennifer Jason-Leigh), who becomes the killer's third victim during the narrative. Frannie and Pauline share a father, who left both of their mothers and who haunts both women's fantasy and dream life. Frannie struggles with her suspicions about Malloy, who she believes is the man she has watched being fellated in the basement of a bar and who is, therefore, likely to be the serial murderer. Malloy's sexual sensitivity and personal mystery seems to suggest the murderer's romantic modus operandi of placing an engagement ring on each victim's left hand. Frannie narrowly escapes death at the hands of the real killer – Malloy's partner, Rodriguez (Nick Damici) – whose easy-going exterior hides a violent, misogynistic killer. Frannie saves herself by shooting him with the gun she finds in Malloy's jacket, which she is wearing.

In commenting on the scenes of desire between Frannie and Malloy, there is a constant interplay between Campion the writer-director and Campion the woman, still musing on how the mechanics of sexual relationships can work. She appears preoccupied with a recurring figure of the man who is sexually proficient and understands his female partner and her needs completely, potentially a kind of wish-fulfilment figure in a heterosexual, romance story. Malloy is in an inheritor of this from Baines, and this figure will appear again in Johnno (Thomas M. Wright) in the first series of *Top of the Lake*. It is important to note that there is consistency between Campion's commentaries and her views towards her male characters, particularly the way in which they break with heteropatriarchal norms in their ability to pay attention, to express vulnerability and their own emotional vulnerability in sexual relationships. Therefore, in a conventional auteur study, Campion's remarks on romance add hermeneutic value; however, there is also another kind of affirmation at work. Regarding a difficult scene between Frannie and Malloy, in which Frannie rejects his attempts at comfort after Pauline's death, Campion states: 'I love in the end, y'know, people get to these pitches at times and these strong places of complete emotional desperation. And they have the compassion to look past it' (Campion and Parker 2003, n.p.). She comments on Frannie's behaviour as unfair towards Malloy here, albeit in her state of grief. Parker concurs, stating friends had told her how 'the guys who are watching [the film], they identify with the character [Malloy], and they feel [his] anxiety [about] making things okay' (Ibid.). Campion frequently demonstrates such sympathy with men's emotional positioning as much as with her female protagonists. She comments on one highly-charged scene that 'it transcends that original aggressive impulse and turns into – because he sees through it – that she needs this kind of grief-fuck; his knowing of that is the real love' (Ibid.). Over one scene in which Frannie confesses she fears that she wants too much from a romantic relationship, Campion discusses the meaning of this from the male perspective: 'It's painful, to be this man, [. . .] a lot of men think they're failing women' (Ibid.).

This understanding extends to Campion's evaluation of her actors. She discusses Mark Ruffalo's performance and his emotional investment in the role, as well as Harvey Keitel's realisation of Baines in *The Piano*. Moreover, she is equally prepared to discuss her own attraction to the male characters or the male actors that she has worked with. Campion again demonstrates her personal frankness about how sexuality functions for her and this acts as an unusual and confident statement for a public woman auteur, bringing herself as a desiring woman into her discussions. She is recurrently interested and gets on well with:

> [R]eally guy guys, tough guys, but as long as they have a feminine side. A lot of tough guys really do have a strong feminine element to themselves because they're very confident about their masculinity and they can afford to relax.
>
> (Ibid.)

She admires Sam Neill's 'handsomeness and diffidence and strength' (Campion and Chapman 2000, n.p.) and she interrupts Parker during one sequence to comment that Damici is 'looking so handsome, so good-looking' (Campion and Parker 2003, n.p.). Campion's active performance of her own attraction to her actors is part of a new public expression of desire directly from the woman, not the director. Therefore, Campion's paratextual speech demonstrates a consistent belief system regarding heterosexual romance. As part of her feminist intervention, Campion repeatedly emphasises the importance of men who listen, who engage in sex as an emotional exchange. She acknowledges her own attraction to her male actors on-screen and, thereby, accentuates how this desire functions for both the woman and the director.

CAMPION IN PARATEXT: DISCUSSING WOMEN INTIMATELY

Equally important, given the content of Campion's films, is the way in which she speaks with her collaborators about women's relationships on-screen. In assessing her own relationship to desire and fantasy, Campion separates herself from *The Piano*'s protagonist and yet she frequently refers to Ada's characteristics as an expression of her own fantasy and her imagining of the greatest possibilities for women's desire on-screen. This paradox adds a positive dynamic because, as exemplified in the following exchange, it shows Campion expressing some of her own repressed feelings through her female protagonist:

Campion: We grew up in a time when there was a lot more attention given to the fact that women didn't have as many rights. I don't think it's really changed, you know [She laughs]

Chapman: Yeah, it's changed on the surface but not fundamentally. [. . .] I remember you were very attracted to characters like that who were

Campion: rebellious, deeply

Chapman: rebellious, and stubborn and strong

Campion: I think I admire it. I'm sort of jealous or envious because I feel in my normal life [. . .] I eat so much compromise and, in fact, compromise is the way to some sort of a life. But in a poetic sense, I find it really moving and quite deep that there are some people that don't

Chapman: Who act their feelings in a very instinctive and direct way

(Campion and Chapman 2000, n.p.)

Campion's statement adds weight to the element of fantasy, being an intimate revelation of the filmmaker's own desires, unlived in life through necessary social compromise. Her separation is an important disassociation of the author with the screen surrogate, an ability to separate her own psychical biography from that of the character. In thinking of this as part of the 'complex conjunction of text, institution and author' as Grant states, the paratext thus shows the complexity of Campion's engagement with fantasy and her personal struggle. It also reflects her consciousness of women's continued struggle with speaking in public space. Ironically, as she expresses these contradictions – importantly in a dynamic and laughter-filled conversation with Chapman – she is successfully performing a woman speaking about desire in public. Campion is thereby disturbing the natural order, of the typical content of the auteur DVD commentary, and as these can be characterised as regimes of speaking, it is a powerful feminist intervention.

What is emerging through a close analysis of Campion's paratextual statements is the interaction of form and content. As an Irigarayan reading will demonstrate more fully later, the dynamic of the conversations adds to the aura of intimacy for the film viewer. This is, therefore, a development of both Grant and Klinger's work on the 'rhetoric of intimacy' in the DVD extra that has specific feminist potential not only in what they say but in the comfortable, conversational – intimate – way that they speak together. This is important in relation to how the commentaries develop Campion's feelings about women and women's relationships with each other. Campion and Parker discuss the love between the two sisters, Frannie and Pauline, in *In the Cut*. Again, there is power in both the content and form of these discussions. Campion discusses the importance of the scene in which Frannie tells Pauline again – it is clearly a ritual in their relationship – about how their father met Pauline's mother. The scene is shot hand-held, the women moving from a moment of lying together on the sofa to an affectionate, slow revolving dance – lightly touching hands – as if enacting an echo of a courtly dance between a man and a woman. At this point, Campion discusses the preparation made by the two actors for representing this relationship; how she as a director asked them to write down what they most feared for their sister. As we watch Ryan and Jason Leigh move on-screen, this commentary works as a hermeneutic explanation of character and of performance process. However, it adds two more layers of female sociality, between Ryan and Jason Leigh and now between Campion and Parker. The director and producer discuss how Ryan, as Frannie, fears for Jason Leigh, as Pauline, and her impulsive nature; in return, Pauline fears Frannie's distance. These actors have thought about each other as if they were sisters, creating a psychic reality to their interaction. Campion and Parker's words add a further interaction between women talking openly and honestly with each other. Thus, again, the DVD commentary space becomes a place for intimacy, reinforced as it is a doubling: Frannie and Pauline on-screen, Campion and Parker on the soundtrack. Campion underlines this association by sharing her own experiences, describing the:

> love and tenderness that underpin my relationships with women; what compassion we have for each other, and the soul journey that we share. And, I guess, by association, what we would like it to be with the men in our life.
>
> (Campion and Parker 2003, n.p.)

Parker agrees, citing the way in which women have 'no artifice' with each other. As with her male actors, Campion also expresses her love towards her female actors. She saw herself as on an adventure with Holly Hunter in *The Piano*, as sisters; she is passionate about Meg Ryan's acting abilities, her ability to cry and show emotion. As a result, the DVD consumer is arguably drawn into a new 'rhetoric of intimacy', included and addressed through Campion's expression of desire, or of love, so that the commentary activates their own memories and experiences. Their voices, present in the threshold space in cinema, overlay and interact with the film's images creating a bridge between the text and the audience, potentially reinforcing female spectators' affective connection with the film's exploration of romance.

The previous analysis, necessarily, isolates commentary so that a fluid and fluent conversation is schematised and categorised for academic purposes. Having demonstrated the ways in which Campion establishes the paratext as having subversive potential through becoming 'women's space', Luce Irigaray's theoretical work provides the means to see and explore Campion's talk in paratext further as a dynamic interplay, an important part of its power. The suggestive nature of Irigaray's theory is consonant with the lively exchange so evident between the two women speaking in each case and, in the following section, provides a theoretical framework for thinking through the potential of this 'women's talk' more fully.

IRIGARAY AND *PARLER FEMME*

Parler femme is a concept by which Irigaray (1985) reimagines subjectivity formation through the action of language; it denotes forms of discourse between women through which feminine subjectivity could be formed in and of itself, rather than as a negative mirror image of the male psychical story, as perpetuated by conventional psychoanalytical discourses. In this work, Irigaray both draws on and then breaks away from the work of Jacques Lacan on subjectivity formation through and in language. Irigaray's contention is that women cannot find themselves in the discourses constituted in the dominant social order in which masculine economies of exchange have become naturalised and the norm. Irigaray's concept of *parler femme* can be literally translated as 'speaking (as) woman', interpreted by translators Catherine Porter and Carolyn Burke as the action to 'disrupt or alter the syntax of discursive logic' and to 'express the plurality and mutuality of feminine difference and mime the relations of "self-affection"' (Irigaray 1985, 222). Public acts of enunciation or 'systems of exchange' which could be 'speaking (as) woman' might disrupt naturalised patterns of engagement, ones which serve a dominant economy. Women's talk in public, within the paratext, has the potential to be part of a new set of 'rites' and new 'systems of exchange' between women (Irigaray 1993, 79), ones in which they can establish (in Irigaray's words) 'another "syntax"' and "grammar" of culture', something she regards as 'crucial' (Irigaray 1985, 143). Luce Irigaray looks specifically at women's social position as part of her philosophy of *parler femme*, asking: '[W]hat rites and what systems of exchange can be set up among women? Today? In the future?' (Irigaray 1993, 75) and asks for a 'currency of exchange, or else a nonmarket economy' (Ibid. 79). Whereas scholars have focused on the film representations in terms of identifying these 'rites' and 'systems of exchange' to great effect, the exchanges of women in paratext are a further potentially powerful 'system of exchange'. For example, Jane Campion's revelation of biographical details is significant because these stories are so unusual in public space in this intimate form. By such statements, women film authors arguably transform their own experiences – culturally – into 'systems of exchange' creating an artefact of 'exchange' in a 'nonmarket economy'.

From an Irigarayan perspective, Campion's films are already a rich source of material for feminist scholars uncovering a language in film which disturbs dominant, patriarchal narrative paradigms. Two such scholars, Caroline Bainbridge and Lucy Bolton, have both explored women-authored film texts utilising Irigaray's theory, and have argued that they contain a specifically female language (indicated by their book titles) – a 'feminine cinematics' (Bainbridge 2008) or a 'female consciousness' (Bolton 2011). Bainbridge's examination of *The Piano* provides an ideal example of this kind of analysis. Bainbridge characterises the relationship of Ada and her daughter, Flora, as one containing a 'highly-charged emotionality' in their 'dyadic unity' whilst underlining 'the importance of their moments of betrayal and distanciation' (Bainbridge 2008, 169). In discovering the energy of the acts of enunciation within the text, Bainbridge explores how women express intimacy and desire between themselves to the exclusion of the male figures in the narrative, particularly through a mother-daughter dyad (though these connections are not without their own conflicts). This doubling, intimacy, and complexity can be found throughout Campion's work and is present again in her paratextual acts of enunciation.

The previous section demonstrated how Campion's persona in paratext reflects her preoccupations with female desire in her stories. This consonance between women and director adds credibility to her paratextual statements. Seen through an Irigarayan lens, the sharing of these thoughts between Campion and her collaborators is an important extension of the narrative of women's desire in the films. In the paratext, however, the protagonists are director and producer in a conversation that redirects and reperforms the material onscreen. Campion and Chapman assess *The Piano* in retrospect as an iconic romance for women, with significant divergences in their viewpoints. Chapman comments on women who have approached her and spoken of the film as understanding the 'female psyche' and their feeling that it appears to communicate in a 'secret language' to them. Campion describes her own ambivalence in 'buying into the myth' of heterosexual romance in writing and creating *The Piano* and questions how they – Chapman and her – might be 'enrolling' their audiences in this myth. She rejects that responsibility with a personal revelation that she, herself, was 'enrolled in it anyway' (Campion and Chapman 2000, n.p.). Campion's comments encapsulate a dichotomy at the heart of the text, as the text's author. She demonstrates both an emotional engagement and an objective distance. The film can be read both as expressing those romantic ideals, a narrative of sexuality and intimate love; however, it also directly confronts abiding questions for women (as Irigaray explores) about their relations among themselves and their wish to move from speaking amongst themselves into speaking to wider society. Campion's narrative identifies herself as struggling with an Irigarayan dichotomy of desire and sexuality. All these factors enhance the role of the paratextual statement as a valid part of the 'systems of exchange' (Irigaray 1993, 75) between women in terms of understanding their shared culture, and acts to 'disrupt or alter the syntax of discursive logic' by the empathy implicit in this revelation (Irigaray 1985, 222). Campion and Chapman and Campion and Parker arguably move the paratextual statement towards something which is able to 'mime the relations of "self-affection"'(Ibid.). Women are able to recognise themselves in these empathic, woman-oriented performances, Campion with Chapman and Campion with Parker. This intimacy mimics the dyadic intimacy – mother and daughter or sisters – visible onscreen.

There is an interplay between Campion as the originator of these images, both as writer and director of the action, with her as an ordinary woman musing with another woman on the whole question of romance in their own lives. In Campion's words, she has 'dressed up in the fantasy-woman way' (Campion and Chapman 2000, n.p.). Therefore, what is also importantly recuperated as part of a public exchange between women is the centrality of women's feelings about sexuality in their own lives. Significant is the idea of the adolescent imagination which occurs elsewhere in these commentaries. There is a recognition that

The Piano might provide a text for all women that returns them to the site of young women's fantasising as a means for developing their own sexuality and subjectivity, of going on their own journey of desire. Gothic literature, as Chapman suggests, often provides the framework for these fantasies. Campion places herself in a dual role as author and female spectator, producing a different kind of 'rhetoric of intimacy' than originally conceived of in Klinger's concept, where it functioned only as part of the marketing of the film. It needs to be noted that Campion is unusual in this intimacy. Discussing female sexuality, and one's own feelings of desire, as a filmmaker, is a bolder enterprise than Campion's easy manner suggests. Irigaray notes that 'if, as a woman, who is also in public, you have the audacity to say something about your desire, the result is scandal and repression. You are disturbing the peace, disrupting the order of discourse' (Irigaray 1985, 145). Campion consistently has the audacity through her discussion of her own beliefs and her own attraction to, and love of, her male and female actors. As it is an intervention, it is particularly significant that these exchanges show little fear and, instead, demonstrate great humour and pleasure in their warm intimacy. Having audacity need not come at the price of losing one's humour and personality. Thus, the act of enunciation itself, the intimate dyad created by Campion and her female producers, is part of the value of the exchange itself, part of the value of *parler femme*, which can offer an alternative paradigm for speaking about film other than that of technical 'mastery'. Campion, when read through an Irigarayan lens, demonstrates the potential for this form of women's talk as an artefact of 'exchange', not least in their humour and intimacy inside the paratextual space.

CAMPION AND CHAPMAN: THE RHETORIC OF INTIMACY

The DVD commentary to *The Piano* was created several years after the film (as part of the release of a special edition) and Campion is heard with her long-time producing partner Jan Chapman. Immediately apparent is the way in which Campion and Chapman's established working relationship and personal familiarity bring a relaxed dynamic to their engagement, considering the film in hindsight together and their experiences of working in the film industry. The exchanges are marked by a 'rhetoric of intimacy' in which humour plays an important role. Campion and Chapman's laughter enacts something familiar to women, of a recognition of the frustration and injustice of the status quo at the same time as it becomes a shared object between them, reinforcing their mutual regard as they speak amongst themselves:

> Chapman: I've always loved the way at the end of the film, she takes on life, she takes on reality. She comes back from the dream, from the fantasy. She's gonna have a go at trying out romance in the real world

> Campion: Well, yeah, maybe not even romance. She's just going to live a life [Chapman: Yeah] and learn to . . . to speak again
>
> Chapman: But have a relationship, you see her with Harvey . . . with Baines. [Campion: Yeah]. Maybe it's the idea, Jane, that life lived without fantasy is possible?
>
> Campion: [Sighing]. . .I don't think so, Jan. [Both laugh]. That's just another fantasy [More laughter]
>
> (Campion and Chapman 2000, n.p.)

Their laughter also acknowledges their difference, as individual women, and their separate encounters with sexuality, an acknowledgement of plurality.

Laughter and self-deprecating humour underpin all these acts of enunciation. What is present in written interviews but emerges much more forcefully in her vocal performances in DVD commentary, is Campion's dry humour. For example, Campion embraces, or arguably consciously performs, her maverick, auteur persona. In the DVD extras for *In the Cut*, Campion comments on her chalk drawing of a lighthouse, to accompany her protagonist's English class on Virginia Woolf's novel, *To the Lighthouse* (1925). She laughs at its obvious phallic style and comments: 'It's my nature. I can't help myself to be outrageous sometimes' (Campion and Parker, 2003, n.p.). Laughter and shared humour contribute a particularly strong dynamic energy to the conversations, and therefore are a key part of the effect of *parler femme* here. In a different, but equally warm, relationship with Laurie Parker, the two share several moments of silliness. The women join in with the song playing on-screen (from a small toy hamster): 'I think I love you, but what am I so afraid of' (Ibid.). They also laugh together about the experience of encountering a flasher whilst shooting the lighthouse scene:

> Campion: He came right up to me and you [. . .] you never stopped talking on the phone. I ran off
>
> Parker: We had the finger pressed on 911. . . we were so scared [. . .] we have to be this scared in the movie.
>
> (Ibid.)

Director and producer also giggle over the choices that had to be made on the prosthetic penis used in an early scene and Campion's own cameo appearance in one sequence as a drunken woman in the bar. It adds to the intimate address and the characterisation of film labour as quite ordinary and manageable in women's lives.

As part of this intimacy, Campion's physical voice is important, as it is warm, Antipodean-accented and often given to laughter. Moreover, this 'rhetoric of intimacy' is a public expression of very private modes of address. Her DVD commentary for *The Piano* also demonstrates a willingness, often through humour, to show vulnerability. Campion and Chapman's meeting with the film's composer Michael Nyman, or her experiences casting well-established actors such as Harvey Keitel, are good examples. In discussing meeting with Nyman, Campion states that we were 'very anxious and nervous', as he was 'for us, such a famous and incredible composer' and 'we wanted everything right' (Campion and Chapman 2000, n.p.). They hired a large concert hall in Sydney with a huge grand piano: 'He sat down at it for five minutes and said, "Do you think we can go shopping?" [Both laugh]' (Ibid.); Campion affirms that 'people are people first rather than technicians' (Ibid.). The same self-deprecation pervades her description of calling Keitel:

> Campion: [It was] exciting and a little scary for me too. I was also insecure about how to direct someone like Harvey, so strong and famously strong. And for me as a director, hardly having done anything, but with a kind of a clear vision and wanting Harvey to co-operate with it [She laughs]
>
> Chapman: [Amused tone] So, how did you achieve that?
>
> Campion: Well, I didn't know if I would be able to. . . I remember doing quite a lot of role-playing with my husband at the time, he had to play Harvey [Both laugh] before I got to ring Harvey up.
>
> (Ibid.)

Through comments like these, Campion demystifies the filmmaking process and demonstrates her desire to explain how difficult and intimidating the act of creativity can be.[7] In a public arena, there is a great danger that any expression of insecurity could undermine women's position in public given that a woman director is still so rare. However, Campion clearly shows confident agency in 'redirecting' and 'reperforming' not just aspects of the text but also aspects of the practice of film direction for the DVD audience.

CAMPION: FILM LABOUR AS A CURRENCY OF EXCHANGE

Even as they laugh about their experiences, their passion for their projects emerges. Jane Campion and Jan Chapman talk in relation to the beginnings of *The Piano* and their inspiration:

Chapman: We had much enormous passion and energy for this film [. . .] You and I had been talking about it for a long, long time even before you made *Sweetie* and *An Angel at my Table*, I wanted to make this film so much. And there was such clarity in the screenplay and even in the treatment when you first showed it to me. And it also reminded me of my love of Emily Brontë and the Romantics. It was sort of like something you also felt, it was kind of like an adolescent imagination come to life, very much about all those things you were talking about [pause].

Campion (interjecting): Love and sex? [Both laugh]

Chapman: Yeah [both laugh]. Female visions of what love is – myths of it as well

Campion: That's right. [. . .] I needed two films to bring my craft up to the kind of sophistication that this film needed

Chapman: You were really clear about that

Campion: I needed to get out of my system the more absurdist, more surrealist aspects of my character [. . .] but I'm still kind of amazed that we had the [. . .] belief creating reality

Chapman: Absolutely

Campion: That we had that idea firmly in our minds that it was possible

Chapman: I mean, I really had no idea where we were going to get the money from, how you actually put together the financing for a film. The two of us wandering around

Campion: We knew we had a story to tell [. . .] all this had to be done in a way we hadn't seen before.

(Campion and Chapman 2000, n.p.)

There are several moments where these women exchange the desire they have felt for the project, the 'passion and energy' as Chapman describes it. This led them to create artefacts to send out, to obtain financing, including not only the scripts but also paintings and other materials. Chapman describes how 'we put them into a little card pack [. . .] beautiful scripts. We'd get really beside ourselves [. . .] it really was a baptism this film for both of us, wasn't it?' Together, ten years after the making of the film, they express a mutual sense of wonder. Chapman comments: 'it was fantastic to be so naïve' (Ibid.). This is a very different kind of 'rhetoric of intimacy' than that described by Klinger, where the secrets were those of the 'mastery' of the film medium. Instead, Campion's performances, with her producers, are marked by the confessions of doubt, of vulnerability in the process, and the importance of 'belief creating reality' (Ibid.). For example, Campion describes the fear of screenings:

> Because making a film or doing a piece of work is my way of really loving other people, trying to give them my best, trying to give to them from the deepest parts of myself. And socially I might seem really casual, like I don't really care but this is coming from a different part of myself, you know, like a soul gift. I think that's why it's very painful for me if people don't like or they don't respond, which of course happens a lot. People don't necessarily like what you do, but because I've got so much emotionalism, or I did have, attached to this effort to make a really lovely gift – it was really crushing.
>
> (Ibid.)

This is a particularly bold, poetic way of speaking about the labour of filmmaking, a 'rhetoric of intimacy' which sees Campion publicly willing to express how filmmaking is an act of love for her. The description of filmmaking as a 'soul gift' is an incredibly personal and moving revelation. It is an important contribution to the idea of a 'currency of exchange', or else a 'nonmarket economy' in Irigarayan terms. It is also important as it sits paradoxically with the characterisation of film labour as ordinary and manageable in women's lives. However, the paradox is part of the exchange present in these conversations; that the filmmaker demystifies the process of filmmaking at the same time as performing its deep, emotional satisfaction. Thus, Campion's paratextual statements are potentially a different answer to Claire Johnston's original feminist call that women's 'collective fantasies' be released in cinema (1973, 30). In the paratext, women exchange their collective fantasies as protagonists, together as director and producer.

CONCLUSION

Therefore, as an act of *parler femme*, the paratext is a complex interweaving of biographical material, interaction between Campion and her producers, and the interaction of the women's talk with the rhetoric of the images. As with her films, these acts of enunciation can form part of a 'currency of exchange, or else a nonmarket economy' in Irigarayan terms. Especially in relation to film labour, these exchanges demonstrate a shift in *'the economy of exchange – of desire'* away from being exclusively *'man's business'* (Irigaray 1985, 176, emphasis in original). In paratext, Campion shows us how the woman auteur can become the hero of her own narrative, establishing women's subjectivity at the centre of an act of narration.[8] In the fantasy medium of cinema, and in the context of the paratext, women filmmakers can be their own subject in a narrative of desire.[9] As an act of agency, within the confines of the DVD commentary and its limited audience, the immediate impact of the paratext is restricted. However, if cinema histories are re-conceived as being communicated through a director's practice, then Campion's attitudes to sexuality are part of that exchange – an inspiration – to future generations. She is a woman freely expressing her own desires within a public space.

This chapter has considered how Campion represents a female auteur speaking with desire in a number of ways, all of which contribute to a more nuanced understanding of Catherine Grant's idea, discussed earlier, of the 'complex conjunction of text, institution and author'. The paratext creates a space for an act of *parler femme*. Talking about their own practice and creativity can become part of a system which women have lacked; a 'social system that reflects their values' through public 'symbolic exchanges' which has (in Irigaray's view) been 'repressed and censored' (1993, 81–2). Irigaray asserts, as part of her argument, that when 'a woman shares her knowledge and experience with a larger female public, this is a contribution to women's liberation' (Ibid., 82). It is part, therefore, of an operation of 'speaking (as) woman' (Irigaray 1985, 135).

Campion is able to speak in this way because she occupies the position of the auteur, within the discipline of film studies and within popular film journalism. Campion's performances in her DVD extras provide a model of a combined kind of agency, one which embraces her work as a filmmaker but also presents her as a socially-situated woman speaking to other women. Campion's work demonstrates her preoccupation with one aspect of women's place in the symbolic order, their difficulty in reconciling their private lives of fantasy with their public lives. Her talk in paratext underscores and reinforces these preoccupations. Thus, she honours an experience of private fantasy which demonstrates great public 'audacity'. In the exploratory, dynamic energy of the exchange she opens up new possibilities of 'speaking (as) woman'. Campion's voice, her laughter and the mutual exchange is a crucial part of a 'transaction' within the paratextual space. As a woman situated within the overriding discourses of the film industry, ones which favour the idea of the 'auteur' with its technocratic, arguably masculinised language, her discussion also disturbs the regimes of auteurist supremacy by speaking about and through her collaboration and relationships. In reviewing Campion's DVD commentaries, it becomes clear that the voice of the female filmmaker moves consciously between the desiring woman, the labouring filmmaker and the intellectual film auteur mobilising new possibilities for speaking about film. Her passion, agency and commitment to doing this in public should be considered as part of her intimate 'soul gift' as a filmmaker.

NOTES

1. For example, Grant (2008, pp. 101–15) and Verhoeven (2009).
2. For example, in 2015, British Film journal *Sight & Sound* produced a special edition entitled 'The Female Gaze'. In his editorial, Nick James commented: 'I've never properly tried to think through the works of either of them in the way I have with Haneke and Tarkovsky [. . .] Tarkovsky made seven features; Denis has made a dozen' (James 2015, 5).
3. These examples are necessarily limited as they represent cis-gendered women and are based around films which largely explore heterosexual narratives in a conventional romance genre form. The potential lies in the possibilities of destabilising discourses that have held strong in relation to film analysis, both popular and academic. In analysing Jane Campion and her collaborators, the intention is to focus on and address a particular speaking position as women, being a role that is socially situated and has, demonstrably, suffered exclusion and prejudice within the film industry. Within the social situation as it exists, it is an identity which can be used – as is argued here – to make an intervention into the still dominant discourses. These hegemonic social structures, which persist as a norm, exclude and regulate, exercising control and preventing fluidity of expression and of social and psychical identities. Speaking as a socially constructed woman, therefore, can be interpreted as one of a number of possible interventionist positions.
4. The epitext, as one subgroup, constituted author-generated 'interviews, conversations and confidences' which Genette contended functioned as a 'fringe' or 'border' which was 'always the bearer of authorial commentary either more or less legitimated by the author' and operated as 'a zone not just of transition, but of transaction' (Genette 1991, 261).
5. For example, Martha Lauzen (2018), 'The celluloid ceiling: behind-the-scenes employment of women on the top 100, 250, and 500 Films of 2017'. Also see Cobb, Williams, and Wreyford (2016).
6. Deb Verhoeven writes of how Campion 'proposes the narcissistic idea of the creative figure who is at one and the same time the object of her own creativity' concluding, however, that her 'origins' and 'creativity' are elusive to the auteur herself (2009, location 2463–5).
7. So Mayer recognised that the accompanying materials in the hands of a filmmaker such as Sally Potter are 'democratising one of the most mystified and mystificatory aspects of the filmmaker's craft' (2016, 197).
8. Sally Potter's question from her film *Thriller* (1979), 'What if I had been the hero?' was reconceived by Sue Thornham (2012) in her study of women filmmakers and their mobilising of the artistic biography as a central narrative.
9. Adapting Teresa de Lauretis's idea that, in conventional narrative structure: 'the itinerary of the female's journey, mapped from the very start on the territory of her own body [. . .] is guided by a compass point [. . .] to the fulfilment of his desire' (1984, 133).

PART THREE

CHAPTER 7

Articulating Feminism(s): Voicelessness, (In)Visibility and Agency in *Top of the Lake*

Adele Jones

Top of the Lake (2013), Jane Campion's first television offering since *Angel at my Table* (1990), is a study of what it means to be female in a patriarchal world structured around male sexual violence against women. The richness of Campion's vision lends itself to a multiplicity of readings but, this chapter will argue, the central concern of the series is an exploration of the meaning of feminism(s) for each of the female characters struggling to articulate her subjectivity within patriarchy. Campion's ambiguous, ambivalent, often thorny relationship to feminism and the question of whether her works engage with feminist politics is well-documented; indeed, it has become almost trite to state this. But although Campion has previously stated that her 'orientation isn't political or doesn't come out of modern politics' (Cantwell 1999, 158), I argue that *Top of the Lake* represents a marked shift from this assertion, as does Campion's own engagement in the discourse around the show.[1] This chapter seeks, then, to read *Top of the Lake* as representative of a discursive shift in Campion's oeuvre. As in all her work, the female experience is central to the meanings generated by and reflected in the series but this time, feminism itself is the organising framework within which the narrative functions.

This may seem a bold claim to make about a director who has periodically problematised the idea that telling female stories is or should be a feminist endeavour. Of *After Hours* (1985), the short she developed with the Australian Women's Film Unit, Campion states, '[it] had to be openly feminist since it spoke about the sexual abuse of women at work. I wasn't comfortable because I don't like films that say how one should or shouldn't behave' (Ciment 1999a, 35). Yet as Dana Polan notes, for all Campion's disavowal of *After Hours*, and her seeming antagonism towards (its) feminist politics, the film encompasses the stylistic and thematic concerns of her earlier student films as well as prefiguring the narrative structures and motifs of her work to date (2001, 76–84). Indeed, this early negation of openly feminist politics is itself an engagement with those politics, leading to a body of work underpinned by representations of the power dynamics between men and women explored in early films such as *After Hours*. The experience of being female in patriarchy preoccupies Campion and informs her protagonists' stories. In fact, she engages with the very same narratives that, in basic terms, drive most forms of feminism. Ironically, it is Campion's exposition of this experience that has led to her auteur status, providing further impetus for claiming her as a feminist icon in a male-dominated cultural landscape.[2]

Given Campion's historical reluctance to being claimed as a feminist, it is all the more notable that *Top of the Lake* represents an explicit and, I will argue, largely positive engagement with feminism than has been present in any of her shorts, feature films, or earlier television work.[3] The series is a direct response to the cultural landscape of the first two decades of the 2000s in which feminist discourse has undergone a shift, culminating in the #MeToo 'moment'. There are a number of debatable and complex issues to consider when talking about what contemporary feminism is, and foremost among those for a consideration of *Top of the Lake* is my contention that while 'feminism' is everywhere – we live in a time when 'empowerment' of women and girls is a buzzword – this ubiquity is only one side of a double-edged sword. In fact, the (hyper)visibility of feminism is, I suggest, partly the result of a point in time at which systems of both patriarchy and capitalism have recognised the value in co-opting discourses of feminism and have strategically done so. This is not a ground-breaking observation because the efficiency with which systems of power encompass, absorb, and seek to delegitimise movements that risk their dominance has been well-theorised.[4] The difference for the argument made in this chapter is that in our networked age the battle between feminism and patriarchy and capitalism is played out in what Sarah Banet-Weiser calls an 'economy of visibility' (2018, 2),[5] against a cultural landscape that now often feels defined by the conflict between – in pop culture terms – #MeToo and #NotAllMen.

In fact, Banet-Weiser's conception of popular feminism (and its inevitable counterpart, popular misogyny) draws on and speaks to the 'critical object[s]' of postfeminism and neoliberal feminism that have characterised much feminist theory since the mid-1990s (Banet-Weiser, Gill, and Rottenberg 2020, 5).[6] This theory emphasises the primacy of visibility within these modes of feminism: Rosalind Gill identifies a 'hostile scrutiny of women' at the centre of postfeminism (Ibid., 4–5); Catherine Rottenberg asserts that neoliberal feminism introduced a 'new feminist vocabulary, where happiness, balance and "lean in" were replacing key terms traditionally inseparable from public feminist discussions' (Ibid., 7); and Banet-Weiser sees the hypervisibility of popular feminism as resulting in the obscuring of 'expressions that critique patriarchal structure and systems of racism and violence' (Ibid., 9). Although these modes of feminism are in a 'cultural conversation with each other' (Ibid., 10), building what is widely thought of as a resurgence of feminism's popularity, they are also, perhaps more importantly for any consideration of the progress made by feminism, mediated in and through the cultural texts that (re)produce them.[7]

As Karen Boyle points out, 'the discursive construction of feminism has only ever been partly within feminists' control' (2019, 3) and in this sense, current feminist discourse clearly speaks to the discourse of backlash explored by Susan Faludi in the early 1990s. Far from being an easily identified movement, the mechanics of backlash 'are encoded and internalised, diffuse and chameleonic' (1992, 13) and its politics make use of (in)visibility to hide in full view. The hypervisibility of current modes of feminism exists on a continuum with this backlash, functioning within a patriarchally sanctioned economy of visibility that serves to control the workings of contemporary feminisms.[8] This link is important to acknowledge because the paradox of (in)visibility is central to our understanding of the #MeToo movement and the feminist politics that underpin it. Banet-Weiser worries that '[t]he visibility of popular feminism [. . .] is important, but it often stops there, as if *seeing* [. . .] feminism is the same thing as changing patriarchal structures' (2018, 4, emphasis in original); this has a direct impact on #MeToo where the 'spectacularly visible' risks undermining the focus on systemic violence (Ibid., 17). Boyle develops this argument, noting that the concept of visibility and women's articulations of male sexual violence are inherently connected; she asks whether the tension between naming – making visible – men like Harvey Weinstein and the often unspoken (and thus, invisible) trauma of women masks the 'structural nature of men's violence' (2019, 12).

It is, I argue, this tension between (in)visibility and the (in)ability to articulate described by Boyle that both masks and exposes the distressing truth at the centre of *Top of the Lake*. Although the first series precedes #MeToo by five years, it both deftly enacts and subverts the processes – central to any understanding of #MeToo – through which women are subjected to violence and forced into a silence which prevents them from articulating any response to that trauma. Campion's pre-empting of the cultural and social #MeToo moment simply reinforces the pervasive ahistorical presence of male sexual violence, and the series is part of a groundswell of cultural representations exploring that systemic violence. Talking of #MeToo, Campion says:

> Right now, we're in a really special moment. I'm so excited about it. It's like the Berlin wall coming down, like the end of apartheid. I think we have lived in one of the more ferocious patriarchal periods of our time, the 80s, 90s and noughties.

(Muir 2018, n.p.)

Through *Top of the Lake* Campion charts a history of feminist thought and challenge to dominant patriarchal discourses from the second wave through to #MeToo. The series creates a thematic space in which dialectical movements between visibility and invisibility, articulation and voicelessness, violence and agency are explored. This chapter will focus on reading the representations of the community of older women that takes up residence in Laketop, the detective character, Robin Griffin (Elisabeth Moss), and the abused child, Tui Mitcham (Jacqueline Joe). It will consider the archetypes and stereotypes of feminism used by Campion, arguing that in linking these representations with the wider thematic concerns, Campion creates new paradigms of female articulation for a paradoxical cultural moment. Ultimately, this chapter asserts, Campion gives us a female-focused series for voicing the particular dualities of twenty-first-century female subjectivity.

THE FEMALE VOICE

Top of the Lake represents a complex generic blend that moves between (among others) detective story, female gothic, and Scandi-noir. Robin Griffin has returned to Laketop, her childhood home, to visit her dying mother when she is recruited by the local police department to interview a pregnant twelve-year-old, Tui Mitcham, who then goes missing. Robin's investigation into Tui's disappearance takes place against a background of violence and criminality perpetrated, in large part, by Tui's family, who run a drug production ring and resent the appearance of a women's camp on land they covet. The parallels between Robin and Tui are strengthened as the series progresses – Robin's teenage gang rape at the hands of local men, as well as her drugging by the local police chief, Al Parker (David Wenham), speaks to the violence inherent in this small, male-dominated community that is also visited upon Tui. The series ends with Robin exposing the child abuse ring run by Parker; if not dismantled then the abusive power dynamics at play are at least made visible, with Robin and Tui both able to move towards articulating their truth. Thus, *Top of the Lake* sets itself up as a narrative that examines the interplay between the 'spectacularly visible' and often invisible systemic patriarchal violence.

Charlotte Brunsdon and Lynn Spigel argue that '[p]aradigms of visibility have been an organizing element of feminist television criticism from its earliest days', concerned with the 'over-visibility' of certain kinds of women and the marginalisation of others (2008, 22). Campion knowingly employs and plays with these critical paradigms from the opening credits of *Top of the Lake* which, as Kathleen McHugh points out, function as paratext, 'invok[ing] aesthetic, narrative, philosophical, and feminist motifs. Surface and depth, prominence and obscurity, the transformations of developmental life forms (girl to fetus) and representational media (painting to animation to photography) all shape this' (2015, 19). Thus the paratext functions to make clear to the viewer the focus on (in)visibility. These themes also characterise the opening sequence, in which the camera follows Tui cycling through the landscape of Laketop; the wide shots privilege the majestic New Zealand backdrop, presenting Tui as a tiny object, emphasising her child-ness and creating a sense of solitude. Tui, then, is visible to the audience but also obscure(d), with the viewer not yet aware that she is a pregnant – and, therefore, an abused – child. The gothic representation of the landscape and the sense of (male) violence characterising the domestic space from which Tui emerges invoke a sense of flight or escape, which comes into focus with Tui's arrival at the lake.

When Tui wades into the lake, fully clothed with fists clenched, Campion establishes the representational thread used to link the female characters throughout the series, with the lake as the central image. The space of the lake is characterised as a paradox by the paratext and Tui's immersion in the water imbues her with the same ambiguities. The first full close shot of Tui's face happens as she becomes submerged to the shoulders, so the viewer sees her for the first time at the same moment that she is disappearing into the lake. In addition, Tui is largely mute throughout the first episode (indeed, throughout the whole series). Thus, Campion allows Tui to evade both the visual and sound structures through which an audience would seek to characterise her, signalling a more complex path to subjectivity. Tui's silence leads So Mayer (2017) to identify her with the Kristevan *chora* through her association with a different kind of aurality; for example, despite her voicelessness – Tui will not, or cannot, speak the name of her assailant – later in the season she howls to express her anguish. Mayer draws on Kaja Silverman's analysis of the ways in which 'the female voice is as relentlessly held to normative representations and functions as [. . .] the female body' (1988, viii), arguing that Campion, through this alternative articulation, allows Tui to escape these normative representations in the same way as Ada (Holly Hunter) in *The Piano* (1993).

I want to extend Mayer's analysis here to suggest that the lake of Laketop is Campion's visual representation of the psychical space of the *chora*, and that it extends non-normative representation beyond Tui's aurality to Robin and the community of women who set up Paradise. For Kristeva, the *chora* is a sort of container for the semiotic, a mode of signification that exists prior to language and can function to disrupt language; this is significant for women because language is ordered according to patriarchal norms. The *chora*, Kristeva states, is a 'receptacle, unnameable, improbable, hybrid, anterior to naming, to the one, to the father, and consequently maternally connoted' (1981, 133).[9] Kelly Oliver's succinct explanation of Kristeva's understanding of the structure of language (and, therefore, society) is useful in understanding the importance of the semiotic:

> The Symbolic order is the order of signification, the social realm. This realm is composed of both semiotic and symbolic elements [...] the semiotic is part of the Symbolic. Which is not to say that it is confined within the Symbolic – although certainly we cannot talk about it except within the Symbolic order, because we cannot talk about anything outside of the Symbolic order. The semiotic moves both inside and beyond the Symbolic. The semiotic, however, does not move within the symbolic. Within signification, the symbolic is heterogeneous to the semiotic. The symbolic is the element within the Symbolic against which the semiotic works to produce the dialectical tension that keeps society going.
>
> (1993, 10)

Thus, it can be said that the semiotic functions both within and beyond language and is characterised not by words but by drives. These drives are inherently corporeal and libidinal because they are connected to the time and space before the subject acquires language, existing as a body at one with the mother. Two parts of this construction of the *chora* are significant for Campion's characterisation of the lake: the notion that it acts as a receptacle for potentially subversive semiotic drives, and the assertion that it is maternally connoted.

In basic terms, Tui, Robin, and the women of Paradise are associated with the lake in a way that strengthens their subjectivity, and the men of Laketop are frightened of or harmed by the lake. This is not to say that Campion performs a simple association of femininity with fluidity or presents us with a stereotyped monstrous femininity; rather the lake becomes the focal point for an examination of the ways in which female and male subjectivities function within a patriarchy organised through the Symbolic Order. Because of Tui's immersion in the lake water, her pregnancy is discovered and her abuse made known, though Tui cannot name the perpetrator, writing 'No One' on a piece of paper when asked by the police for his identity. Her voicelessness leads to the emphasis of her pregnant body as an object of intense focus, and Campion establishes a paradox that speaks to the concerns of both Banet-Weiser and Boyle: the spectacle of visibility represented by Tui's pregnancy threatens to obscure the male violence that has caused the spectacle. At the same time, however, although Tui does not (cannot) speak, her voicelessness does not mean she is unheard, because she is linked through the thread of lake imagery with Robin and the women of Paradise.

This thread allows Campion to create a semiotic space in which, although female voices might be literally silenced by a patriarchal Symbolic Order, the women speak to one another through the chain of visual imagery of the lake. The first shot of Robin comes as she takes a phone call asking her to investigate the pregnancy and the lake fills much of the background immediately associating her with Tui. In the third sequence of the first episode, we are shown the establishing of the women's camp – made of shipping containers – on the shores of the lake. That the lake is a space outside normative social constructions is reinforced by one of the women noting that GJ (Holly Hunter) – as the 'leader' of the camp – 'won't allow more [buildings] because she says we'll play house'. Thus the alternative domestic space is in direct contrast to the house Tui has left, which is dominated by men and their aggression. The gnomic GJ is both a 'self-ironizing surrogate for the director herself' and 'a form of cinematic self-haunting' (Thornham 2017, 109): as well as doubling Tui's father – the sinister, brooding Matt Mitchum (Peter Mullan) – as the head of a domestic space, GJ also invokes *The Piano*'s Ada (Holly Hunter having played Campion's protagonist in a critically lauded performance). This invocation emphasises that the space in which she operates directly challenges the restrictions of Symbolic Order because the female voices silenced by the men of Laketop can surface in Paradise (just as Ada's voice can be heard through her piano). Indeed, Sue Thornham also suggests that Paradise and its residents are a spatial rather than a narrative presence, emphasising that the visibility of women's (naked) bodies allow the space to stand apart from Laketop and lead the men to 'invest Paradise with its mythical stories'; it also offers, she argues, an 'ironic inversion' of the Oedipus narrative played out by the Mitchum family (2017, 108). I want to suggest here that viewing Thornham's characterisation of Paradise through the lens of the Kristevan *chora* highlights the way in which Campion does more than invert a male-dominated narrative; rather, she creates a female space in which women are not subjugated to patriarchal silencing.

Characterising the *chora* as a space of female articulation is strongly linked to Kristeva's assertion that the *chora* is 'maternally connoted'; it contains semiotic drives which are libidinal and connect the subject to the space she inhabits before she must submit to language, which initiates her into a patriarchal Symbolic Order, breaking apart the mother-child dyad. The father represents this break and so the symbolic (as a mode of signification) and the Symbolic Order (the ordering function of language and society) are strongly associated with maleness and masculinity. Tui's voicelessness and the fact that she is motherless symbolises the violence of this initiation. She is essentially alone in a house dominated by aggressive men (a microcosmic representation of patriarchy itself) and has been raped (by No One). There is no female space or relationship in which Tui can take refuge and she is, therefore, alienated from the semiotic, and the brutality of her initiation into female subjectivity has literally taken her voice. It is notable, then, that she finds words when she visits Paradise, which she does for the first time following the discovery of her pregnancy. Tui sits with the women listening to their tales of heartbreak and subjugation, though GJ's story is typically cryptic and we find out only that she experienced a 'calamity [. . .] as if [. . .] hit by lightning'. Tui asks, 'How come you're alive?', to which GJ replies, 'I don't think I am.' This is a figurative answer to a literal question and encompasses the state of all the women seeking refuge in the liminal space of the camp. Indeed, the question could easily be the other way round, for GJ's words indicate the futility for the women of Laketop in attempting to live only within *or* outside silencing patriarchal structures: Tui lives solely within patriarchal structures and is unable to speak; GJ lives within a women's space but is unsure whether she is 'alive'. This is indicative of Campion's paradoxical approach to female subjectivity. She does not encourage a withdrawal from the world of men but emphasises the importance of relationships between women in challenging the oppressive effects of maleness and masculinity.[10]

This position is accentuated by Tui's return to Paradise for advice from the women before she gives birth, and Robin's later arrival at the camp after facing her traumas at the hands of men, as well as the loss of her mother. It is interesting that neither directly communicates their needs through words but that their bodies are used to represent the distress – Tui is dirty, small, and vulnerable, and Robin is drunk, bleeding, and crying. In this lakeside space characterised by the semiotic, though, communication can take place beyond language and voicelessness does not mean an inability to articulate or be heard. GJ recognises what both are saying, and her advice is as corporeal as their communication (and we are reminded here of the ways in which Hunter's Ada communicates despite her muteness): 'follow the body', she tells Tui, 'it'll know what to do'; and to Robin she states, 'Sleep like a cat. Heal yourself. There is no match for the tremendous intelligence of the body.' Tui leaves the camp to give birth before Robin's arrival, and Robin leaves to continue her quest to find both Tui and her abuser. Their actions strengthen the suggestion that Campion is not advocating for a retreat from patriarchy; rather, she is suggesting that listening to the ways in which the female body speaks the violence of patriarchy is possible within female spaces and thus, these spaces pose a challenge to the very functioning of patriarchy. The 'maternally connoted', then, is an archetypal rather than literal spatial construction within Laketop.

This notion is reinforced by the wider function of Paradise within the community. It is at the camp that the mothers of Laketop find themselves grieving for the loss of Tui's friend, Jamie (Luke Buchanan), and the women working for Matt Mitchum finally turn against him because of the loss of this child. While the interactions within Paradise are intergenerational, none of the women is easily a mother figure: GJ displays none of the stereotyped characteristics of motherhood although both Robin and Tui are motherless (Robin's mother dies in episode five); Robin's daughter, born after Robin's rape, was adopted at birth; and Tui is about to give birth after being abused. The only explicit, yet difficult, mother-daughter relationship in the camp is between Bunny (Geneviève Lemon) and Melissa (Georgi Kay) and their (mis)communication is stilted and affected by Melissa's relationship with her father. Like Tui, Melissa is largely wordless, though episode six sees her rendition of Björk's 'Joga' (1997) with the refrain – 'state of emergency' – seemingly embodying the 'emotional landscapes' ('Joga') of all the women before they enter the camp.[11] And like Tui, Melissa finds a form of articulation in the music through which she can express the pain of patriarchal violence within the space of Paradise and the lakeside. Paradise, then, is a place where the 'maternally connoted' comes to mean a space which privileges the importance of female articulation, not as a place in which some kind of essential maternal identity operates. The women return to a state where their communications with one another are differently articulated than in the male spaces, which either silence them or disavow their truths. This state recalls the wholeness of the subject before initiation into the patriarchal Symbolic Order; thus, articulation and the corporeal are strongly linked.

THE FEMALE BODY

This link is emphasised by the presence of whole, naked female bodies unashamedly taking up space in the frame in the wider shots of Paradise, despite most of the women in *Top of the Lake* being subjected to unspeakable male violence: physical, emotional, and symbolic. The women who occupy Paradise are, for the large part, older and therefore characterised by the men of Laketop as less than women ('Is she a she?') and probably lesbians. This derogatory language, however, is not enough to ensure male control of those bodies, particularly as they function within the semiotic space of Paradise. And as Robin and Tui are subjugated to sexual violence in order to ensure their submission to patriarchal norms, so Matt Mitchum sets out to date Bunny (the woman funding the camp) in episode three, 'The Edge of the Universe' (a telling title because the women are indeed dangerously at the edge of this male-dominated universe). By accident he finds himself going home with Anita (Robyn Malcom), though they do not have sex – 'play[ing] together' instead – because he needs warning in order to 'take [his] pills'. The date precipitates Mitchum's self-flagellation at the grave of his mother, where he screams at Anita for 'fucking standing on her'. These scenes contain several intersections that reinforce Campion's focus on the power of female space and the subversive and frightening potential of women articulating their own bodies; as Kristeva (1984) might say, the challenge that the libidinal, corporeal drives of the semiotic pose to the organising system of the Symbolic Order has transformative promise.

For Matt Mitchum that challenge is emasculating, signalled by his inability to get an erection without 'chemicals'. But beyond the physical, Campion signals just how threatening female subjectivity can be through Mitchum's jump from 'playing' (like a child) with Anita to taking her to his mother's grave. In terms of the dialogue while Mitchum and Anita are in bed, the distance between the two women (Anita and Mitchum's mother) is collapsed, crucially, through his proximity to the female body and he says: 'You're so beautiful. Want to meet Mum? [. . .] You're beautiful.' Thus, the identification between would-be lover and mother is established and when Mitchum and Anita reach the grave, he descends into hysteria, screaming at Anita and promising to bring his mother 'home' to the land on which Paradise is established. For Mitchum to engage in sexual play with a woman from Paradise, then, undermines his whole sense of self and leads him instinctively back to his mother, as if a child. If, however, the mother reminds the male subject of the maternally connoted *chora*, he is threatened with a privileging of the semiotic over the symbolic, precipitating alienation from the Symbolic Order and his position of power within it: any woman has the potential to cause this threat. The strength of the risk to Mitchum's male and masculine identity is reflected in his use of the language of the abject when he storms to Paradise the next day, full of rage:

> You won't last in this land. Shit's coming out of your mouth [. . .] Shit, just shit, you have shit for brains [. . .] Where do you put your piss and your shit? You put it in my fucking land! That's where you fucking put it [. . .] Your fucking menstrual waste [. . .] You're unfuckable [. . .] You're a dry, useless, fucking bitch! [. . .] Unfuckable. Utterly unfuckable!

As Oliver notes, Kristeva asserts that 'abjection of the maternal body' is necessary in order to function in the Symbolic Order (1993, 87), and Campion literalises this in Matt's attempt to run over Anita in his van.

This sense of connection between Anita and Matt Mitchum's mother is reflected in Robin and Tui. There are numerous instances of doubling between the two in each episode of the series, which not only emphasise Campion's focus on the dynamic between women but also speak to their shared knowledge of attempting to come to a sense of self while living through male-inflicted trauma. This leads to the realisation, for the viewer, that male violence against women *is* the story of *Top of the Lake* and that rather than allowing spectacle to obscure the experience of women, Campion uses it to expose the systemic and pervasive nature of that violence. This exposure is often paradoxical within the series precisely because of the concerns voiced by Karen Boyle, noted at the start of this chapter: does naming and, thus, focusing on a perpetrator, she asks, mean that both women's trauma and the systemic nature of male violence remain invisible? Two of the clearest examples through which Campion explores this notion occur with Robin confronting one of the perpetrators of her gang rape and the discovery of video footage of Tui in the home of a convicted child sex abuser, Wolfgang Zanic (Jacek Koman).

Episode four sees Robin talking with Al Parker about being raped at fifteen years old by multiple men. Parker tells her that the gang was given 'a hiding' at the time by him, Mitchum, and other men of the town and that most people know about the rape. Later in the episode, Robin meets one of her rapists, Sarge (Oscar Redding), in a bar and stabs him in the stomach with a broken bottle before being led away by Johnno (Thomas M. Wright). Johnno, at the beginning of episode five, assaults Sarge and makes him leave town. In these interactions, Robin's trauma is subsumed into a patriarchal script in which Al and Johnno play both saviour and avenger: Robin's story becomes little more than an object used by them used to exert power and control, reinforcing their masculinity, negating her voice, and undermining the action she takes in hurting Sarge. This is emphasised by Al's comment that he and Mitchum stepped in because '[Robin's] father wasn't around to teach those dirty little shits a lesson', bolstering the notion that the rape is an affront to the men linked to Robin. Johnno uses the opportunity to punish Sarge in order to assuage his own guilt at knowing the rape was happening but being too afraid to do anything at the time, though it is notable that he takes action now that he and Robin are in a sexual relationship. This treatment of Robin by the men speaks to the ways in which both Gayle Rubin (1975) and Luce Irigaray (1985) characterise the exchange of women in patriarchy: women, they conclude, are the currency through which men transact their own relationships. Thus, the men's reactions to Robin's rape exemplify the way in which *what* has been done to Robin is less important than *who* has done it, because *who* has done it (dis)orders the power relationships between men.

THE FEMALE GAZE

Tui's story is told in direct contrast to Robin's story in the sense that it is always filtered to the viewer through women, and so becomes divorced from the political economy that serves to reify the male subject position. Tui's story, then, is always already part of the semiotic space set up through the image of the lake. Robin and Tui are doubled through their relationship to the lake, which remains the focal point to which they both return, letting the viewer know that their stories are entwined from the start. That entwining solidifies at three points in the series when it becomes clear that the doubling between the two is also part of the semiotic challenge to a Symbolic Order that is less concerned with the abuse of Tui than who has committed that abuse. Sue Thornham (2017) provides a comprehensive analysis of the complexity of Robin's gaze in *Top of the Lake*, and I want to extend that analysis here to suggest that Robin's gaze is part of the Kristevan impulse of Campion's representations. The challenge of this gaze also serves to place Tui's story at the centre of a narrative which destabilises a Symbolic Order that consistently seeks to silence the women of Laketop.

When Robin first sees Tui, it is through the one-way glass of the police station, where she is being observed – objectified – by the male officers. The spectacle of Tui's pregnant, child body has already been established, and she is further sexualised and demeaned through Parker's description of her inability to speak: 'She's tight as a clam.' However, Tui's position as object of the (male) gaze is undermined by the next shot, which shows Robin looking at Tui and also at her own reflection in the glass – the symbolism of Robin as mediator and disrupter of the male gaze is immediate.[12] The relationship between Robin and Tui established by this shot is compounded by the fact that Robin persuades Tui to write the identity of her perpetrator: 'No One'. This naming bypasses the male-focused narrative applied to Robin's rape because Tui's voicelessness enables her to keep her story among the women, shifting the balance of power. It is, in addition, an obvious nod to the viewer that Tui's story is also Robin's story. Later, when Robin discovers video footage of Tui at Zanic's cabin, her role as mediator of the narrative is consolidated. The video footage of Tui dancing and playing prefigures Robin's final, horrifying discovery of the abuser's identity, but her influence over Tui's narrative is tightened as her viewing of the video leads her to begin thinking more clearly about the identity of No One. Thornham argues that in this moment of gazing at the footage of Tui, Robin is in 'a position, *too close* to the object of her gaze, that corresponds, writes Mary Ann Doane, to Freud's vision of femininity, which is too self-absorbed for subjecthood and knowledge' (2017, 110, emphasis in original). Robin overcomes this closeness, Thornham states, when she enters Al Parker's basement in the final scene, using her camera to film the abuse, thus achieving 'distance' rather than being 'an over-empathetic reader of images' (Ibid.). While this is, of course, true, I argue that the space of Paradise allows the closeness – or entwinement – between Robin and Tui to be revalued as a mode of articulation, an expression through semiotic impulses that provides a challenge to the denial of selfhood, and ultimately leads to the discovery of what has happened to Tui.

It is in the final episode that the extent of the sexual abuse occurring in Laketop is exposed when we view it through Robin's camera. Walking into Al Parker's basement, Robin sees the paraphernalia of abuse scattered around, a slurring Al Parker, and a man dragging an unconscious young girl across the floor. It is immediately clear that 'No One' means multiple men, and the series tips decisively into the exposing of male violence as systemic and endemic. Naming the abuser here will not lead to further silencing of the victims of the abuse (the concern raised by both Boyle and Banet-Weiser) because, the camera tells us, this is not one man but a system of patriarchy being exposed. Although the distance constructed by the view through the camera is crucial for the sense of cold (yet heartbreaking) objectivity, the repeated image of a camera-view also invokes earlier moments from the preceding episodes; those points at which Robin has viewed Tui through a lens and the first scene in which we meet GJ, being filmed by one of the Paradise women as they set up camp. This visual invocation means that No One also refers to the women of *Top of the Lake*: it is not that one woman has been abused, all the women have in some way been touched by what Robin's camera exposes. 'No One', then, is a shattering of the singularity of the patriarchal Symbolic Order through the visual summoning of all the women into this scene. This creates a subversive multiplicity that challenges the silencing of these women.

DISCOURSES OF FEMINISM

Ending a reading of *Top of the Lake* with an emphasis on multiplicity highlights the paradox of Campion's vision. This is an ending that implies the suffering of all women in patriarchy but is also one which considers the privileging of female relationships and the necessity of female articulation. This brings me back to the space in which this chapter began: with a consideration of Campion's engagement with #MeToo, the notion that the series is structured within a feminist framework, and the assertion that Campion offers us an appraisal of current feminist discourse. The women's camp at Paradise is an obvious play on second wave feminist practices of women-only spaces and consciousness-raising groups. Victoria Hesford argues that representations of second wave feminism – women's liberation, in particular – very often 'both evoke [. . .] and elide [. . .] the complex array of feminist movements' that emerged in and since the 1960s (2013, 1). These elisions are often used to homogenise feminism and to contain it within its historical moment, undermining any effects of feminism that may exceed its own historicity. So it is that backlash politics empties feminist discourse of its power, producing and reproducing stereotypes and tropes that break the ties between the personal and the political.

Campion's representation of the women's space might actually be considered parodic and implicated in this discourse (especially given her own career-long problematisation of her work's engagement with feminisms) if it were not for the ways in which she contemporises the space of Paradise through its engagement with Robin and Tui. Her characterisation allows the influence of the second wave to open up space for the younger women, undermining the elision of the second wave in postfeminist and neoliberal economies of visibility, and insisting on the importance of the link between women's material and lived experiences. Through opening up Paradise as a space in which both Robin and Tui are able to articulate the traumas enacted upon their bodies, the series underlines the importance of recognising not a chronological, over-and-done-with feminism, but a cyclical, timeless feminism. The spectacular visibility of the post-menopausal, 'unfuckable' women's bodies are linked through the space of Paradise to Robin and Tui's abused, motherless, childbearing bodies; all these bodies are allowed and allow expression of the women's experiences that are otherwise silenced.[13]

Robin's quest to speak the truth in the face of both physical and symbolic silencing speaks to both Banet-Weiser's and Boyle's analyses of #MeToo and post-#MeToo, and is Campion's answer to the fear that structural change cannot take place while violence is made spectacle. In fact, the series foregrounds the female body as spectacle, its hyper-visibility threatening to undermine its subjugated place within patriarchy, and then links that visibility to articulation in order to expose how patriarchy seeks to control and silence. Both Robin and Tui, then, can be said to function as receptacles of violence and agents of change. Although *Top of the Lake* concludes with the seeming dismantling of Paradise (as GJ walks off into the distance) and a sense of uncertainty in the silence between the women, 'No One' has indeed changed the structure of Laketop. The viewer is left with a sense of the importance of both seeing and doing: seeing violence and listening to women's voices, and using those stories to challenge the silence that allows that violence.[14] Ultimately, this work represents an acknowledgement that feminism and the relationships between women engendered by feminism are the key to women's survival.

NOTES

1. It is reported that Campion joked at a press conference for *Top of the Lake* that she hoped the series is 'not just feminist but fallopian' (Furness 2017, n.p.). Joking aside, I argue that Campion's overt engagement signals a discursive move.
2. I use the term 'auteur' as shorthand for Campion's cultural standing, though I do recognise the problematic associations of this term and the paradox of using it to describe Campion.
3. Wherever I use the word 'feminism' I am actually thinking not of feminism as a monolithic or linear movement but of multiple moments and positions, implying the 'feminism(s)' of the chapter's title.
4. Two of the best longstanding analyses of this process are (in my opinion) Derrick A. Bell, Jr (1980) and Susan Faludi (1992). In addition, Manuel Castells (1997) explores how power operates in a 'network society', adapting to technological innovations, becoming diffuse with even greater potential for dominating social movements.
5. The introduction to *Empowered: Popular Feminism and Popular Misogyny* provides a comprehensive overview of the visibility of both 'popular feminism' and 'popular misogyny', with numerous examples of both in popular culture (television, advertising, celebrity culture, and social media platforms for example).

6. Rosalind Gill uses this term to describe her relationship with postfeminism in discussion with Banet-Weiser and Catherine Rottenberg. The three also highlight the links and differences between these three models of contemporary feminism, providing a useful overview of what we might say feminism 'is' today.
7. Karen Boyle (2019) gives an overview of this current resurgence in the opening chapters of *#MeToo, Weinstein and Feminism*.
8. Banet-Weiser (2018) re-visions the feminism/backlash relationship in her exploration of the symbiotic links between popular feminism and popular misogyny (1–40).
9. I also want to note here that, in basic terms, because the semiotic is associated with the mother and the pre-linguistic realm, it is also strongly associated with the female and femininity; the symbolic is the realm of language and is predicated on acceptance of the Law of the Father – thus, it is associated with maleness and masculinity.
10. This notion is present in her oeuvre from her early output (*After Hours* (1985), *A Girl's Own Story* (1984), and *Sweetie* (1989), for example).
11. For a reading of Björk's song in the series, see Susannah Radstone (2017, 87–94).
12. An intuitive (or perhaps knowing) nod to Laura Mulvey's foundational theorising (1975, 6–18).
13. Julia Erhart (2019) makes an interesting link between Campion's representations of aging women and her own aging; she terms it the "fictional-biographical overlap" (68).
14. With *Top of the Lake* Campion paved the way for other women to produce prestige television that unashamedly focuses on women's stories and voices and flooded onto our screens in the latter half of the 2010s: see, for example, *Big Little Lies* (HBO, 2017–2019), *The Handmaid's Tale* (Hulu, 2017–current), *Little Fires Everywhere* (Hulu, 2020), and *Mare of Easttown* (HBO, 2021).

CHAPTER 8

Jane Campion's Palimpsestuous Gothic: Kinship in *Top of the Lake: China Girl*

Johanna Schmertz

Drawing on her background as an undergraduate student of anthropology, director Jane Campion examines notions of family with an anthropological eye. Her female protagonists come from fractured or dysfunctional families, and their adventures and investigations highlight larger flaws in the social systems in which they participate. In the two seasons of Jane Campion's *Top of the Lake* (2013, 2017), protagonist Detective Robin Griffin (Elisabeth Moss) investigates crimes against younger women while suffering herself from the trauma of being raped by a group of men in her youth and bearing a child as a result. Beyond exploring rape culture, Campion's anthropological approach bears witness to the fracturing of patriarchal kinship structures based on incest taboos that structure the exchange of women between men (Lévi-Strauss 1969). In the second season in particular (subtitled *China Girl*), the sex and illegal surrogacy trades in Australia point to the disintegration of these structures.

Kathleen McHugh has observed that Campion's interest in family structures is apparent from the very beginning of her career, noting that the opening credits of her student film *Peel: An Exercise in Discipline* (1982) contain a Lévi-Strauss kinship schematic – a triangle containing the names of its three actors showing how their characters are linked with one another – followed by the phrase 'A True Family' in scare quotes (2007, 27–8). McHugh also examines the opening credit sequence of the first season of *Top of the Lake*, in which cast and crew names emerge and disappear alongside images of stag antlers, girls, and foetuses. McHugh argues that these images are a paratext, enabling us to read the series as gesturing towards possible versions of 'family' unencumbered by patriarchal structures (2015, 23). Similarly, the opening credits of the second season, *China Girl*,[1] perform a similar manoeuvre, appearing to sweep the so-called nuclear family off to sea. In this chapter, I argue that Campion violates incest taboos as a way of flouting male kinship structures. She does this in two ways: through a use of the Gothic in which Campion's female characters break taboos themselves and work as signifiers of the undoing of the patriarchal management of women, and through a set of aesthetic practices that blur lines between characters and fuse their familial roles.

BLUEBEARD'S KIN

The influences of Campion's education resonate throughout her work. Part of Campion's anthropological education included studying under a professor who had worked with Lévi-Strauss (Ciment 1999a, 31). As an anthropologist and ethnologist, Lévi-Strauss (1969) postulated that kinship structures in all cultures rest on the necessity of creating exogamous relations that ensure peace between families and tribes, and that taboos against incest are necessary in creating these structures, although who counts as 'family' or 'kin' – and therefore what counts as incest – varies across cultures and times. Campion's educational background arguably would have brought her into contact with Sigmund Freud's *Totem and Taboo* (1913), in which Freud reworks the Oedipus myth. Freud suggests that entailed in the father's prohibition of his sons' incestuous sexual desire for the mother is a primal ur-father who will hoard all the women for himself unless his sons rise up to kill him, which would then allow for the exchange of women between brothers. Implicit in Freud's description of the incest taboo is the desire to violate it; in other words, men can avoid incest only by giving women away to other men. In addition, during the time Campion was at university, early formulations of feminist theory located the roots of patriarchal power in the same social structures laid out by Freud and Lévi-Strauss. For example, Gayle Rubin noted that in a kinship system based on female reproduction and the prohibition of incest, women play the role of 'gift' in marriage transactions made by men, and can only be the object, not subject, of exchange in creating these kinship systems. The exchange of women between men, Rubin argued, 'imposes the social aim of exogamy and alliance upon the biological events of sex and procreation' (1975, 173).

Campion's women struggle against the cultural expectations Rubin describes. This struggle is often refracted through the tropes of the Gothic, in which the Bluebeard figure may be seen as representing the mythic primal ur-father of Freud's *Totem and Taboo*, whom the sons must kill in order to take his place. In Campion's films, tropes of Bluebeard and the Gothic have appeared together with the theme of the traffic in women at least since *The Piano* (1993), when Ada's (Holly Hunter) introductory voiceover tells us she is being sent by her father to cross oceans to meet and marry a man she has never met, in a quasi-origin story for a Europeanised New Zealand. A 'gift' exchanged between men to solidify an alliance, Ada's removal from one family structure and placement into another represents both paternal protection and sexual threat. The threat embedded in the exchange figures most prominently in a Bluebeard shadow play performed by the local church that foreshadows a later scene when Ada's husband, Alisdair Stewart (Sam Neill), chops off her finger as punishment for giving herself to another man.

In the first season of *Top of the Lake*, Campion's Bluebeard figures are Al Parker (David Wenham), Robin's commanding officer, whom she ultimately learns has been running an undercover child sex trafficking ring, and local drug kingpin Matt Mitchum (Peter Mullan). Matt has had sexual relations with many of the townswomen and fathered an unknown number of its residents – a patriarch who has seeded (and polluted) the town's roots. Buried in secrets that trace back to the troubled origins of its occupants, Laketop operates like a dysfunctional family. The first season of *Top of the Lake* ends with the discovery of Al's sex-trafficking ring, paralleling a brothel populated by Southeast Asian women at the centre of season two. In the second season, set in Sydney, Australia, Robin's familial role shifts from daughter to mother, as she attempts to reconnect with the child she gave up while a teenager in Laketop. In *China Girl*, Al returns in a wheelchair for part of an episode to attempt his patriarchal revenge on Robin for exposing his sex trafficking, having largely escaped punishment in season one. However, Campion's primary Bluebeard figure in this season is not Al but Alexander, who is referred to as 'Puss' (David Dencik), because he is always surrounded by both cats and women. Puss is the landlord of a brothel populated by Southeast Asian women and a self-proclaimed feminist who claims he supports the cause of women by permitting an avenue for undocumented women to make money (prostitution is legal in Australia, but undocumented women are not covered by legal protection and are thus still vulnerable). Like Al and Matt, he traffics in women, both through his connection with the brothel and by facilitating a subsidiary illegal surrogacy ring in which some of the prostitutes are carrying babies paid for by wealthy (mostly white) Australians.

Noting that Campion's films have 'repeatedly used the Bluebeard story as a myth underpinning [their] narrative structures', Sue Thornham suggests that Matt Mitchum in season one represents the continual failure of patriarchal culture to maintain itself (2017, 102); Matt prostrates himself before his mother's grave, is abandoned by the women who produce the drugs he sells, and is ultimately killed by his daughter in the final episode. If, as Thornham suggests, Matt signifies the failure of the Oedipal quest and of its concomitant patriarchal control of women and their reproduction, I argue that Puss, the Bluebeard figure in *China Girl*, both reflects and comments on that failure performatively.[2] Through Puss's trafficking, and through his own wry and sententious observations that he is merely a symptom of a culture that has produced him, *China Girl* illustrates the potential for disruption in the traditional family created by its roots in the exchange of women between men.

GOTHIC MOTHERHOOD

> I wanted to go deep into the uterus of a woman [. . .] from creation to appropriation. It was always in my mind that the ocean is the major uterus of the whole thing. It's a feminine space.
>
> (Vineyard 2017, n.p.)

Campion has said that her approach to *China Girl* was 'ovarian' and 'fallopian', jokingly deflecting questions about her feminism (Ibid.). By this, Campion seems to suggest that feminism cannot ignore the role that maternity plays in shaping women's destinies, even and especially when those roles are outsourced to other women. From the outset of *China Girl*, Campion associates female reproduction with danger and death. The opening credits of each episode show a shoreline of the sea, onto which a series of images is superimposed: an ovum, a sperm penetrating it, a foetus, and finally the waves washing over the foetus and absorbing it, such that the sea seems to contain the whole human life cycle from birth to death. A few scenes after this title sequence, we see a suitcase slowly descending into the ocean. In a subsequent scene we see a bit of hair escaping the case – that of the eponymous 'China Girl', who is later revealed to have been a prostitute in a Sydney brothel that traffics exclusively in Thai women, as well as pregnant surrogates for wealthy white Australian women.

This early image of an object descending into water harks back to a closing scene in *The Piano* where Ada's piano sinks slowly, ethereally, into an amniotic ocean, with Ada freeing herself from it at the last minute. By beginning a new life with Baines, Ada has been able to find a place in society for both herself and her daughter. But as a non-white immigrant prostitute, 'China Girl', who goes by her street name Cinnamon (Thien Huong Thi Nguyen), cannot create a space for herself within existing kinship structures. Unlike Ada, she does not survive her descent into the water.³ Instead, she – like Tui (Jacqueline Joe) in the first season of the series, who at one point appears to be considering drowning herself in a lake – becomes the starting point of a Gothic mystery to be solved by Robin Griffin. Cinnamon, Tui, and Robin are all mothers who have had their bodies used against them in ways that place them on the margins of society, forced to carry children outside accepted kinship systems, children whose mere existence points to the problems underlying these systems.

Claire Kahane has observed that motherhood is at the 'secret center of the Gothic structure, where boundaries break down, where life and death become confused, where images of birth and sexuality proliferate in complex displacements' (1985, 338). Registered visually in the ocean waves that overlap images of fertilisation, gestation, and death in the opening credits, this 'secret center' generates Campion's plot points. Cinnamon is trapped in both the sex trade and the surrogacy trade, merging birth and sexuality. These themes pervade Robin's story as well, as her prior rape has resulted in her serving as a kind of surrogate, carrying a baby (Mary, played by Campion's own daughter Alice Englert) who is ultimately destined to be adopted by another couple. Feeling a loss of identity because Robin has not responded to her request for contact, Mary too participates in the displacements Kahane describes. Mary accuses her adoptive mother, Julia, of having a womb where 'nothing ever lives, where everything dies', and Mary masochistically replicates women's 'destiny' through her boyfriend Puss, who is involved in the same sex and surrogacy trade that has led to Cinnamon's death.

While the 'China Girl' at the secret centre of this story dies, the (white) female characters that survive her express both their pain and their relative privilege under male kinship systems by breaking up marriages, thwarting legal and biological definitions of family, and generally disrupting cultural norms. Most emblematic of this disruption of cultural norms is Miranda (Gwendoline Christie), Robin's police partner and ultimately Robin's closest emotional bond. Miranda engages in an affair with their boss, who is married and has a son. She has sex with Robin's brother Liam (Kirin J. Callinan), wears his clothes as a disguise in the series' climactic manhunt, and fakes a pregnancy that is in fact carried by one of the surrogates in the illegal surrogacy ring managed by Puss. Despite her many transgressions, Miranda is the series' happiest and most emotionally connected character, believing in sex, love, and connection beyond any patriarchal laws. But whatever new paradigm her choices may usher in is left on hold, as she ends the series in a coma. In short, in *China Girl* and in much of Campion's work, maternity is Gothic. Sexuality has been constrained by patriarchal kinship structures based on the incest taboo, and the exchange of women's bodies produces its own counterforce that struggles against that culture.

DISRUPTING THE FAMILY ROMANCE: INCEST AND THE MATERNAL

In its most basic form, the prohibition against incest ensures that fathers will not have sex with their daughters, protecting their 'purity', but will instead bestow this privilege upon men who are not blood-related, thereby creating exogamous alliances between tribes. In Western traditions the incest taboo is encoded in rituals like the father walking the daughter down the wedding aisle to be given away (or 'gifted') to the groom, purity balls, and the father-daughter high school dance, which plays a prominent role in an episode of *China Girl* discussed later in this chapter. While these rituals enshrine the father's role of protecting his daughter from a rapacious male culture, they also displace the mother, rendering her obsolete once she has provided the daughters that are the medium of exchange. The prohibition against incest is also encoded at the level of the individual psyche: in psychoanalytic accounts of child development, the child must break the maternal bond in order to gain access to language and a sense of an independent self. Campion undercuts such accounts of social and psychological development. As Campion scholars have frequently noted, the law of the father is countered in her work by the mother's return in the form of the pre-Oedipal realms of the semiotic and the imaginary.[4] In this pre-linguistic realm, incest does not exist, cannot exist, because difference – including gender difference – does not exist; desire is undifferentiated and there are no distinctions made between familial and sexual touch.

Hilary Radner observes that one of Campion's recurring themes is 'the reworking of what Sigmund Freud calls the family romance' (2009, 8). Given Radner's insight and given the role that the semiotic plays in Campion's work, it is important to note how incest functions in Campion's stories. Incest occurs fairly explicitly in Campion's early films *A Girl's Own Story* (1984) and *Sweetie* (1989).[5] In later, more commercial work, incest is less overt, appearing as a kind of polymorphous chain of displacements. For example, in *The Piano*, sexual and familial touch are merged, disrupting the Oedipal order meant to break the bond between mother and child. While Ada explores her sexuality by trading sexual favours for her piano with a man she is not married to (Baines [Harvey Keitel]), Flora's (Anna Paquin) sexuality is likewise unleashed in what Richard Allen has called a 'string of metonymic substitutions' (1999, 60). After spying Ada and Baines having sex in his cabin when they are supposed to be having piano lessons, Flora participates vicariously in the primal scene she has just witnessed by rubbing herself on trees. Continuing the substitutions engendered by her sexual relations with Baines, Ada caresses Flora in bed at night, awakens shocked by that caress, and in the next scene transfers her touch to her husband, its 'rightful' owner.

Incest emerges as a major theme in both seasons of *Top of the Lake* largely through Robin, who suffers from sexual trauma and fractured family bonds. She attempts to repair her psychic damage by forging sexual relationships with men who also represent family. In the first season, Robin comes back to Laketop and renews her relationship with Matt's son Johnno (Mark Leonard Winter), a boyfriend from her past who was a silent witness to her rape. Through investigating Matt, she learns that her mother had sex with Matt around the time Robin was conceived. Nevertheless, she initiates sex with Johnno after telling him they may be brother and sister and ponders whether their social fate would be worse than that of a gay couple in the town (Johnno initially participates, then pulls away). By pushing past the incest taboo, Robin and Johnno re-enact a primal scene, much like Flora in *The Piano*, with Robin having sex as (and with) her mother in a 'family romance' in which Johnno doubles for their father Matt. They are, and perhaps Flora is as well, trying to both replicate and rewrite their family origins. In violating the incest taboo, Robin may be seen as refusing a social order that severs the bonds between mother and daughter and that erects in its place a system of male exchange of women.[6] Her incestuous act may be seen as a revision to her own troubled family history, but also as Campion's commentary on the problematic place of women in the larger culture.

Top of the Lake's theme of incest continues in *China Girl* because its main characters are all displaced in one way or another from traditional family structures and in a sense are not answerable to its taboos. Elisabeth Moss, who plays Robin, notes in an interview that the first season never fully concludes that Johnno is not, in fact, Robin's half-brother: 'But we're not sure if they're related still? I *don't* understand why this is being brushed under the rug. I don't feel this has been resolved?! It was for the best that we stopped asking questions' (Saraiya 2017c, n.p., emphasis in original). Moss's phrase 'brushed under the rug' echoes the kind of Freudian punning and wordplay that often drives Campion's plots (McHugh 2007, 46), suggestive of why the 'question' of incest perpetually reshapes itself to emerge in new ways.[7] Bonded by a shared desire to rescue Mary (tellingly nicknamed 'Baby') from the grips of forty-two-year-old boyfriend Puss, Robin and Pyke (Mary's adoptive father, played by Ewen Leslie) become sexually and romantically involved. Taking Pyke as her lover allows Robin to merge with her lost daughter and combine father figure and lover into one man, the mother seeking to insert herself into the daughter's family structure (a reversal of the Flora-Ada pattern in *The Piano*). On one level, Robin may be seen as stealing Mary's father for herself, rupturing the nuclear family with its false promises. On another, she is rewriting both herself and Mary into its structure, 'marrying' legal and biological definitions of kinship, as she claims parenthood by biological right while Pyke can claim that right by law.

Robin's re-configuration of the family romance is captured in an image that blurs Mary, Robin and Pyke into a tangled triangle of flesh. On a swimming outing at Bondi Beach, Puss has bitten Robin's nose for being a 'nosy bitch' regarding his involvement with the brothel from which Cinnamon has disappeared. Pyke and Mary run to Robin's rescue and the three of them merge into each other's arms and bodies in the right foreground, with Puss in the left middle ground of the frame, out of focus (Figure 8.1). A focus pull then places Puss in sharper focus (Figure 8.2), with Pyke, Robin, and Mary now blurred, so that Puss may be seen looking jealously at the trio, who have found 'family' at his (perceived) expense. Campion's use of rack focus literalises, through its blurring of boundaries, that 'family' is paradoxically both incestuous and dependent on exclusion for its meaning.

Figure 8.1 Family in Focus, in *Top of the Lake: China Girl* (2017)

Figure 8.2 Puss in Focus, in *Top of the Lake: China Girl* (2017)

PUSS IN THE FAMILY WAY

Although Campion's female characters fight against patriarchal kinship systems by pushing at the boundaries of the incest taboo, in *China Girl* it is the male antagonist Puss who articulates this fight. In Puss, Campion transforms the traditional Bluebeard figure of the Gothic into 'a kind of theorist [. . .] a politicized socialist' who wants to 'get up in the noses, deliberately, of the middle classes' (Vineyard 2017, n.p.). Campion notes that the three primary characters of *China Girl* are 'interestingly kind of matched' (Ibid.). Mary is the product of Robin's rape at the age of sixteen in Laketop, and immediately released for adoption, and Puss's mother was raped by her employer. Campion says:

> So they've all got this kind of lack of ease in what I would call 'straight society'. He was the result of rape, Mary was the result of rape, and Robin was raped. And so that makes them all pariahs in a way.
>
> (Ibid.)

Puss is, as he tells Mary, 'the bastard son of a rape' and thereby angry both at being excluded from a man-made kinship system and at the system itself. If 'legitimate' families are formed by fathers bestowing daughters in ways intended to create exogamous alliances with other families, Puss is unable to participate in the creation of family either as a father or as a suitor. Codified as a bastard and (later) a bigamist, according to the social norms he critiques, he ironically performs a series of received male roles that expose or subvert the law(s) of the father. In several scenes, he attempts to insert himself into family structures and thereby disrupt them.

In the first of such scenes, Puss plays the role of male suitor asking the father for the daughter's hand in marriage. Mary invites Puss to a family dinner with Pyke and Julia (Nicole Kidman) at their house, despite her parents' disapproval of their age difference (Puss is forty-two and Mary is seventeen). Puss resists, saying the meeting will end in 'class warfare', but goes to dinner anyway. The dinner goes as badly as predicted; he alienates Julia by claiming to be both a feminist and an intellectual, both characteristics that Julia would like to claim for herself. After dinner, Puss gets Pyke alone in a room while Mary, headphones on, dances by herself in an adjoining hallway, pretending not to be the object of their discussion but clearly visible to both men. The character blocking within the *mise-en-scène* depicts the bonding of two men through a woman who is both outside the bond and central to it, a bonding Luce Irigaray has called 'hom(m)osocial' (1985, 171). Puss then asks Pyke for permission to marry Mary. The tradition of asking a father's permission to marry his daughter presumes an understanding between men that women are property to be exchanged between them in order to create and preserve paternal lineages. But as this is a 'right' that Puss as a 'bastard' does not possess, it is a dramatic gesture bound to fail, solidifying Puss's anger against middle-class values and social mores. Pyke expresses his disgust at the request, refusing this male bond.

A subsequent scene shows Puss still trying to insert himself into Mary's family, this time by announcing his ability to provide for her economically. In an attempt to prompt Mary to break things off with Puss, Pyke has invited them to dinner at a restaurant with him, Julia, and Isadore (Julia's lover), planning to confront Puss with a bigamy charge. Puss enters the restaurant without Mary, dressed in a suit and tie but unwashed, unshaven, and with his tie loose. After noting that the chandelier at the restaurant was made by slave labour – 'Elegance, but at what cost?' – he looks at the three huddled together at a table and asks: 'Is this gang of three here to confront me?'. Pyke lies, saying that they want to welcome him into the family. Puss responds, 'Nothing pierces an illegitimate boy's heart like the word "family"', underscoring his status outside the conventional constructs of that word. He begins to wave an engagement ring in a box in front of Julia, asking if she approves of it – simultaneously flaunting and flouting another gendered middle-class cliché – and she pushes it away, refusing to look at it. Drawing attention to the middle-class pretensions of securing a good economic match for one's daughter, the index of which is an expensive and showy ring, Puss suggests that perhaps Julia only wants to know more about his bank account. He assures her that he is a landlord and can provide for Mary. However, Julia pushes the ring box away and Pyke confronts him with papers that prove Puss's bigamy. Since Pyke has tried to embarrass him, Puss responds in kind, loudly announcing to the entire restaurant that he took pity in college on a girl who was bullied because of a lame leg, proposed to her in front of her bullies to make her look good, and followed through on his own charade after the girl told him that her father had accepted his proposal. He has, he suggests, been an unwitting victim of the patriarchal exchange of women in his effort to empower a woman he felt sorry for, getting the raw end of the deal, and Pyke and his middle-class rules are obligated to put things right.

After this second rejection, Puss gives up on the possibility of a male bond and a proper role in the kinship system. He retreats to his apartment above the brothel with his harem of cats, taking pills and refusing to eat or see Mary. Mary attempts to feed him through a cat door (Campion's visual pun on his name), but he seems to have lost interest in the game of inserting himself into her family until he asks her why she is dressed up and she says it is for a father-daughter dance that Pyke has been looking forward to. This gives him the idea for one last performance. He determines to rise up against the father figure by attending the dance himself. 'But wait', he says, 'aren't I your old man?'. Playing on a phrase that means both father and husband, he continues speaking in a quasi-syllogistic series of verbal substitutions that draws an equivalence between himself and Pyke: 'This old Puss is your old man. I mean, I think it's true! This old cat is your old man.' His play on words enables Puss to gain pity and reassurance from Mary, and enables Campion to point out the inherently incestuous nature of rituals like the father-daughter dance and how its assumptions are culturally embedded in and reflected through language. In agreeing to let him accompany her to the dance, Mary accepts his syllogism, seeming to acknowledge him as both lover and father.

In the scene that follows, Puss crashes the father-daughter dance with Mary, attempting to displace Pyke or (in Freudian terms) 'kill' the father who won't release his daughter to him. As Pyke and Mary dance, Puss grabs a drink and looks on angrily, and after a few slow-motion glamour shots of fathers dancing with daughters, he cuts in, saying 'Hello baby. It's my turn.' Like the term 'old man', the term 'baby' linguistically collapses familial and sexual relationships, and allows him to transpose roles with Pyke. Pyke responds 'I'm dancing with my daughter' but Puss repeats 'It's my turn' and pulls Mary away. As in the scene at the restaurant, Puss then draws the attention of the whole room through a theatrical performance, moving in exaggerated ways and biting Mary's neck. An off-screen voice asks, 'Oh my God, is that someone's dad?', and Puss yells 'Who's your Daddy? Come to Daddy, Baby', shoving his head under Mary's dress as they both go down in a heap (a visual pun recalling a scene in *The Piano* in which Stuart witnesses Baines performing cunnilingus on Ada, and also a reminder of where all 'daddies' come from). In a final act of revenge against the symbolic father, Puss encourages Mary to go 'breast-to-breast' with her 'sisters' in the sex trade, stealing the father's (socially sanctioned) role of distributing daughters and converting it into daddy-as-pimp. Given his role as pseudo-social theorist, Puss is the fly in the ointment that proves the ointment (the whole arrangement whereby sex, blood, and family are legally interlocked in ways that create vilified Others) was bad to begin with.

CAMPION'S PALIMPSESTUOUS AESTHETIC

The topic of incest parallels Campion's film practices, which I describe as palimpsestuous.[8] One example of Campion's 'palimpsestuous' film practices is her use of opening credit sequences as paratexts, as noted by Kathleen McHugh (2015). In *China Girl*, the opening credits paratextually amplify Campion's agenda of exploring and exploding traditional kinship structures based on the incest taboo. In these credits, we can see a series of dissolves in which the ocean tide obliterates the signifiers of the traditional nuclear family. The credits appear over a shoreline where waves ebb and flow at the water's edge. The first shot contains an ovum framed by the names of the female leads. The water dissolves into another shot in which we see a sperm penetrating the ovum, the names of the male leads replacing the female ones. The names of the male leads are likewise washed over by waves and replaced by a foetus, over which appear the names of the producers. In the last shot, the foetus too has been washed away. Nothing remains but the ocean, and Campion's name, as the director's credit. As Campion has stated, the ocean represents a maternal space in *China Girl*. It is also a space where sexual difference is erased, a place where familial and sexual desire are merged, and incest therefore does not yet exist. The water has seemingly erased mother, father, and baby, consigning them all to the ocean, which blurs difference as soon as it appears. Like her incestuous characters, Campion is obliterating origin stories, making room for different ways of belonging in the world and building connection.

In addition to the dissolves in the title sequence described above, some of Campion's signature techniques may be regarded as palimpsestuous because they bring together things that we tend to think shouldn't belong together. These include decontextualizing close-ups, point-of-view shots that implicate the viewer, nondiegetic inserts, uncomfortable visual parallels and juxtapositions, and soundtracks that 'reframe' the shots and scenes they bridge. These techniques create overdetermined signifiers that disrupt the narrative and displace the viewer, compelling logics of association based on similarity and difference rather than a unity of action or cause and effect. Such techniques also blur boundaries between characters, uprooting them from the family structures where they 'belong'. For example, a key signifier in *China Girl* is the knock on the door, a kind of repeating knock-knock joke with different, surprising answers, with the plot moving to a new direction that depends on who is on the other side of the door. The series ends on one such knock heard from Robin's perspective, and since it is heard in the final shot, the viewer never gets the answer to 'Who's there?'. The knock could be from Pyke, coming to retrieve his only DVD of Mary, but it could just as easily be one of several other people who have visited Robin's apartment before.[9] Campion's knock-knock joke that has no answer disrupts fixed familial and sexual roles. Narrative ellipses, both within and between scenes, deconstruct the family and frustrate the viewer's desire to know what happens behind closed doors, to witness the primal scene and become part of the family romance.

A scene that erodes sexual difference as well as distinctions between sexual and familial intimacy occurs in a narrative ellipse between the fourth and fifth episode. With the exception of Robin herself, whose hair is short, the major characters have long brown hair, creating the possibility of visual confusion. Near the end of episode four, Robin is shown in close up, surrounded by bedsheets, singing 'I've Got You Under My Skin' as she holds a traumatised Mary, who has been rescued from Puss. Pyke enters the door bringing groceries for them. A subsequent close-up shows two sets of long hair bending over Robin in bed as she sleeps, bodies out of frame, and the scene ends. It appears we are seeing the possibility of a happily reconstructed family romance. Puss has been excised from the picture, and biological mother and legal father are now able to construct a union through their daughter. Episode five begins with a similar shot of two people bending over Robin in bed, visible only by their long hair, as a few soft words are exchanged off-screen. We assume, based on the absence of any long shots to suggest otherwise, that we are seeing the same characters from the previous episode, that Pyke and Mary have spent the night at Robin's apartment and have now got up to care for her in some way. However, the last shot of the scene shows Mary exiting Robin's apartment not with Pyke but with Puss, who has somehow managed to get Mary back. Gender difference has been erased through the close-ups of long hair, but so have familial roles – in the Oedipal triangle of mother, father, and child, roles appear interchangeable. Robin could, in theory, have been 'sleeping' with any of them.[10]

A key element of Campion's palimpsestuous aesthetic is her use of ironic juxtapositions, seen most clearly in a scene from episode four, 'Human Sacrifice'. Mary's eighteenth birthday becomes the final contest between Pyke and Puss. Anxious to share the day with her, Pyke follows Mary into the bathroom in the morning and asks her what she and Puss will be doing later to celebrate it. Mary drily responds, 'human sacrifice'. The depiction of the actual evening of Mary's birthday begins with a non-diegetic shot insert of a shelf of waving Chinese Lucky Cats, which are associated both with the brothel and – in continuation of the wordplay on his name – with Puss himself. The cat/Puss/pussy connection layers the meaning of the Chinese Lucky Cat onto a connection between cats and cu(n)ts that Campion previously established with *In the Cut* (2003), where, as Bowler explains, Campion invests in the 'transformative power of the linguistic breach' (2018, 109). The image of the Lucky Cats thus condenses multiple meanings into a rupture in the narrative, a 'cut' that gives birth to a sequence that literalises Mary's 'human sacrifice'.

After the non-diegetic insert of the Chinese Lucky Cats, Campion cross-cuts scenes of Mary being initiated into prostitution by Puss with a scene of Pyke waiting for her at home to return to celebrate her birthday. First, we see Mary in Puss's apartment displaying herself in a streetwalker outfit as Puss remarks approvingly that she is 'going for cutesy-pie'. They drive to an area known for prostitution and learn the going rate for a 'suck-off'. When Mary loses her nerve, Puss slaps her and tells her that this is the worst thing she is likely to experience on the job. The scene then cuts to Pyke waiting hopefully at home with Julia and Isadora for Mary to appear for her birthday dinner. As it seems she will not show up any time soon, Pyke bides the time by playing a home video of Mary dancing at her birthday party when she was a little girl. The scene cuts back to Mary, now out on the streets without Puss, experiencing her first encounter with a customer, who throws her out of his car back onto the streets.

These scenes of Mary at home and in the streets are juxtaposed for ironic contrast, underscoring the idea that Mary has 'come of age' by displacing a man who loves her (a good father), for men who only want to exploit her. However, the soundtrack Pyke has dubbed onto the video of little Mary suggests that Campion's irony goes further than this, that the line between Mary's two choices is not so clear-cut, because being born female, she will always be a kind of 'human sacrifice'. The song is 'A Little Ray of Sunshine' (1970), whose lyrics suggest male ownership of women and romanticise the father-daughter relationship. At the end of the series, Puss exits the country with the pregnant surrogates and Mary returns home to her adoptive parents, while Pyke and his wife Julia have agreed to reconcile. But the family, especially the daughter's role within it, remains under threat. In the closing scene, Robin has borrowed Pyke's home video of Mary, and 'A Little Ray of Sunshine' is heard once more, as part of the video's soundtrack. But with the unseen knock at the door that ends the series, the closing credits begin, and the diegetic version of the song slides non-diegetically into composer Mark Bradshaw's more sinister-sounding modern reinterpretation of the song.[11]

CONCLUSION

If the incest taboo provides for an 'outsourcing' of sex and procreation for the sake of cultural and geopolitical alliances, surrogacy is an extreme case of reproductive outsourcing that destroys its entire purpose. Reproduction is distilled to the simple matter of biological processes separate from sex or intimacy, no cultural overlays or niceties, and the 'guest mothers' (as Campion notes they are called) who bear the children are erased from the family picture once their job is done. If Gayle Rubin critiques the practice of mapping law and culture onto sexuality and female reproduction through incest taboos, Campion's exploration of the outsourcing of reproduction through surrogacy deepens Rubin's argument. Harnessing the disruptive potential of Gothic themes, *China Girl* critiques social structures created through exclusion and division rather than attachment, proscription rather than connection. In the ocean's ebbs and flows, in its liminal spaces that signify birth and return to origins, the mother returns to threaten the patriarchal structures in order to reclaim her child. Campion's palimpsestuous approach to exploring the family explodes family kinship structures, so that new ways of 'making kin' can take place.

By layering and fusing the lenses of anthropology and film, Campion gains both a model of cultural interpretation and an aesthetic strategy. The topic of incest enables Campion to question the structure of the family around which female identities are based. And aesthetically, Campion breaks taboos of narrative film by dissolving conventional shot and scene boundaries through dissolves, counterintuitive shot juxtapositions, and jarring sound correspondences, replacing narrative continuity with discomfiting 'family resemblances' that disturb the viewer's scopic pleasures. Perhaps the most disruptive of the film taboos Campion breaks is the casting of her own daughter Alice Englert as Robin's daughter, and the inclusion of footage from Alice's birthday party at two different parts of the narrative. Like Puss, who 'confesses' to his crimes in a self-made video in which he implicates entitled white women for the existence of an under-the-table baby market in which he has participated, Campion implicates herself in her own narrative. She is both protagonist and critical theorist,[12] transacting with the medium of film in ways that transform both her own understanding and the medium itself.

NOTES

1. I refer to season two as simply *China Girl*, both to distinguish it from the first season and to follow Campion's pointed reference to David Bowie's song about the anonymising and fetishising of Asian women.
2. There are also some would-be (or perhaps fallen) Bluebeard figures in *China Girl*, a group of young men who gather in a café to discuss prostitutes and rate them on a website. Like Al and Puss, they traffic in women, but they are unable to communicate with women they do not pay for. They are dangerous in their own way – one, Brett, aims to get himself in the news as Cinnamon's avenger and shoots three people along the way – but, like Matt, their need for control is arguably rooted in fear of the maternal.
3. Cinnamon is one of several allegorically named characters in the series. Her pseudonym refers to her colour and is meant to promote her as spicy and hot to potential customers. However, the name also points to her status as a commodity, referencing the spice trade routes that once connected Asia to the Western world. In a similar way, Silk 41, the brothel where Cinnamon worked, points to the silk road that connected East to West.
4. See, for example, Richard Allen (1999, 44–63); Caroline Bainbridge (2008); Jaime Bihlmeyer (2005, 68–88), and Stephen Crofts (2000, 135–61).
5. In *A Girl's Own Story* (1984), a young girl is impregnated by her brother as part of a sex game. In *Sweetie*, Campion's first feature film (1989), the title character's relationship to her father is perceived to be incestuous by her sister Kay, as Kay sees 'Sweetie' bathe her father's naked body.
6. This reading is consonant with the position taken by Sue Thornham, who argues that Campion replaces the myth of Oedipus, where the child's desire for the mother is cut short, with the myth of Proserpine. In that story, Proserpine's mother Demeter rescues her from Hades, a representative of a rapacious male culture who has stolen her away from home. Such a primary mother-daughter bond would subvert Lévi-Strauss's kinship model. See Thornham (2017, 102–17).
7. In slang terms, the word 'rug' has been used to refer to women's pubic area.
8. The term 'palimpsestuous' is borrowed from Linda Hutcheon (2012), who uses it to play on the verbal similarity between the words 'incest' and 'palimpsest', suggesting that all texts are intertextual rather than self-contained.
9. Elisabeth Moss and Gwendoline Christie, who play Robin and her detective partner Miranda, say they have no idea who is on the other side of the door, but that they hope it is Miranda, returned from the coma where the series left her, bearing Chinese food. See Saraiya (2017, n.p.).
10. There are many instances in *China Girl* where uncomfortable equivalencies are drawn between characters because of how scenes are edited together. For example, Brett, Cinnamon's customer turned psycho-killer, is at various times connected with Robin, Mary, and the audience itself, through matches on action and/or ellipses. Also, shared fantasies

or dreams about lost babies join both Robin and a woman whose inability to bear children has driven her mad. These equivalencies, as I argue, uproot characters from preconceived structures and layer them into new ones.
11. In some streaming versions, Bradshaw's version may be cut from the closing credits. Alexia L. Bowler notes that in *In the Cut*, Campion performs a similar manoeuvre by replacing Doris Day's version of 'Que Sera, Sera' with the more sinister Pink Martini version (2018, 98).
12. McHugh argues that Campion uses her work to engage in 'self-conscious theorizing' about the nature of film itself (2009, 151).

CHAPTER 9

Photosensitive Primetime: Race and Recovery in *Top of the Lake: China Girl*

Blythe Worthy

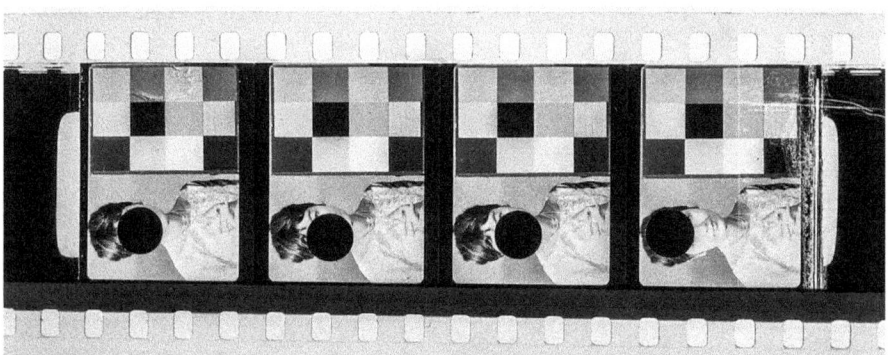

Figure 9.1 From a 35mm print of Masahiro Shinoda's film *Pale Flower* (1964) from Janus Films. Submitted by Rebecca Lyon, courtesy of the Chicago Film Society's Leader Lady Project.

In an interview with *The Guardian*, Jane Campion candidly discussed 'being on the verge of closing a deal to shoot an adaptation' of Rachel Kushner's 2013 art world novel *The Flamethrowers* (Pulver 2014, n.p.). Reno, the protagonist, is an emerging land artist who gets by on her secretarial job as a film lab 'China Girl' and the novel details her experiences of liminality as she is used to better service the artmaking of others. However, after a year of media speculation, all discussion of the Kushner adaptation ceased and it was announced in March 2016 that Campion would instead produce a follow-up series to her crime drama *Top of the Lake*, intriguingly subtitled *China Girl* (O'Connell 2016). With this follow up to the first season, Campion and co-writer Gerard Lee interpret facets of Reno's story across two character doubles to focus again on a missing, pregnant young woman of Thai extraction, this time named Cinnamon (Thien

Huong Thi Nguyen), and Senior Detective Robin Griffin (Elisabeth Moss), the Caucasian detective intent on solving her case. Produced by the Sydney-based production company See-Saw Films (*Lion* (Garth Davies, 2016) and *Widows* (Steve McQueen, 2018)), *Top of the Lake: China Girl* balances the two characters to reflect on the cast at large, imitating the central conceit of *The Flamethrowers*.

While it is not uncommon for projects (like the Kushner adaptation) to be abandoned, given that it is such a coincidental and particular moniker imbued with a history of malfunction and exploitation, I see the *China Girl* subtitle of *Top of the Lake: China Girl*, and the woman it represents, as demanding critical attention, especially because of how infrequently any Chinese women, let alone Asian women, feature on Australian primetime television. Though it is filmed and set on the land of the Gadigal people in Sydney, Australia, the international broadcast of Campion's second season explores the liminal Antipodean space between Australia, New Zealand and the nearby Southeast Asian region. Though 'China Girl' refers to the first episode discovery of the body of the pregnant Cinnamon, an undocumented immigrant from Thailand, it also crudely precludes her narrative function, the nickname referencing celluloid film colour and laboratory aim density (LAD) development and processing. A woman's portrait (termed a 'China Girl') is commonly cut into film leaders (Figure 9.1). As has been explored by Genevieve Yue, LAD 'China Girls' were celluloid portraits shot by laboratory technicians which were used for colour and density-corrected control when posted on celluloid leader tape, and were never seen on screen and thus never credited, their existence no more than a marginalised record to the conventional hermeneutics of popular film, forming racialised, shadowed histories.[1] Campion's strategic use of the provocative term 'China Girl' to represent a Thai woman, then, provokes considerations of the marginalisation of Southeast Asian women in Australia, one component of a series of racial issues in film studies that has been explored by Yue. As such, this chapter will interrogate commentary on the China Girl and her representations, as well as considering the geographical positioning of Australia in comparison to its popular representations in visual culture, the critical racial discourse surrounding Campion's work, and the use of undocumented or 'erased' women in crime dramas writ large. Using the work of Campion scholars as a springboard, I will continue the work of rescripting Women of Colour back into Campion studies to better hear those who 'struggle to be heard from the margins' and reflect the local landscapes that inspire the director's television (Pihama 1994, 239).

THE COMPLEX IRRITATION OF THE 'CHINA GIRL'

As a New Zealand filmmaker working between her home country and Australia, Campion has long operated in a transitory space to unearth uncomfortable underlying schemes of postcolonial stasis, focusing on difficult characters she has called 'Suburban Queens' (MIFF Talk 2017, n.p.). From a single episode of the 1986 young adult series *Dancing Daze* (ABC) to telefilm *Two Friends* (1986), to the 1990 auto-biopic miniseries *An Angel at My Table* and the two *Top of the Lake* series, the director and her collaborators present unconventional plot trajectories and character pairings. These pairings are often (though not always) white women juxtaposed with People of Colour, who challenge foregone local paradigms of white supremacy within suburban limits. Though her films often follow a classical narrative framework with only brief moments of inactivity, Muriel Andrin sees Campion's 'strange' television as diverging into distinct 'breathing spaces' to stall plot progression via technical decisions related to shot composition and temporality to 'create a space in which the self is "allowed to live"' (2009, 28–9). Campion herself has acknowledged these diversions, stating in an interview with *Variety*, 'I wanted to get [my storylines] all rubbing against each other, one way or another. You could call them too many coincidences, but [. . .] That's the way the story is told', while also suggesting the strategy was 'irritating' (Saraiya 2017a, n.p.).

Though she is commonly seen as an auteur of cinema, Hilary Neroni argues that television hosts Campion's long-term career interests well, especially her preference for stories that 'wander' or skirt classical narrative trajectories favouring a white viewpoint (2017, 115). With a densely layered interpretation of *The Flamethrowers* connected to the mundane textures of pedestrian Sydney life, *Top of the Lake: China Girl* is one such wandering story, juxtaposing the city's well-documented underbelly of human trafficking and illegal Southeast Asian surrogacy flows with the white middle-class family unit of Sydney's wealthy North Shore (McCloud 2016, n.p.). In order to comment upon the treatment of Thai migrants within national media and popular paradigms in Australia, *Top of the Lake: China Girl* traverses (using techniques common to Swedish crime dramas) what Steven Peacock calls crime drama's 'distinct borders', focusing on the suburban vs the transnational (2014, 17). Peacock maps these transitions as 'moving from the page to screen; moving from [nation states]' and 'across boundaries thematically, within the texts themselves' to form new ways of approaching the limits of the genre (Ibid.). Though billed as an Australian crime drama, *Top of the Lake: China Girl* hones Campion's New Zealand transnationalism which as Leoni Pihama has argued, has obscured her ability to 'belong' and 'identify' to a single nation, unfolding diverse stories of transition and migration within the neighbourhood of a single plot (2000, 114). The 'wandering' narrative has been used in many of Campion's works, in which characters move restlessly, either from their rural homes to the city or internationally, reflecting Deb Verhoeven's consideration of Campion's own colonial positioning as 'a migrant in a history of migration' given 'her own endemic movement is always already global' (2009, 121).

Though the body of Cinnamon is found and a search for her killer inspires much of what happens in *Top of the Lake: China Girl*, Campion's dense narratology spirals to focus on the 'global' Robin, returned from her first season sojourn in New Zealand. Robin investigates Cinnamon's death while working in a masculinised police force which insensitively dubs the dead woman 'China Girl', to the detective's chagrin. The effect of transplanting an Australian back from New Zealand gives Robin an odd foreign-ness, doubled by Cinnamon's sensitive case and the male-dominated team. Neroni argues Robin's alienation exposes the sexism rife in law enforcement and also, I argue, racism, in 'society at large', nudging the detective to be more self-reflective about her geographical and psychological positioning (2017, 117). Surrounded by men who see her as little more than a sexual conquest and foreigner, Robin is haunted by her encounters with the Thai women who force her to reflect on her own everyday complicity in the objectification of 'China Girls' (Ibid.). The friction from these perspectives 'rubbing against each other' creates existential plot holes throughout the series, as Cinnamon's identity hovers behind the narrative. As Yue says of the figure of the 'China Girl', 'she is not the invisible other buried *within* the visible image but something that remains *outside* the field of vision afforded by the screen', as though waiting to emerge (2015, 108, emphasis in original).

Aligning with a real-life 'China Girl' existence, Cinnamon's animated corpse refuses to remain a portrait in the film leader; instead, her haunting figure frequently disrupts Robin's efforts to reconnect with her biological daughter Mary (Alice Englert). Where Sue Thornham sees Robin as a 'Gothic investigator' whose investigation is 'simultaneous with her own potential victimisation' (2019, 102), Cinnamon also confronts Robin with her implicit absence. Historically, many Campion scholars have avoided racial commentary, with not enough arguing for the importance of recognising that the director's Australian and New Zealand television works often do explore racialised anxieties in some form, even if these tensions are oblique.[2] Tania Modleski, though, argues that colonial strains were evident in the 'blackgrounds' of Campion's 1993 film *The Piano*, in which Māori extras provided little genesis or acceleration to the film's narrative engine (1998, 38). In this sense, Modleski argues, 'the lives of people of color, as is the case in the crassest of Hollywood films, are of no intrinsic interest; their main role is to take interest in the lives of white people', complicating the film's connections to the postcolonial (Ibid.). Alison Wielgus contends that similar issues are present in *Top of the Lake: China Girl*, arguing that while the 'ultimate victim' is Cinnamon, 'the emotional locus of *China Girl* is Mary', tracing an inherent racial tension in the series' narrative trajectory (2019, 88). Within her detective plot, Campion embeds this 'emotional locus' through the claustrophobic family melodrama in which Robin attempts to reconnect with her daughter after eighteen years of estrangement, replicating other issues in *The Piano* noted by Lynda Dyson, whereby '"natives" provide the backdrop for the emotional drama of the principal white characters [. . .] located on the margins of the film' (1995, 268). The 'Suburban Queen'

Julia (Nicole Kidman) and her ex-husband Pyke (Ewen Leslie), an architect, make up the white, middle-class family unit, the specific means through which the affluent, aspirational society of the North Shore seeks to represent itself. Julia embodies the middle-aged, white second wave feminist, reflecting Modleski and Dyson's critiques, wherein 'the narrative focus [is] on a white victim' (Wielgus 2019, 88). Wielgus contends it is 'the exchange of a white woman' such as Julia or Robin with 'postcolonial sex trafficking' that primes the audience to consider 'the impact of globalization on women' (Ibid.). I see these tensions between characters like Mary, Robin, Julia, and Cinnamon as also drawing attention to issues surrounding feminism not just in relation to globalisation, but more in terms of how white women (many of whom consider themselves feminist) marginalise Women of Colour, a relationship rarely critiqued on television.[3] In producing work that actively problematises this white supremacy, Campion and her production team work to better understand the painful, inherent racism of many white Australian feminists.

Through the 'top' and 'bottom' of Campion's narrative 'lake', the director contrasts the middling visibilities of Robin and Mary, and Cinnamon and her baby, characters poised against one another to expose what, through the words of W. E. B. Dubois, Kara Keeling argues is screen culture's 'common sense problem of the color line' (2007, 89). When compared with Robin and the teenage Mary, who shirks familial connection and attention, Cinnamon and her baby's animated corpse refuse to remain behind the film's action, instead frequently intruding through dream sequences, photography, and morgue scenes. The spectre of Cinnamon reflects and confirms the absence of Women of Colour in the white Australian psyche and that of the next generation of privileged white children who continue this paradigm. Cinnamon and her baby evolve from an unknown corpse to fully-fleshed characters in these sequences, jostling the other characters for narrative attention to recover their space on Australian TV (Figure 9.2), a place Australian TV personality Yumi Stynes argues is 'great until you notice [the Asian faces] missing. And once you notice that absence, it becomes all you see' (2020, n.p.). As the series continues, the racial underpinnings of the characters' interactions begin to unravel the plot as various Thai surrogates disappear with the foetuses they hold, forcing the white couples employing them to contact the police to admit their own complicity in the surrogates' oppression. Accentuating plot inconsistencies and anti-formulaic experimentations, *Top of the Lake: China Girl* culminates in an abrasive scrutiny of presuppositions underpinning the ordinariness of white supremacist Antipodean cultural values, as white characters who believe themselves to be 'good' are confronted with their past epistemological violence.

Ignored by criticism and scholarship thus far but capturing much of the series' thematic concern, the series' subtitle, 'China Girl', has a triple fold significance that exemplifies these complex racial tensions. 'China Girl' is a

Figure 9.2 Brett Iles (Lincoln Vickery) and Cinnamon (Thien Huong Thi Nguyen). Photographer: Sally Bongers. © See-Saw (TOTL2) Holdings Pty Ltd.

complicated, orientalist signifier, encompassing debates over Australia's imagined fear of encroaching East Asian identities and paradigms. Ien Ang remarks on the geographically influenced racial dynamic in the region: 'Whereas in Britain the term "Asian" implicitly and explicitly refers to South Asians, in Australia the key component for "Asianness" is arguably East Asian, perhaps more explicitly Chinese', given Australia's historic avoidance of cultural association with Southeast Asia and high numbers of Chinese international students (2000, xxiii). Furthermore, *Top of the Lake: China Girl* connects the fragile, feminised traits of china dolls with domestic violence, with advertisements depicting Moss topless with a gun, cracks forming across her bare back, and cuts and bruising on her face. Finally, as I have noted above, the term alludes to the anonymous, elusive process of the celluloid 'China Girl', the photographic portraits of women (often film laboratory secretaries chosen at random) who held density charts used to calibrate film stock. As she is unseen by an audience unless a projectionist loaded the reel incorrectly, at which point her visage might flash on-screen to signal technical failure, the 'China Girl' symbolises the structural and pervasive character of ubiquitous exploitation. Unwelcome and on the margins, if the 'China Girl' appears it is only momentarily to signal, as Yue says, 'a kind of glitch, a momentary breakdown [. . .The China Girl] brings to light, to visibility, all the previously unseen processes, both cultural and technical, that attend its image', to signal something mechanical, indeed fundamental, has gone wrong (2015, 108).

BROADCASTING THE CIRCLE OF COLLUSION

Through Cinnamon, Campion seeks to accentuate this fundamental injustice within the televisual apparatus, gesturing to the distinct absence of the *China Girl* of the series' subtitle, which clashes with Moss's explicit whiteness. Attention is drawn to specific social mechanisms of exploitation within *Top of the Lake: China Girl*, whereby white women crowd out the stories of Women of Colour even after death. Given Yue argues the complex encoding of historical white 'China Girls' creates an 'ideal' which is then transmuted into a 'norm' to '[produce] a fiction of a single color against which all others must be measured', the advertising for the series plays on the racial title and this obscured filmic history (2015, 104). As a paratext, the importance of similar themes in the original *Top of the Lake* series' opening titles has been explored by Kathleen McHugh (2015). McHugh has argued images such as a New Zealand mountainous lake, a foetus, and stag heads in the first series' animated opening sequence are important symbols to the inter-series plot as they 'reference and incorporate distinct "parafeminist" frameworks' (Ibid., 18). Due to the title sequence's 'liminal composition and transactional function as an advertising paratext', these frameworks operate through Campion's reputation as 'creator', as well as in appropriations of the crime and mystery genres, and through the series' 'critical reception' as a prestige drama series (Ibid.). Frontloading such complex signifiers in the second season's advertising extends these features; posters of Robin as the cracked 'China Girl' with Campion's name were highly visible throughout Australian and New Zealand cities in the lead up to the season's premiere at the Melbourne International Film Festival. Cinnamon's absence in the advertising highlights a historical filmic white supremacy. Despite their racialised moniker, Yue has traced a 'shadow history' whereby most LAD China Girl subjects were white, a historical truth reflected in the racialised title of the series and its majority-Caucasian cast (2015, 99).[4] Mary Anne Doane, comparing the China Girl 'avant-garde face' with the china doll, argues the term 'is also a Western stereotype referring to the racist belief that Asian women are docile, submissive, the simple carriers of meaning – the screen for its display' (2011, 222). This process of control is also reflected in the series' casting, with all leads of the series being white. Cinnamon is primarily displayed on a mortician's slab surrounded by white people, or on camera and phone screens held by Robin's hands, enclosed and trapped by a white frame (Figure 9.3). In this way, Campion's casting interprets Sydney's postcolonial features, whereby the Southeast Asian geographical positioning of Australia is overwhelmed by a colonial mindset which is, as Ang shows us,

> An avid managerialist discourse [. . .] fought over the heads of Asian Australians. They are being reduced to objects to be counted, and to be

held in check too often [. . .] voiceless pawns in the public discussions about the present and future shape and formation of Australian culture.

(2000, xiv)

Within these public discussions, stereotypes have often shaped many popular representations of Asia on Australian television, with popular soap opera *Neighbours* (Seven, 1985–2022) portraying the Lims (Diane Bakar-Coleclough, T. S. Kong, and David Tong), a Hong Kong family, as being under suspicion for eating the family dog in 1993, and war series like the ABC's *Changi* (2001) and *Curtin* (2007) positioning apathetic portrayals of Japanese characters against heroic 'Aussie Diggers'; Benjamin Law's comedy *The Family Law* (SBS, 2016–2019) is essentially the only sustained exception. Representations of Asian women beyond Cinnamon in *Top of the Lake: China Girl* are similarly limited to other sex workers, all named with exotic signifiers such as 'Caramel' (Merlynn Tong), 'Honey' (Cynthia Ng), 'Sinn' (Lynda Ngo), and 'Jade' (Sereena), raising questions as to whether this 'feminist' series really serves all Australian women.[5] In order to examine 'the aesthetic, industrial, and cultural traffic' of *Top of the Lake: China Girl*, and 'the way the texts, and their characters, embrace, resist, and embody pluralism', as Peacock argues crime dramas often do, it is necessary to examine the Sydney of *Top of the Lake: China Girl* as a city with unique cultural and geographical features underrepresented in local television (2014, 17).

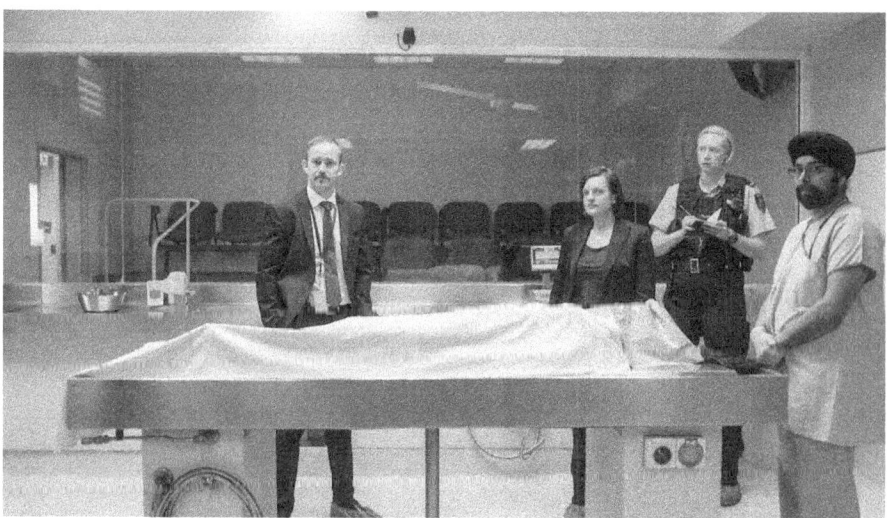

Figure 9.3 Stally Watkins (Christiaan Van Vuuren), Robin Griffin (Elisabeth Moss), Miranda Hilmarson (Gwendoline Christie), and Mo (Sumit Singh). © See-Saw (TOTL2) Holdings Pty Ltd

The intricate title of *Top of the Lake: China Girl* is clearly reliant on the cultural tensions around controversial representations of Asian cultures since the turn of the century, when the cultural implications of Australia's regional Asian context began to antagonise what Ang sees as a tradition 'insistent on its espousal of racial and cultural whiteness as the core of Australian identity' (2000, xvii). The ordinariness of television's status as a cultural form is rendered problematic in *Top of the Lake: China Girl*. The dynamic characters and dense, at times uneven, narrative divert narrative flow from predictable configurations. Campion and Lee obscure their storyline, leading prominent critics to condemn the series as having a 'strange confusion' that had 'gone very wrong' (Gilbert 2017, n.p.). Having spent much of the past decade living in Sydney, where around five per cent of the greater population comes from a Chinese background, Campion, in accordance with Stynes, argues that 'Sydney is a very Asian city . . . and you don't often see that' (Chang 2017, n.p.; Saraiya 2017a, n.p.). Especially interested in how Asian women are racialised by Antipodean men, Campion suggests:

> They like Asian women [who they hope are] more docile [and] compliant brides [. . .] there's a habit among certain types of Australian and New Zealand men to go over and get [themselves] an Asian bride [. . .] things don't always go as well as they hoped.
>
> (Saraiya 2017a, n.p.)

Revealing in the same interview that she believes a manipulated and depressed Cinnamon in fact committed suicide, Campion gestures at Cinnamon's death as a refusal to play her assigned role of surrogate to the impotent colonial saviour, the series resisting and challenging feel-good narratives that rely on white salvation.

The continuity between seasons reflected in these elements is reinforced by the ways in which the majority of the plot revolves around the exploitation and disappearance of Cinnamon, resonating thematically with the first series. Centring on Tui Mitcham (Jacqueline Joe), a pregnant twelve-year-old adolescent of Thai extraction who mysteriously vanishes, each end credit sequence of *Top of the Lake* features a scribbled note of Tui's, 'No One', alongside a China Girl-esque school portrait of the teen used in the media coverage of her disappearance. Campion's focus on the Thai diaspora in both seasons maps a purposeful path through the geographical lives of Antipodeans to Southeast Asia, a creative decision McHugh argues also '[refuses] the codes of racialized value that have persistently informed the gender politics of this genre and its affective appeal' (2015, 20). As Yiyan Wang argues, social tensions associated with Australia's Southeast Asian neighbours need not be seen only as a toxic and deadly force, especially since easy notions of assimilation or integration serve to obscure the resistances, contestations and uncomfortable mutual adjustments that inevitably accompany the 'working out of modes of coexistence', and their creative transnational potentials (2000, 108). Though Tui's rape and Cinnamon's pregnancy and death are scrutinised by Robin, a relationship that symbolises the similarity of the detective's experiences with those of the cases she works, her race complicates her relation to Tui and Cinnamon. Recovered from the margins of television, the faces of Tui and Cinnamon encompass the China Girls of Kushner's *The Flamethrowers*, in which Reno recounts her lack of visibility:

> If the projectionist knew what he was doing, loaded the film properly and wound it past the leader, viewers did not see me. If they did see me, my face strobed past too quickly, leaving only an afterimage, like those pulsing colors that mosey across the retina after you stare at a light bulb. Me then gone, me then gone.
>
> (2013, 86).

As 'pulsing colours', Tui and Cinnamon represent the 'China Girl' 'afterimage', a visual illusion of the human eye wherein retinal impressions attempt to replicate a pattern or colour that has been removed. This afterimage is racialised in Robin and Mary, who replace Tui, Cinnamon, and their babies to make palatable (for a majority white audience) the traumas of Women of Colour through their figures of white femininity. In the final episode, as Mary's older brothel-owner boyfriend Alexander, or 'Puss' (David Dencik) ushers a group of pregnant surrogates onto a plane back to Thailand, the biological white Australian parents of the foetuses watch a decoy film made by Puss that lectures them on their complicity with his corruption, completing the circle of settler participation in subaltern exploitation. Along with Robin and Mary, the biological parents function as afterimages, surrogates themselves for the audience's consumption of cultural exploitation, Campion mapping the circle of collusion ever wider.

These white couples who are serviced by the Thai women working at Silk 41 as sex workers while also moonlighting as surrogates suggest 'sex work' does not always occur in a brothel. Campion has explained her pervasive interest in surrogacy as a distinctly Antipodean issue, given the region has criminalised commercial surrogacy:

> It's very difficult [. . .] family creation in Australia [. . .] by the time you've discovered you maybe have fertility issues, you may well be over the age where it's easy to be considered an adoptive parent [. . .] the desperation that makes people go to get surrogacy, or have babies through surrogacy overseas in Thailand – which is now illegal – or in India, which is now also really difficult. It can be really abused as well.
>
> (Saraiya 2017b, n.p.)

This distinctly Antipodean issue becomes an intercultural tool to highlight the abuses experienced by poor Thai migrants at the hands of the white middle class, accurately reflecting the region's shockingly high rate of modern slavery, in which out of an estimated 1,619 victims of labour, sex trafficking, and forced marriages, only one in five was detected by authorities in 2017 (International Labour and Walk Free Foundation 2017, n.p.). Though Campion and Lee's Australian crime drama is populated almost entirely with Caucasian couples who represent this exploitative reality, the 'China Girl' remains at the centre of the narrative, representing the reported 24.9 million people living in modern slavery in the Asia Pacific region (Ibid.).

THE ANTIPODES ARE NOT ASIAN

The distinction between Cinnamon's markedly complex figure and her death is explored as a televisual representation of the subaltern 'out there', with the audience safe and substantially 'still here'. This achievement occurs through their witnessing of the subaltern (in this case, Cinnamon's death) as mediated by Robin, first via her camera lens and then through her retelling and understanding of Cinnamon's death. Displacing the central Woman of Colour in each series with an inverted, white afterimage, *Top of the Lake* raises questions as to whether these so-called feminist (Campion has gone as far as to describe her series as 'ovarian') interventions truly provide a qualitative rupture in the television of Australian racial homogeneity and gender essentialism (Vineyard 2017, n.p.). Many cultural critics, including Ang (2000), argue this homogeneity is implicit in the media packaging of Australia as multicultural in much of its digital and broadcast cultural products, a white supremacist utopianism that glosses challenging but productive intercultural tensions. The specific multiculturalism introduced to Australia in the 1970s by a range of Asian migrants was, Ang posits, far more challenging to the pre-existing 'mainstream mode of nationalism hinged on Europeanness' (Ibid., xvii). It is not surprising then, Ang reasons, that the spectre of an 'Asianisation' of Australia is widely experienced by Anglo-Saxon television audiences as a threat or unwelcome presence (Ibid.). Though such diverse cultures cannot be equated nor compared, Ang argues the 'Australian cultural embrace of Asia at least at a superficial level' may just be a matter of time (Ibid.). However, Ang cautions, the sense of danger associated with 'Asianisation' is,

> [M]ore than a question of cultural xenophobia: it is intensified by the paradoxical geographical positioning of Australia, far from Europe and on the margins of Asia, an isolation that is manifest in persistent popular discourses on the 'distance' of Australia from the US and

European cultural and political power and influence and on public debates on the 'place' of Australia 'in' or 'out' of Asia as quintessential to the nation's selfhood.

(Ibid.)

Cinnamon's body – as Ang's 'spectre of Asianisation' – works to bring *Top of the Lake: China Girl*'s audience into contact with cultural xenophobia, positioning the Caucasian foetus discovered within her womb as a symbolic paradoxical positioning of Europe within Asian regional margins; the Thai woman, though she is within Australia, still planted with the coloniser's seed. Robin's recurrent time spent with Cinnamon's body in the morgue pulls these racial tensions into forensic focus, imitating the layered 'CSI Image', wherein the morgue, viewing glass and detective's prying eye coalesce into a complex and absurd inquisition.[6] The recovery and prime positioning of the 'China Girl' in *Top of the Lake: China Girl*, though, forms what Yue argues is 'a kind of shadow history to [. . .] the development of standardisation methods for the film industry', extending and questioning the identities concealed within Cinnamon's post-mortem body (2015, 99). This violation causes Cinnamon to commit suicide, sacrificing herself. Considering the Australian cinematic canon, Olivia Khoo notes that 'despite various political and economic positionings (or posturings) of Asia as Australia's "nearest neighbour" and "friend" [. . .] the encounter between Asians and Australians inevitably results in violence and ends with the sacrifice of the Asian character' (2006, 46). As a result of these sacrifices, Khoo argues that it is clear Australia's genuine Asian regionalism is unseen, the sacrifice of Asian characters birthing a warped national identity 'formed through a distinction from its regional "Other"' (Ibid.). Instead of sacrificing Cinnamon further, Robin's dedication to recovering her life reveals the desperation of the white colonial oppressor to right past wrongs, a desire Susannah Radstone has likened to repairing traumatised landscapes and bodies (2017, 89). As such, *Top of the Lake: China Girl* compromises a history of sexist crime dramas masquerading as feminism to face racial traumas and begin 'the journey [to] dig deeper', that Indigenous filmmaker Rachel Perkins has said brings 'layers of history, race and feminism to the [television] form' to better understand its present (Hopewell 2018, n.p.).[7]

'FEMINIST' CRIME DRAMA?

This televisual historical recovery is new. Popular shows often praised for their 'feminism', such as Alan Cubitt's *The Fall* (BBC Two, 2013–2016), expressly erase murder victims to trade on feminism as a blanket ethos, whereby declaring something 'feminist' immediately denotes it as such. In response to criticism, Cubitt claimed his intention was to 'explore some aspects of this phenomenon of violence against the female body' through allusions to the BBC's *Prime Suspect* (ITV, 1991–2006) (Cubitt 2018, n.p.). Accordingly, the series does engage Gillian Anderson (a well-respected actress similar in reputation to Helen Mirren of the now infamously transgressive crime drama *Prime Suspect*) as DSI Stella Gibson, a blonde, high-heeled female detective chasing a handsome serial killer, Paul Spector (Jamie Dornan), through a series of murders. *The Fall*, however, lacks the sociocultural complexity of *Prime Suspect*, in which diverse demographics are interrogated to showcase various communities, and murder victims are lensed carefully. Instead, first episode murder victim Sarah Kay (Laura Donnelly) is shown by cinematographer Ruairí O'Brien in close-up and mid-shot, sanitised with bathing and suggestively posed in a soft filtered light. Paul is sexualised as a deadly date, sketching and photographing his victims, his murders disturbingly intercut with Stella's sex scenes, which distance and sexualise femicide.

Top of the Lake: China Girl risks being read in such generic terms. However, this risk is mitigated by the choices of Germain McMicking, the cinematographer for *Top of the Lake: China Girl*, who uses intensive telegraphic techniques to lens Robin's 'painful fixation' on Cinnamon. In Cinnamon's discovery scene in episode one, McMicking uses an 80mm Super Baltars and Panavision Primo zoom lenses to focus on Cinnamon's decomposing body, which has washed up on Bondi Beach bound within a turquoise suitcase (Martin 2017, n.p.). These heavy lenses show Cinnamon's putrefying face in key focus, photographed in close-up by Robin, who uses a digital single-lens reflex camera with zoom in direct contrast to Paul's careless photographs of Sarah with a cheap virtual camera in *The Fall*. For the second episode morgue scene, McMicking changes to an intensive deep focus, digital screen display and prolonged mid-shots of Cinnamon's body in its entirety as the detective and pathologist Ray (Geoff Morrell) carefully perform her autopsy. These technical choices do not shy from the abjection of the corpse, romantic renderings such as posed photographs or drawings common to detective narratives that Julia Kristeva argues encourage 'corpse fanciers' and 'unconscious worshippers of a soulless body' to obscure the horror of decomposition (1982, 109).

McMicking changes perspective again to a shallow focus of Cinnamon's face and hands, an effect obtained by a larger aperture, close viewpoint and larger image sensor, registering brief expressions on Cinnamon's decomposing and immobile face, showing an exposed lower jaw in a death grimace and a yellowed body left to wrinkle in the sea. Robin takes countless photographs. Her attention gives 'clothed and naked, bloodied and bruised, tortured and decomposing, in close-up and in long shot, the corpse [. . .] whether haunting the margins of text and screen or, intermittently, centre-stage', an intention Deborah Jermyn has noted was pioneered in *Prime Suspect* (2008, 58). As Robin's piercing blue eyes penetrate Cinnamon's portrait on her camera, there is a sense of rebellion and resistance to letting the dead woman drift into obscurity. Ray assures Robin the nickname 'China Girl' is only 'temporary' before pouring water over Cinnamon to wash her of sand, analysing every aspect of her body from her hair to her teeth and skin and then cutting into Cinnamon's womb to find a foetus, which he holds out to the detective. Robin gravely enquires what the coroner will do with the foetus, to which Ray replies he will expedite the ID process before 'sew[ing] him back in nice and neat where he belongs'. This careful consideration of Cinnamon, beyond her body's function to the plot, is particular to *Top of the Lake: China Girl*. Despite the need for ever more young, nude actresses to play cadavers in the production of increasingly popular crime television, Cinnamon and Nguyen are not disposable. At a certain point, the increase in popular crime drama production feeds a decrease in significance and respect to the communities who frequently feature as cadavers, young white women, sex workers, and Women of Colour. Ironically, as Joanna Dillman has argued, at the same time that female labour is increasingly vital to the global economy, elite entertainment television is undervaluing the contributions of women in order to frame them as disposable and exploitable if it is not trading off feminism as a commodity (2014, 2). *Top of the Lake* refuses this narrative.

GIVING THE 'CHINA GIRL' A BREATHING SPACE

As with the China Girls of LAD, women are depicted as negligible objects who, in the globalised world of work, reinforce the images and storylines of the single-purpose function subaltern. There is neither a removal of certain disadvantages for these communities, nor restoration of consideration nor meaning to their deaths; the ironic end result of this emphasis on production makes an increasing demographic, namely female extras, temporary 'China Girls', fascinating only in the forensic dissection of their corpses. Dillman argues the proliferation of violence against and erasure of women in crime dramas can be traced to anti-feminist sentiments, arriving at this distinction by arguing that series such as *The Fall* remain exploitative by operating via a 'contradictory logic that recognises feminist goals and speaks through feminist codes, but that ultimately serves the status-quo, androcentric, dominant culture' (2014, 3). This culture is intent, as is Puss, on male power being produced at female expense, the death rattle of a neoliberal economic order that requires, says Dillman, 'an ever-expandable, exploitable, individualised – and some might say feminized – labor force' (Ibid.). To the creative team behind *Top of the Lake: China Girl*, though their names may reflect their racist context, Cinnamon, Caramel, Honey, Sinn, and Jade matter. Attempting to cajole Robin into having dinner with him after the autopsy, Ray jokes she is 'enlivened by dead matter' as though she is indeed one of Kristeva's 'corpse fanciers'. Distracted, the detective looks pained: 'I care what happened', she replies flatly.

The superficial accuracy of representations of crime drama cadavers in their most conservative sense is an expectation that their function relates only momentarily to the narrative. Cinnamon's identity and the details of her death remain a mystery. Campion and Lee instead halt the narrative repeatedly to explore the turbulent interiority of the characters left pondering her absence, as the wild landscape of the first season is turned inward. These sequences function to destabilise the narrative apparatus, showing surreal representations of Cinnamon in dreams. A dream sequence of Robin's operates as what Andrin terms a moment of 'stasis [. . .a] strange [. . .] breathing [space]' (2009, 28–9), in which Robin, lying in bed, sees a woman's fluorescent blue-green silhouette (the colour of the suitcase Cinnamon was found in) with a baby walking down her hall to sit on her bed. Cinnamon's bright silhouette is an inversion of a shadow, shown lit from within in opposition to the typical dark *a contre jour* or 'against the light' silhouettes. The inversion figures as a strip of undeveloped, photosensitive film burning a hole through the on-screen tableau, Cinnamon's inverted silhouette displaying her absence as a data loss. Later, an imagined Cinnamon wanders into Brett's bedroom and embraces him, giving him comfort in his loneliness and grief. Though we cannot know Cinnamon, her character's multiple visual facets represent an abundance of subjectivities that refute what Grace Chang's book title refers to as the 'disposable domesticity of immigrant women workers in the global economy'; workers who (in the case of Cinnamon) as surrogates, enable wealthy and infertile middle-class couples to have children, or adopt, or have the release of sexual pleasure (Chang 2000).[8] Campion's work has always, argues Laleen Jayamanne, contained various experimentations of the 'fantastic', surreal elements that both disrupt and frame narrative realism (2001, 26). Cinnamon, as the recovered 'China Girl' in a series she graces with her name, rejects complicity in the censoring of her image by transmuting herself into a disruptive and fantastic element, and living plot hole.

In moving to the surreal from what Campion has termed the 'mundaneness of life', Cinnamon's televisual portraits reveal poignant racist moments in the white Australian everyday (Young 2013, n.p.).[9] Campion has said of her surreal televisual 'breathing spaces',

> To go outside of what's really real, we only do that because something's really interesting. When we veer off reality it's for very good gains. The rest of the time we say 'but we really know how things are, the mundane-ness of life is well known to us'.
>
> (Ibid.)

Therefore, given Cinnamon's portrait is animated repeatedly 'outside of what's really real', she represents a presence behind or through the 'reality' that is shown on screen. I see the 'very good gains' of *Top of the Lake: China Girl* as a glimpse of the subaltern 'China Girl' too often invisible to the eye of prestige drama, her decaying visage a living reality of modern slavery too close for white Australia to see. Within their Australian context, these surreal flickers of identity double as what Ang identifies as the 'presence of Asians [as a] blemish on the ideal image of the white Australia continent', and Campion problematises the cultural narrative of white supremacy dominant since the inception of the White Australia policy, a racist immigration legislation that was enforced officially from 1900–1949, with reverberating effects beyond the 1970s (Ang 2000, xiii). Since she would have been prevented from coming to Australia a short half-century ago and is now invited purely to service the sterile white middle-class, Cinnamon's resurfacing on Bondi Beach represents not only, as Neroni argues, 'the ocean [as] dangerous and [unable to] contain the trauma of female subjectivity' (2017, 123), but also the ocean of trauma and exploitation risked to gain the transnational hypermobility promised by neoliberal capitalism. Just as Reno is never seen by a filmgoing audience unless a projectionist loaded a film reel incorrectly, Cinnamon's presence exists in *Top of the Lake: China Girl* to indicate to those middle-class white families using her womb that what they are doing is wrong.

THE SUBALTERN AND A SOPHISTICATED SUPPLICANCY

Indeed, Campion commented in a 2018 interview that 'capitalism is such a macho force', admitting she felt 'run over' and 'caught in a sophisticated supplicancy' in which the world of consumerism masquerades as feminism (Muir 2018, n.p.). Given Southeast Asian women are 'the world's increasingly mobile women' as Dillman argues, it is imperative that their increasing presence in crime dramas accrue them more attention than it currently does (2014, 2). While Cinnamon is arguably quite mobile, Robin struggles to trace and understand her death independently, as she exhibits little inclination to seek help from the Asian women of Silk 41. This inability to listen to the voices of the oppressed is a character trait noted by So Mayer (2017) after the first season of the series, and given that Robin tries and fails again to listen to the subaltern, it is possible Campion and Lee are indicating the role of detective is not hers to play in this instance. In a manner similar to the first series, the central plot concerning the mystery of Cinnamon's death deviates as Robin learns the truth about her investigation from Puss, an unreliable antagonist. This unsatisfactory resolution leaves an uneasy, existential end to the series; there is no 'answer' to what Ang calls the 'Asian problem', then, especially when it is viewed through the Caucasian afterimage of Robin (2000, xvii). After the climactic reveal of illegal surrogacy networks via Southeast Asian sex workers, Robin chases Mary and Puss, who have kidnapped the Silk 41 surrogates, only to see their plane leave.

After spending the series eschewing collective action necessary to the feminist project, the fiercely independent detective is left staring at an abandoned panda bear stuffed toy at Sydney's Kingsford-Smith airport, its inert slump revealing little more than its abandonment. Robin's patently white feminism is shown to be profoundly unsuccessful, as she is caught in the 'supplicancy' of 'macho' capitalism; she does not know the panda, a gift from surrogate hopefuls Miranda (Gwendoline Christie) and Police Chief Adrian Butler (Clayton Jacobson), has been discarded by Sinn, a Silk 41 surrogate (Figure 9.4). Cinnamon's mystery remains so, as Reno states of her function as a 'China Girl' in *The Flamethrowers*, 'I would be looked at, but by people who didn't know who I was. I would be looked at and remain anonymous' (Kushner 2013, 177). Having herself given up Mary as a baby, Robin potentially sees something of herself in the anonymous surrogates, her strained relationship with Mary's family reminding the detective that she is herself caught in an unending transnational flow of 'sophisticated supplicancy'.

Campion gestures to the futility of solving problems not necessarily in need of solving by the well-meaning white feminist, reflecting Gayatri Spivak's consideration of feminists of the first world who she sees as limiting their considerations of feminism to themselves as privileged women (1981, 156–7). Mary, Robin, and Julia, in different ways, characterise the well-meaning but profoundly misguided first world feminism buffeting the primetime viability of subaltern narratives. In *Top of the Lake: China Girl*, Campion and Lee seem resolute: there is no way to solve this 'Asian problem', or purport to show someone who might, or even, it seems, find an entry point with which to begin. Despite the

Figure 9.4 Robin Griffin (Elisabeth Moss) and the panda. © See-Saw (TOTL2) Holdings Pty Ltd

white characters only too happy to take her narrative space, serving as lynchpin to both *Top of the Lake* series is the redacted silhouette of the marginal woman, and it is the problem of her absence that causes Robin's investigation to ultimately come undone. Campion's meditation on corporeal commodification reflects on the 'China Girl' afterimage, what Kushner terms an unstable, 'pulsing' colour. It is Cinnamon's non-European immigrant status that, Ang argues, inspires 'near hysterical mainstream public opinion' (2000, xiv), with Campion again using the complexities of her central protagonist to reference the intercultural tensions of Australia's reluctantly multicultural society.

NOTES

1. Genevieve Yue has written extensively on 'The China Girl on the Margins of Film' for *October Magazine* (2015, 96–116), and her work is influential on the ways I understand Cinnamon's and Robin's placements as racialised 'China Girls'.
2. Of the several books produced on Campion's films there are (as far as I can see) no sustained considerations of race or postcolonialism in Campion's television work (there is some consideration of postcolonialism in her film work but even this is limited). Lynda Dyson has noted how discourse surrounding *The Piano*, for example, 'constructed *The Piano* as a feminist exploration of nineteenth-century sexuality and tended to ignore the way in which "race" is embedded in the text', terming the film a 'fantasy of colonial reconciliation' to allay settler anxieties (1995, 267).
3. In a 2019 survey (*Who Gets to Tell Australian Stories?*), of 19,000 news and current affairs items broadcast on free-to-air television during two weeks in June 2019, it was found that 'more than 75 per cent of presenters, commentators and reporters have an Anglo-Celtic background' (Soutphommasane 2020, n.p.).
4. I have used Yue's article to extend my own understanding of race within the 'China Girl' image and am indebted to her research. Though it was published too late for proper research to be conducted for this chapter, Yue has published a new book on film and feminism (*Girl Head: Feminism and Materiality*, 2020) with an extensive consideration of 'China Girls'.
5. One exception is Linda (Michelle Lim Davidson), a Scarlet Alliance representative who serves as a one-off, clear-eyed consultant to Robin over sex worker union issues.
6. Karen Lury has documented the popularity of the 'CSI Image' in her book *Interpreting Television* (2005).
7. In this instance, Perkins is discussing the racial and feminist underpinnings of her show *Mystery Road* (ABC, 2018–). See Hopewell (2018, n.p.).
8. Chang also refers to the statement of Wendy Perkins: *Towards a Disposable Workforce: The Increasing Use of 'Contingent' Labor: Hearing before the Subcommittee on Labor of the Committee on Labor and Human Resources*, 113th Cong. 4 (June 15, 1993).
9. Claire Young's film, *From the Bottom of the Lake* (2013), documents the work of Campion and her crew.

Afterword: Unsettling Feminism

Annabel Cooper

Jane Campion's much-fêted return to film in 2021's *The Power of the Dog* marked a turn away from her career-long preference for female leads but left her firmly in the familiar territory of ambiguous sexual politics. As the contributors to this volume observe, Campion first asserted in 1989 that she did not want to be seen as a 'feminist' director, and she has reiterated an arms-length distance from feminism over the decades since (Ciment 1999a, 35). Nevertheless, her films and her way of working with other women have proven irresistibly attractive to feminist critics. The 'feminist problem' with Campion therefore naturally engages this collection.

In 1989, Campion appears to have held a quite prescriptive view of feminism, involving telling people 'how they should behave' (Ibid.). Since then, time and cultural politics have moved on and so has Campion's career. It is not irrelevant that for most of her career-building years, to submit to the classification of 'feminist filmmaker' would likely have delimited her reputation and restricted her access to funding. Moreover, her refusal to be pinned down may have left her freer to create complicated and unheroic female leads, and a character like *The Piano*'s (1993) sympathetic but also somewhat creepy Baines (Harvey Keitel). So, even while much in her oeuvre proclaims her a close fellow traveller, Campion has managed to avoid being labelled, and therefore held to account, as a feminist.

Having emerged as a filmmaker through a brief window of unusual possibilities for women, as Zachary Zahos demonstrates (see Chapter 2), Campion has more than paid forward her own opportunities, maintaining close and supportive relationships with other women filmmakers throughout her career. She applauded the #MeToo campaign and the changes and new opportunities it has helped to effect. Her selection of Ari Wegner as cinematographer for *The Power of the Dog* – a major stepping-stone for Wegner's career resulting in an

Oscar nomination – is only the latest in a series of productive female collaborations (Campion's first feature, *Sweetie* (1989), saw Sally Bongers become the first female director of photography in Australian feature filmmaking). Rona Murray's study of female conversation in paratexts demonstrates the integration of female working relationships in Campion's practices (see Chapter 6).

As this collection shows, Campion's films – until now – have consistently placed women's experience at their centre, evicting the glamour of cinema in favour of the peculiarity and awkwardness of everyday life. Adele Jones (Chapter 7) argues that these feminist-like patterns through Campion's career converged in explicitly feminist productions in *Top of the Lake* (2013 and 2017). She points to an extensive engagement with feminism, supported by Blythe Worthy's argument that in the second season, Campion engages with an overtly feminist focus on the significance of the 'China Girl' in film production (Chapter 9). Has a long career as a fellow traveller, then, finally brought Campion into the fold?

In this afterword, like Alexia L. Bowler in Chapter 5, I consider *The Power of the Dog*, taking up themes traversed throughout this volume. First, the film invites further exploration of the uneasy sexual politics in Campion's work. Her detailed attention to embodiment, discussed especially in Catherine Fowler's essay (Chapter 3), is again evident in this film and central to its elaboration of power. Second, I address Antipodean feminist critics' disquiet over indigenous representation in *The Piano*, in light of *The Power of the Dog*'s adaptation from Thomas Savage's 1967 novel of the same name.

[1]

Stephen Kuster (Chapter 1) observes that the label 'feminist' is frequently attached to Campion despite her tendency to evade it. He demonstrates her insistence from the beginning of her career on women-centred 're-vision' – but that in the female lives of her characters, 'nice, neat narratives with clarity do not exist' (p. 32). Indeed, Campion's work leaves viewers wrestling with ambiguities and omissions in one production after another. One thinks of the obscure hints of incest in *Sweetie*, and Ada's muteness and Flora's paternity, both unexplained. As early as 1992, Campion spoke about a dedication to such complexity:

> I think that the subliminal effect of *Sweetie*'s shooting style is that you are unable to create strong simple emotional relationships with the characters. It continually insists that you feel *and* think [. . .the critic] is saying that she's attached to catharsis and clear emotional release experiences, whereas I feel it's more complex than that.
>
> (Bilborough 1992, 100, emphasis in original)

In light of this predilection for uncertainty, ambiguity, it is not hard to see how Thomas Savage's novel, a story which confounds easy understanding, attracted Campion.

But Campion takes us into muddier waters than Savage. While her adaptation echoes Savage's subtle transfer of power from Phil (Benedict Cumberbatch) to Peter (Kodi Smit-McPhee), the film makes its audience work harder than the novel's readers – what exactly have they witnessed in the closing scenes? We have to retrace our way through the minimal clues, and only on a rewatch will most viewers recognise Peter's opening voiceover ('For what kind of a man would I be if I did not help my mother?'). The contributing plot threads are necessarily fewer in the shorter format of feature film, but also sparer with clues. Gone are Savage's many hints – Phil's contempt for gloves and the cuts on his hands. The history of Bronco Henry and Phil remains a trace, rather than a mystery uncovered, and Campion offers no judgement. These are classic Campion moves: hints rather than explanations. By the end of the novel, no ambiguity remains, but Campion's audiences are frequently blindsided by the conclusion. She follows Savage in channelling expectation then producing an unexpected twist but is far more at home with ambiguity – asking that we 'feel *and* think' (and flounder, too).

If ambiguities of plot and sexual politics signal Campion's resistance to ideological clarity, her persistent fascination with destructive patriarchy marks a clearer affiliation with feminism (as Jones observes): we think of the cold control of adolescent girls in *A Girl's Own Story* (1984), the transacting of Ada (Holly Hunter) in *The Piano*, the cruel manipulation in *The Portrait of a Lady* (1996), and sexual murder in *In the Cut* (2003). *The Power of the Dog* is not Campion's first film to expose the hollow core of masculine power, as Bowler explains, but is the first to focus primarily on the damage done to men themselves.

In the masculinist world of rural Montana in the early twentieth century, the three white men of *The Power of the Dog* suffer in different ways from the regime they inhabit. Phil's sexuality turns cruel through grief and concealment: vicious hypermasculinity is a good cover for same sex desire. George (Jessie Plemons), in outward form a wealthy, successful rancher, has retreated into defensive, persecuted loneliness. Peter suffers privately also – a loner by virtue of his effeminacy, self-contained and driven by single-minded purpose. The regime shapes Rose (Kirsten Dunst) too, as she escapes the fragile existence of widowhood only to find herself the object of Phil's misogynist fire. Campion's eye for the working of sexual power in private worlds, then, is readily recognisable as feminist insight.

Feminism's long interest in embodiment, encompassing bodily vulnerability, resilience, dominance and submission, abuse, and the physical occupation of space, offers a further alignment with Campion's work. The awkward, odd-angled bodies or body parts Catherine Fowler discusses are sometimes shockingly un-cinematic. (And is there another director outside the porn industry whose oeuvre features so many urinating women?). The shedding of glamour is insistent, persistent from the beginning. A correlative, as Leanne Weston observes, is the frequently reported visceral responses to Campion's films (Chapter 4). No surprise, then, that Campion turns from Savage's relatively spare use of dialogue to the portrayal and interaction of bodies in her adaptation to the screen. Hyper-masculine control mobilises Phil's dominance of space, as he maintains a threatening, audible presence in the shadows of the house to erode Rose's fragile sense of self and sets out to taunt Peter. Measured, stealthy, predatory as a hawk, Cumberbatch captures the meanness of knowingly deployed masculine entitlement. George's stiff containment betrays a lifetime of persecution: awkward and cautious, his courting of Rose is an act of difficult bravery. Johanna Schmertz's analysis of kinship and incest (Chapter 8) alerts us to sources of disquiet in Jesse Plemons's buttoned-in demeanour, the brothers' too-close relationship, and George's discomfort with the topic of Bronco Henry. Rose's initial, emotional generosity – embodied in her invitation to George to dance, an invitation to loosen up – gives way to vulnerable, nervy disintegration.

The Peter-and-the-Wolf story plays out in stance and movement. Stick-thin, pale, and full-lipped, Smit-McPhee's movement is both unconscious and (like but unlike Phil's) measured. Waiter with napkin over his arm, creator of paper flowers, he is already exposed. The hotel dining room scene which precipitates the plot is a study in embodied power relations: George, silent at one end of the table; Phil, hoovering up attention, leaning back, burning the flowers, erupting in anger at other diners; Peter, open and innocent until, suddenly, he is a target. Peter's gathering resilience is figured through movement too. The strange scene in which he hula-hoops with intense concentric focus is a distinctively Campion addition (like the echoing twirl Phil gives to his chair before leaving, quietly linking the two). The superb flat-footed walk as Peter runs the gauntlet of wolf-whistling hired men at the haymaking – deliberately, twice – confirms a shift: he is tougher than we thought. From such a disregard for torment, Peter moves to calculated seduction. The 'love scene', as Campion has described it (Ward 2022, n.p.), is played out through precise movement in close-up: the tightening of the rope against Phil's taut, tense hips as – we and he may imagine – he draws Peter in; Peter's seductive knowingness and dissembling as he brings the cigarette to Phil's lips. As Rose falls apart, Peter comes together.

[11]

The theme of race and colonialism is addressed in chapters by Kuster and Worthy (Chapter 9), who discuss *Passionless Moments* (1983) and *Top of the Lake: China Girl* (2017) respectively. At opposite ends of Campion's career, both works encompass an oblique handling of race and colonialism in Australia. Both were collaborations with Australian writer and filmmaker Gerard Lee. Kuster delineates Campion's subversion of the codes of ethnographic film in *Passionless Moments*: this gently mocking film, using its lens not to examine a native other but to defamiliarise suburban Australian life, critiques the genre and its colonial imperative. (The chaotic final scenes of *Sweetie*, where Dawn's naked, blackened, and outdoor-dwelling body disrupts the white Australian suburban setting, echo this subversive colonial shadow theme.) Worthy's focus is on the 'China Girl' image used to control colour and density in film labs. Investigating Campion's use of the term to represent a Thai woman, who is both central to the series' second season but persistently absent from view, Worthy demonstrates the nuance Campion brings to the racial politics of what and who remains 'outside the field of vision' (p. 163). As Worthy points out, in both series of *Top of the Lake* women of the Thai diaspora – Tui (Jacqueline Joe), Cinnamon (Thien Huong Thi Nyguen) – disappear both literally and from screen time, their stories effectively eclipsed by those of the white characters. Schmertz's discussion of Cinnamon's exclusion from the circle of kinship also borders on these questions.

In the context of contemporary feminism, concerned as the movement now is with intersectional perspectives, how can we assess Campion's handling of race, colonialism, and whiteness? This aspect of her work has aroused most criticism from feminists – as Worthy explains – especially in New Zealand and Australia, where pride in Campion's achievements is mixed with unease and sometimes sharp critical comment. The critique was first raised in relation to *The Piano*.[1] Margaret Jolly's analysis of the gaze and colonialism and the mixed reception of *The Piano* is the most extensive discussion of these reservations. She writes:

> My ambivalence derives from a tension between a qualified sympathy for Campion's feminist revisioning of gender and sexuality and my distaste for the way in which Māori are represented, despite Campion's expressed cross-cultural intentions.
>
> (Jolly 2009, 100)

'We were the blackdrop' says Māori actor Cliff Curtis, who was cast in the film early in his career (Curtis 2018, n.p.). Like many in New Zealand I echo this unease with the film. Campion had lived outside New Zealand for the sixteen years prior to *The Piano*'s production and seemed out of sync with cultural shifts in process from the mid-1970s. It is notable that there is no aboriginal presence in the outback scenes of *Holy Smoke* (1999). Perhaps the charge levelled at *The Piano* – Māori characters appear but with no story of their own – led Campion to evade the issue.

The obliqueness of the instances above, and the restriction of non-white characters to the margins of the films, suggests a pattern. With the highly arguable exception of *China Girl*, Campion has not dealt with stories of cultures outside white colonial and European societies. A white filmmaker in a settler society walks a minefield, of course, between misrepresenting or appropriating another culture, and ignoring the presence of Indigenous people: Campion's strongest response has been to stick with what she knows. But it is perhaps also pertinent that Campion's context is, as Worthy observes, 'global'. In New Zealand's national cinema, there is something of a division between filmmakers whose primary orientation is to New Zealand film, whose work tends to include Māori characters, who may, increasingly, be Māori or work with Māori crew, and those whose orientation is transnational. Although she works with Antipodean material, Campion belongs more to the latter camp (as the making of a Western confirms).

The concerns of critics signal that questions of race, whiteness, and otherness – taking various forms in different sociocultural settings – have become central to contemporary feminism. Intersectional feminism is now feminism's prevalent politics, and in settler societies the colonial context is a core dimension of its inquiry. What happens if we bring this kind of feminist lens to *The Power of the Dog* – a Western, a genre premised on colonialism and the relationships among peoples and landscapes? Here we need to turn once more to the adaptation.

Watching *The Power of the Dog*, I was like many others enchanted by the beautifully shot landscapes. The film begins and – almost – ends on powerful visual continuities between the bodies ('hides') of people, animals, and land. The cattle ripple through the tussocky landscape at the outset, then we cut to Phil badgering George as they ride. The bodies of Phil and Peter lit with warm browns in the final stable scene cut to the moving, supple chestnut hides of the horses the next morning and the longer shots of the supple, flowing recumbent hillsides. Yet these connections seem to remain visual ones. They are not aligned with the film's thematic structure, and here Campion seems to draw back from the underlying unease about Western expansion and colonial dispossession which resonates through the Burbank story in Savage's novel. The adaptation, in bringing the novel into the scope of a two-hour film, removes a number of backstories, one of which is the history of an Indigenous American father, Edward Nappo and his son, who appear in the film only momentarily as they seek to buy hides, and gift a pair of gloves to Rose.

In Savage's novel, the Nappo family has a story of its own and its presence is a telling component of Phil's downfall. The ranch was once the land of the family's tribe. As a child, Phil watches with satisfaction as they are moved off to a reservation. In the novel's present, Edward brings his son to see the land and to camp. As they approach, however, Phil confronts them and Edward offers him a gift of gloves. Phil refuses the gloves and drives them off, augmenting his domestic tyranny with racial and colonial dominance. The novel's Indigenous story therefore underlies the Burbank wealth and the troubled quality of the ranch. Cruelty and injustice pervade the entire world these characters inhabit, extending beyond sexual and gender dynamics and the industrial-scale exploitation of animals to colonial dispossession. This larger story brings the land, Western expansion, and Native American dispossession into the thematic structure, but this nexus drops away with the omission of this past from the screenplay.

Blythe Worthy argues that Cinnamon's invisibility creates inexplicable plot holes in *China Girl*, and perhaps something similar happens in *The Power of the Dog*. The loss of the Indigenous story leaves its trace in a certain lack of depth in the motifs of gloves/hides/land. The offer of gloves in the novel is made to Phil, not Rose as in the film. Gloves, made from hides, offer a protection that Phil explicitly refuses, at the moment of cruelly turning away the Nappo family. Symptom of his defensive hypermasculinity, the lack of gloves will be his undoing. His scratched hands are open to the anthrax – a poison deriving from the once-Indigenous land – which enters through Peter's substituted hide. The thematic and plot significance of the land and its former inhabitants in Phil's fate disappears with the Indian story, and Phil's dismissal of them and their gift. In Savage's structure, the permeable bodies of humans, the bodies and hides of animals, and the land and its history and dispossession are interwoven in this plotting: in the film, these resonances are largely confined to the visual structure.

CONCLUSION

Campion's assertions over decades, made in one form or another, that she is 'not political', must be taken seriously. She has spent her career evading capture by anyone who might seek to pin her down. Yet like any film, hers repeatedly speak to their cultural-political moment. In respect of the cultural politics of gender, sexuality, and embodiment they sometimes seem in the vanguard; at other times, especially as feminism's intersectional orientation consolidates and in the light of profound changes in Indigenous politics, less so. She has never been content with characters who sit safely in their worlds, or plots that follow a conventional path. She is perfectly willing to dispense with glamour and conventional beauty. A fellow traveller, in some respects ahead of debates and sometimes oddly trailing them, Campion's uneven fit with the seismic shifts of feminism looks set to trouble a generation to come.

NOTE

1. See, for example, Pihama (1994, 239–42; 2000, 114–34); Orr (1999, 148–60), and Dyson (1999, 111–21).

Bibliography

Agence France-Presse. (2019) 'Lack of female directors in Hollywood an "embarrassment": Geena Davis', *France 24*, 10 October. Available at: https://www.france24.com/en/20190910-lack-of-female-directors-in-hollywood-an-embarrassment-geena-davis (Accessed: 11 July 2022).

Allen, J. and Young, I. M. (eds) (1989) *The thinking muse: Feminism in modern French philosophy*. Bloomington: Indiana University Press.

Allen, R. (1999) 'Female sexuality, creativity and desire in *The Piano*', in Coombs F. and Gemmell, S. (eds) *Piano lessons: Approaches to The Piano*. Sydney, NSW, Australia: John Libbey Cinema and Animation, pp. 44–63.

Alleva, R. (2009) 'Dying light: Jane Campion's *Bright Star*', *Commonweal Magazine*, 23 October. Available at: https://www.commonwealmagazine.org/dying-light (Accessed: 25 March 2022).

Andrin, M. (2009) 'Her-land: Jane Campion's cinema, or another poetic of the inner sense', in Radner, H., Fox, A. and Bessière, I. (eds) *Jane Campion: Cinema, nation, identity*. Detroit: Wayne State University Press, pp. 27–38.

Ang, I. (2000) 'Introduction', in Ang, I., Law, L., Chalmers, S., and Mandy, T. (eds) *Alter/Asians: Asian-Australian identities in art, media and popular culture*. Sydney: Pluto Press, pp. xiii–xxx.

Anon. (1986) 'Other people's children: *2 Friends* helps kick off the 1986 season of ABC telemovies', *Cinema Papers*, January. Available at: https://issuu.com/libuow/docs/cinemapaper1986janno055 (Accessed: 3 August 2022).

Appler, M. (2021) 'Jane Campion and Benedict Cumberbatch discuss toxic masculinity and the American frontier at "The Power of the Dog" NYFF premiere', *Variety*, 2 October. Available at: https://variety.com/2021/scene/news/jane-campion-benedict-cumberbatch-the-power-of-the-dog-nyff-premiere-1235079496/ (Accessed: 29 April 2022).

Attwood, F. (1998) 'Weird lullaby Jane Campion's *The Piano*', *Feminist Review*, 58(1), pp. 85–101. HTTPS://DOI.ORG/10.1080/014177898339604.

Australian Film and Television School (2020) *Our history*. Available at: https://www.aftrs.edu.au/about/why-aftrs/our-history/ (Accessed: 29 April 2022).

Bainbridge, C. (2008) *A feminine cinematics: Luce Irigaray and film*. London: Palgrave Macmillan.

Balsom, E. (2020) 'In search of the female gaze', *Cinema Scope*, June. Available at: https://cinema-scope.com/features/in-search-of-the-female-gaze/ (Accessed: 11 July 2022).

Banet-Weiser, S. (2018) *Empowered: Popular feminism and popular misogyny*. Durham and London: Duke University Press.

Banet-Weiser, S., Gill, R., and Rottenberg, C. (2020) 'Postfeminism, popular feminism and neoliberal feminism? Sarah Banet-Weiser, Rosalind Gill and Catherine Rottenberg in conversation', *Feminist Theory*, 21(1), pp. 3–24. https://doi.org/10.1177/1464700119842555.

Barcan, R. and Fogarty, M. (1999) 'Performing *The Piano*', in Coombs F. and Gemmell, S. (eds) *Piano lessons: Approaches to The Piano*. Sydney, NSW, Australia: John Libbey Cinema and Animation, pp. 3–17.

Barthes, R. (2005) 'The death of the author', in Caughie, J. (ed.) *Theories of authorship: A reader*. London: Routledge, pp. 208–213.

Bell, Jr, D. A. (1980) 'Brown v. Board of Education and the Interest-Convergence dilemma', *Harvard Law Review*, 93(3), pp. 518–33. https://doi.org/10.2307/1340546.

Berger, L. (2022) 'Watch the women behind "The Power of the Dog" discuss the evolution of the film', *Women in Hollywood*, 8 March. Available at: https://womenandhollywood.com/watch-the-women-behind-the-power-of-the-dog-discuss-the-evolution-of-the-film/ (Accessed: 25 March 2022).

Beugnet, M. (2004) *Claire Denis*. Manchester and New York: Manchester University Press.

Bihlmeyer, J. (2005) 'The (un)speakable femininity in mainstream movies: Jane Campion's *The Piano*', *Cinema Journal*, 44(2), pp. 68–88. https://www.jstor.org/stable/3661095 (Accessed: 6 October 2022).

Bilborough, M. (1992) 'Different complexions: Jane Campion, an interview', in Dennis, J. and Bieringa, J. (eds) *Film in Aotearoa New Zealand*. Wellington: Victoria University Press, pp. 93–105.

Bolton, L. (2011) *Film and female consciousness: Irigaray, cinema and thinking women*. Basingstoke: Palgrave Macmillan.

Bordwell, D. (2006) *The way Hollywood tells it: Story and style in modern movies*. Berkeley: University of California Press.

Bourdieu, P. (2001) *Masculine domination*. Translated from the French by R. Nice. Cambridge: Polity.

Bowler, A. L. (2018) '"Killing romance" by "giving birth to love": Hélène Cixous, Jane Campion and the language of *In the Cut*', *Feminist Theory*, 20(1), pp. 93–112. https://doi.org/10.1177%2F1464700118804445.

Boyle, K. (2019) *#MeToo, Weinstein and feminism*. Switzerland: Palgrave Macmillan.

Brayton, T. (2009) '2 friends', *Alternate Ending*, 6 August. Available at: https://www.alternateending.com/2009/08/jane-campion-2-friends-1986.html (Accessed 29 April 2022).

Brunsdon, C. and Spigel, L. (eds) (2008) *Feminist television criticism: A reader*. Berkshire and New York: Open University Press.

Bruzzi, S. (1995) 'Tempestuous petticoats: Costume and desire in *The Piano*', *Screen*, 36(3), pp. 257–66. https://doi.org/10.1093/screen/36.3.257.

———. (2006) *New documentary*. London: Routledge.

———. (2020) *Approximation*. London: Routledge.

Butler, J. (1999) *Gender trouble: Feminism and the subversion of identity*. New York and London: Routledge.

Campion, J. (1993) *The Piano*. London: Bloomsbury.

Campion, J. and Parker, L. (2003) 'Commentary', *In the Cut*. Screen Gems, 2003.

Campion, J. and Chapman, J. (2018) '*The Piano* at 25', in *The Piano 25th Anniversary Edition*. Studiocanal.

Canfield, D. (2021) 'Jane Campion finally made a new movie. She gave it "everything"', *Vanity Fair*, 23 August. Available at: https://www.vanityfair.com/hollywood/2021/08/awards-insider-first-look-jane-campion-power-of-the-dog (Accessed: 25 March 25 2022).

Cantwell, M. (1999) 'Jane Campion's lunatic women', in Wright Wexman, V. (ed.) *Jane Campion: Interviews*, Jackson: University Press of Mississippi, pp. 153–63.
Cartmell, D. (ed.) (2012) *A companion to literature, film and adaptation*. London: John Wiley and Sons.
Castells, M. (1997) *The power of identity*. Chichester: Wiley-Blackwell.
Chang, C. (2017) 'How Asian are we really? What Australia's census 2016 showed us', *News.com.au*, 29 June. Available at: https://www.news.com.au/national/how-asian-are-we-really-what-australias-census-2016-showed-us/news-story/2f055e32e74cbe4341953006379b6394 (Accessed: 3 August 2022).
Chang, G. (2000) *Disposable domestics: Immigrant women workers in the global economy*. Cambridge, MA: South End Press.
Chapman, J. (2002) 'Some significant women in Australian film – a celebration and a cautionary tale', *Senses of Cinema*, 21–22, 22 October. Available at: https://www.sensesofcinema.com/2002/australian-women/chapman/ (Accessed: 3 August 2022).
Cheshire, E. (2000) *Jane Campion pocket essentials*. Harpenden: Oldcastle Books.
——. (2018) *In the scene: Jane Campion*. Twickenham: Supernova Books.
Chion, M. (1999) *The voice in cinema*. Translated from the French by C. Gorbman. New York: Columbia University Press.
——. (2007) 'Mute music: Polanski's *The Pianist* and Campion's *The Piano*', translated from the French by C. Gorbman, in Goldmark, D., Kramer, L., and Leppert, R. D. (eds) *Beyond the soundtrack: Representing music in cinema*. Berkeley: University of California Press, pp. 86–96.
——. (2009) 'La femme désarticulée: La folie chez Jane Campion', *Positif*, 581/582, pp. 49–51.
Ciment, M. (1999a) 'Two interviews with Jane Campion', in Wright Wexman, V. (ed.) *Jane Campion: Interviews*, Jackson: University Press of Mississippi, pp. 30–44.
——. (1999b) 'A voyage to discover herself', in Wright Wexman, V. (ed.) *Jane Campion: Interviews*, Jackson: University Press of Mississippi, pp. 177–85.
Clare, C. (2017) 'We spoke to the feminist director who's making audiences faint', *TimeOut*, 6 April. Available at: https://www.timeout.com/london/film/we-spoke-to-the-feminist-director-whos-making-audiences-faint (Accessed: 3 August 2022).
Clifford, J. (1994) 'On ethnographic allegory', in Steidman, S. (ed.) *The postmodern turn: New perspectives on social theory*. Cambridge: Cambridge University Press, pp. 205–28.
Cobb, S. (2012) 'Film authorship and adaptation', in Cartmell, D. (ed.) *A companion to literature, film and adaptation*, London: John Wiley and Sons, pp. 105–21.
Cobb, S., Williams, L., and Wreyford, N. (2000–2015) *Calling the shots? Counting women filmmakers in British cinema today*. Available at: https://callingtheshots138740090.wordpress.com/home/ (Accessed: 3 August 2022).
Connell, R. W. (2005) *Masculinities*. Cambridge: Polity Press.
Connell, R. W. and Messerschmidt, J. W. (2005) 'Hegemonic masculinity: Rethinking the concept', *Gender and Society*, 19(6), pp. 829–59. doi: 10.1177/0891243205278639.
Coombs, F. (1999) 'In the body of *The Piano*', in Coombs, F. and Gemmell, S. (eds) *Piano lessons: Approaches to The Piano*. Sydney, NSW, Australia: John Libbey Cinema and Animation, pp. 83–96.
Cook, P. (1993) 'Border crossings: Women and film in context', in Cook, P. and Dodd, P. (eds) *Women and film: A sight and sound reader*. Philadelphia: Temple University Press. pp. 9–23.
——. (2007) *The cinema book*. London: BFI.
Corrigan, T. (1990) 'The commerce of auteurism: A voice without authority', *New German Critique*, 49, pp. 43–57. https://doi.org/10.2307/488373.
Cowie, E. (2011) *Recording reality, desiring the real*. Minneapolis: University of Minnesota Press.

Crofts, S. (2000) 'Foreign tunes? Gender and nationality in four countries' reception of *The Piano*', in Margolis, H. (ed.) *Jane Campion: The Piano*. Cambridge: Cambridge University Press, pp. 135–61.

Cubitt, A. (2018) '*The Fall*'s writer Allan Cubitt on women and violence in TV drama', *The Guardian*, 8 June. Available at: https://www.theguardian.com/tv-and-radio/2013/jun/07/the-fall-allan-cubitt-women-violence (Accessed: 3 August 2022).

Curtis, C. (2018) 'ScreenTalk short: Cliff Curtis', *NZ on Screen Iwi Whitiāhua*. Available at: https://www.nzonscreen.com/interviews/screentalk-short-cliff-curtis (Accessed: 4 August 2022).

Davis, N. (1999) 'Two Friends', *Nick's Flick Picks*. Available at: http://www.nicksflickpicks.com/2friends.html (Accessed: 27 April 2022).

D'Cruz, D. (2006) 'Textual enigmas and disruptive desires in Jane Campion's *Sweetie*', *Australian Feminist Studies*, 21(49), pp. 7–22. https://doi.org/10.1080/08164640500470578.

de Lauretis, T. (1984) *Alice doesn't: Feminism, semiotics, cinema*. Basingstoke and London: Palgrave Macmillan.

del Rio, E. (2003) 'Re-thinking feminist film theory: Counter-narcissistic performance in Sally Potter's *Thriller*', *Quarterly Review of Film and Video*, 21(1), pp. 11–24. https://doi.org/10.1080/10509200490262424.

Dillman, J. (2014) *Women and death in film, television and news: Dead but not gone*. London: Palgrave Macmillan.

Doane, M. A. (1999) 'Film and the masquerade: Theorising the female spectator', in Thornham, S. (ed.) *Feminist film theory: A reader*. New York: New York University Press, pp. 131–45.

———. (2011) 'Screening the avant-garde face', in Butler, J. and Weed, E. (eds) *Question of gender: Joan W. Scott's critical feminism*. Bloomington: Indiana University Press, pp. 206–29.

Doland, A. (2007) 'Where are the women? Jane Campion is the lone female director in Cannes film project', *Brisbane Times*, 22 May. Available at: https://www.brisbanetimes.com.au/entertainment/campion-lone-female-in-cannes-project-20070522-ge8p4q.html (Accessed: 3 August 2022).

Doros, D. (1995) 'Email message to Bill Russo', 12 December, in the contributor's possession.

Dyer, R. (2017) *White*. New York: Routledge.

Dyson, L. (1995) 'The return of the repressed? Whiteness, femininity and colonialism in *The Piano*', *Screen*, 36(3), pp. 267–76. https://doi.org/10.1093/screen/36.3.267.

Erhart, J. (2019) '"But do I care? No, I'm too old to care": Authority, unfuckability, and creative freedom in Jane Campion's authorship after the age of sixty', *Studies in Australasian Cinema*, 13(2–3), pp. 67–82. https://doi.org/10.1080/17503175.2019.1700022.

Fabian, R. (2018) 'Reconsidering the work of Claire Johnston', *Feminist Media Histories*, 4(3), pp. 244–73. https://doi.org/10.1525/fmh.2018.4.3.244.

Faludi, S. (1992) *Backlash: The undeclared war against American women*. London: Vintage.

Farrow, R. (2017) '#OscarsSoMale? Hollywood is biased against female directors, some charge', *Today*, 22 February. Available at: https://www.today.com/popculture/oscarssomale-hollywood-biased-against-female-directors-some-charge-t108442 (Accessed: 3 August 2022).

Fendel, H. (1999) 'How women live their lives', in Wright Wexman, V. (ed.) *Jane Campion: Interviews*. Jackson: University Press of Mississippi, pp. 86–90.

Fileborn, B. and Loney-Howes, R. (eds) (2019) *#MeToo and the politics of social change*. Switzerland: Palgrave Macmillan.

Film at Lincoln Center. (2017) 'An evening with Jane Campion', *YouTube*, 15 September. Available at: https://www.youtube.com/watch?v=y9UWX2pIkPw&t=2768s (Accessed: 3 August 2022).

Flood, M. (2008) 'Men, sex, and homosociality: How bonds between men shape their sexual relations with women', *Men and Masculinities*, 10(3), pp. 339–59. https://doi.org/10.1177%2F1097184X06287761.

Foster, G. A. (2017) 'Girlhood in reverse – Jane Campion's *2 Friends* (1986)', *Senses of Cinema*, September. Available at: https://www.sensesofcinema.com/2017/cteq/2-friends/ (Accessed: 3 August 2022).
Foucault, M. (1992) 'What is an author?', in Marsh, J. L., Caputo, J. D. and Westphal, M. (eds) *Modernity and its discontents*. New York: Fordham University Press, pp. 299–314.
Fox, A. (2011) *Jane Campion: Authorship & personal cinema*. Bloomington: Indiana University Press.
Francke, L. (2000) '*The Piano*' in Margolis, H. (ed.) *Jane Campion: The Piano*. Cambridge: Cambridge University Press, pp. 168–72.
Fraser, K. (1999) 'Portrait of a director', in Wright Wexman, V. (ed.) *Jane Campion: Interviews*. Jackson: University Press of Mississippi, pp. 192–200.
Fraser, N. (2013) *The fortunes of feminism*. London: Verso Books.
French, L. (2014) 'The international reception of Australian women film-makers', *Continuum: Journal of Media & Cultural Studies*, 28(5), pp. 654–65. https://doi.org/10.1080/10304312.2014.942024.
Freud, S. (1990) *Totem and taboo: Some points of agreement between the mental lives of savages and neurotics*. Translated from the German by J. Strachey. New York: W. W. Norton and Company.
Fried, K. (1996) 'Garnering attention', *The Village Voice*. XLI (19), 7 May, pp. 54 and 56.
Furness, H. (2017) 'Inserting "feminist ideology" into films means viewers can "guess the end", screenwriter says', *The Telegraph*, 31 May. Available at: https://www.telegraph.co.uk/news/2017/05/31/inserting-feminist-ideology-films-means-viewers-can-guess-end/ (Accessed: 3 August 2022).
Gaines, J. (2016) 'On not narrating the history of feminism and film', *Feminist Media Histories*, 2(2), pp. 6–31. https://doi.org/10.1525/fmh.2016.2.2.6.
Garner, H. (1977) *Monkey grip*. Victoria: McPhee Gribble.
———. (2016) *The Last Days of Chez Nous & Two Friends*. Melbourne: Text Publishing.
———. (2020) 'Email to Zachary Zahos', in contributor's possession.
Geena Davis Institute. 'MYTH: Things are looking great for females behind the camera', *Geena Davis Institute on Gender in Media*. Available at: https://seejane.org/research-informs-empowers/gender-in-media-the-myths-facts/ (Accessed: 28 April 2022).
Genette, G. (1991) 'Introduction to the paratext', translated from the French by M. Maclean. *New Literary History*, 22(2), pp. 261–7. https://doi.org/10.2307/469037.
Gilbert, S. (2017) 'The strange confusion of *Top of the Lake: China Girl*', *The Atlantic*, 13 September. Available at: https://www.theatlantic.com/entertainment/archive/2017/09/top-of-the-lake-china-girl-review/539367/ (Accessed: 3 August 2022).
Gilbert, S. and Gubar, S. (1979) *The madwoman in the attic: The woman writer and the nineteenth century literary imagination*. New Haven and London: Yale Books.
Gillett, S. (1995) 'Lips and fingers: Jane Campion's *The Piano*', *Screen*, 36(3), pp. 277–87. doi:10.1093/screen/36.3.277.
Gledhill, C. and Knight, J. (eds) (2015) *Doing women's film history: Reframing cinemas, past and future*. Urbana: University of Illinois Press.
Goodfellow, M. (2018) 'Cannes Film Festival pays tribute to industry legend Pierre Rissient', *Screen Daily*, 8 May. Available at: https://www.screendaily.com/news/cannes-film-festival-pays-tribute-to-french-industry-legend-pierre-rissient/5128985.article (Accessed: 3 August 2022).
Gorbman, C. (2000) 'Music in *The Piano*', in Margolis, H. (ed.) *Jane Campion: The Piano*. Cambridge: Cambridge University Press, pp. 42–58.
Grant, C. (2001) 'Secret agents: Feminist theories of women's film authorship', *Feminist Theory*, 2(1)1, pp. 113–30. https://doi.org/10.1177%2F14647000122229325.

———. (2008) 'Auteur machines? Auteurism and the DVD', in Bennett, J. and Brown, T. (eds) *Film and television After DVD*. Abingdon, Oxon: Routledge, pp. 101–15.

Groo, K. (2019) *Bad film histories*. Minneapolis: University of Minnesota Press.

Grosz, E. A. (1994) *Volatile bodies: Toward a corporeal feminism*. Bloomington: Indiana University Press.

———. (2005) *Time travels: Feminism, nature, power*. Durham and London: Duke University Press.

Hahn, K. (2021) '*The Power of the Dog* conversation with Jane Campion, Benedict Cumberbatch, Kirsten Dunst and more', *AFI*, 20 November. Available at: https://www.youtube.com/watch?v=U4BwWLfuNgk. (Accessed: 29 April 2022).

Hal, H. (1990) 'Moody "Sweetie's" twisted roots', *The Washington Post*, 2 March. Section D1.

Hamad, H. (2013) 'Hollywood fatherhood: Paternal postfeminism in contemporary popular cinema', in Gwynne, J. and Muller, N. (eds) *Postfeminism and contemporary Hollywood cinema*. Basingstoke and New York: Palgrave Macmillan, pp. 99-115.

Harrington, C. (2021) 'What is "toxic masculinity" and why does it matter?' *Men and Masculinities*, 24(2), pp. 345–52. https://doi.org/10.1177%2F1097184X20943254.

Hawker, P. (1986) 'A tale of friendships and . . . a few little surprises', *The Age*, 24 April.

Heller, A. and Doros, D. (1995) 'Email message to Lee-Anne Higgins of Jan Chapman Productions', 18 September, in the contributor's possession.

Henkel, C. (2019) 'Screen Australia celebrates its work in gender equality but things are far from equal', *The Conversation*, 29 October. Available at: https://theconversation.com/screen-australia-celebrates-its-work-in-gender-equality-but-things-are-far-from-equal-122266 (Accessed: 3 August 2022).

Henley, P. (2020) *Beyond observation*. Manchester: Manchester University Press.

Hesford, V. (2013) *Feeling women's liberation*. Durham: Duke University Press.

Higgins, L. (1995) 'Email message to Amy Heller and Dennis Doros', 22 September, in contributor's possession.

Hochman, B. (2014) *Savage preservation*. Minneapolis: University of Minnesota Press.

Holden, S. (1996) 'Film review; two buddies whose family life is the nemesis', *The New York Times*, 24 April. Available at: https://www.nytimes.com/1996/04/24/movies/film-review-two-buddies-whose-family-life-is-the-nemesis.html (Accessed: 3 August 2022).

Hopewell, J. (2018) 'Series mania: Rachel Perkins, Greer Simpkin talk "Mystery Road", creating a sense of place', 2 May. Available at: https://uk.movies.yahoo.com/series-mania-rachel-perkins-greer-053041723.html (Accessed: 4 August 2022).

Hughes, J. (2015) 'A work in progress: the rise and fall of Australian filmmakers co-operatives, 1966–86', *Senses of Cinema*, 77, December. Available at: https://www.sensesofcinema.com/2015/australian-film-history/australian-filmmakers-co-operatives/ (Accessed: 3 August 2022).

Hutcheon, L. (2012) *A theory of adaptation*. London: Routledge.

IMDb, *An Angel at my Table*. Available at: https://www.imdb.com/title/tt0099040/ (Accessed: 27 April 2022).

IMDb, *The Portrait of a Lady*. Available at: https://www.imdb.com/title/tt0117364/ (Accessed: 27 April 2022).

Ince, K. (2017) *The body and the screen: Female subjectivities in contemporary women's cinema*. Edinburgh: Edinburgh University Press.

International Labour and Walk Free Foundation (2017) 'Global estimates of modern slavery: Forced labour and forced marriage'. Available at: https://www.ilo.org/global/publications/books/WCMS_575479/lang--en/index.html (Accessed: 27 April 2022).

Irigaray, L. (1985) *This sex which is not one*. Translated from the French by C. Porter with C. Burke. Ithaca: Cornell University Press.

―――――. (1993) *Sexes and genealogies*. Translated from the French by G. C. Gill. New York: Columbia University Press.
Iversen, M. (2003) *Alois Riegl: Art history and theory*. Cambridge, MA; London: MIT Press.
James, N. (2015) 'The anxiety of influence', *Sight & Sound*, 25(10), October, p. 5.
Jayamanne, L. (2001) *Toward cinema and its double: Cross-cultural mimesis*. Bloomington and Indianapolis: Indiana University Press.
Jensen, W. (1903) *Gravida*. Frankfurt am Main: S. Fischer Verlag.
Jermyn, D. (2008) 'Women with a mission: Lynda La Plante, DCI Jane Tennison and the reconfiguration of crime drama', in Spiegel, L. and Brunsdon, C. (eds) *Feminist Television*. Berkshire: Open University Press. pp. 57–71.
Johnston, C. (1973) *Notes on women's cinema*. London: Society for Education in Film and Television.
―――――. (1999) 'Women's cinema as counter-cinema', in Thornham, S. (ed.) *Feminist film theory: A reader*. New York: New York University Press, pp. 31–40.
Jolly, M. (2009) 'Looking back?: Gender, sexuality and race in *The Piano*', *Australian Feminist Studies*, 24(59), March, pp. 99–121. https://doi.org/10.1080/08164640802680627.
Jones, G. (2007) *The Piano*. Sydney, NSW: Currency Press and the National Film and Sound Archive.
Juarez, S. (2022) 'Jane Campion doesn't refrain from "telling stories of men"', *AwardWorld*. Available at: https://awardworld.net/palme-dor/jane-campion-does-not-refrain-from-telling-stories-of-men/ (Accessed: 27 April 2022).
Kahane, C. (1985) 'The gothic mirror', in Sprengnether, M., Kahane, C. and Garner, S. (eds) *The (m)other tongue: Essays in psychoanalytic interpretation*. Ithaca: Cornell University Press, pp. 334–51.
Kalinak, K. (1992) *Settling the score: Music and the classical Hollywood film*. Madison, WI: University of Wisconsin Press.
Kaplan, E. A. (ed.) (2000) *Feminism and film*. Oxford: Oxford University Press.
Kaufman, G. S. and Hart, M. (1934) *Merrily we roll along*. New York: Random House.
Kaufman, M. (1994) 'Men, feminism, and men's contradictory experiences of power', in Brod, H. and Kaufman, M. (eds) *Theorizing masculinities*. California: SAGE Publications Inc, pp. 142–63.
Keegan, R. (2019) 'Governors awards: Honorees Lina Wertmüller, Geena Davis call for gender parity in Hollywood', *The Hollywood Reporter*, 27 October. Available at: https://www.hollywoodreporter.com/news/general-news/academy-honors-geena-davis-david-lynch-wes-studi-lina-wertmuller-1250327/ (Accessed: 3 August 2022).
Keeling, K. (2007) *The witch's flight: The cinematic, the black femme, and the image of common sense*. Durham: Duke University Press.
―――――. (2019) *Queer times, black futures*. New York: New York University Press.
Khoo, O. (2006) 'Telling stories: The sacrificial Asian in Australian cinema', *Journal of Intercultural Studies*, 27(1–2), pp. 45–63. https://doi.org/10.1080/07256860600607587.
Kimmel, M. S. (1994) 'Masculinity as homophobia: Fear, shame and silence in the construction of gender identity', in Brod, H. and Kaufman, M. (eds) *Theorizing masculinities*. California: SAGE Publications Inc., pp. 119–41.
―――――. (2005) *The history of men: Essays on the history of American and British masculinities*. Albany: State University of New York Press.
Kirkland, J. (2022) 'The Power of the Dog director calls Sam Elliott a "bit of a B-I-T-C-H"', *Esquire*, 14 March. Available at: https://www.esquire.com/entertainment/movies/a39281446/sam-elliott-the-power-of-the-dog-comments/ (Accessed: 22 March 2022).
Klawans, S. (2000) 'The Piano', in Margolis, H. (ed.) *Jane Campion: The Piano*. Cambridge: Cambridge University Press, pp. 186–89.

Klinger, B. (2006) 'The art film, affect and the female viewer: *The Piano* revisited', *Screen*, 47(1), January, pp. 19–41. https://doi.org/10.1093/screen/hjl002.

Knight, C. (2006) 'Ada's piano playing in Jane Campion's *The Piano*: Genteel accomplishment or romantic self-expression?', *Australian Feminist Studies*, 21(49), March, pp. 23–34. doi: 10.1080/08164640500470610.

Kohn, E. (2021) 'Palme d'Or winner Julia Ducournau on groundbreaking "Titane"', *Indiewire*, 17 July. Available at: https://www.indiewire.com/2021/07/julia-ducournau-interview-palme-dor-titane-1234652010/ (Accessed: 3 August 2022).

Krishnan, A. (2017) '10 best reverse chronology movies of all time', *The Cinemaholic*, 2 August. Available at: https://www.thecinemaholic.com/best-movies-that-use-reverse-chronology/ (Accessed: 3 August 2022).

Kristeva, J. (1980) *Desire in language: A semiotic approach to literature and art*. Edited by L. S. Roudiez, Oxford: Basil Blackwell.

———. (1982) *Powers of horror*. Translated from the French by L. S. Roudiez. New York: Columbia University Press.

———. (1984) *Revolution in poetic language*. Translated from the French by M. Waller. New York: Columbia University.

Kuhn, A. (2013) *The power of the image: Essays on representation and sexuality*. London: Routledge.

Kushner, R. (2103) *The flamethrowers*. New York: Scribner.

Lauzen, M. (2022) 'The celluloid ceiling: behind-the-scenes employment of women on the top 100, 250, and 500 Films of 2017', Centre for the Study for Women in Television and Film. Available at: https://womenintvfilm.sdsu.edu/research/ (Accessed: 27 April 2022).

Le Bris, V. (2018) 'Interview with Jane Campion', *European Women's Audiovisual Network*, 3 December. Available at: https://www.ewawomen.com/interviews/interview-with-jane-campion/ (Accessed: 22 March 2022).

Leppert, R. D. (1995) *The sight of sound: Music, representation and the history of the body*. Berkeley; London: University of California Press.

Lévi-Strauss, C. (1969) *The elementary structures of kinship*. Boston: Beacon Press.

Lindner, K. (2017) *Film bodies: Queer feminist encounters with gender and sexuality in cinema*. London and New York: I. B. Tauris.

Lury, K. (2005) *Interpreting television*. London: Bloomsbury Academic.

McCarthy, T. (1996) 'Campion's elegant, chilly "portrait"', *Variety*, 9 September, p. 114.

McCloud, F. (2016) 'Human trafficking victims deserve national compensation scheme', *ABC News*, 25 October. Available at: https://www.abc.net.au/news/2016-10-25/anti-slavery-compensation-scheme-needed-for-australia/7960376 (Accessed: 3 August 2022).

Macdonald, M. (1995) *Representing women: Myths of femininity in the popular media*. London and New York: Edward Arnold.

McHugh, K. A. (2001) '"Sounds that creep inside you": Female narration and voiceover in the films of Jane Campion', *Style*, 35(2), pp. 193–218. https://www.jstor.org/stable/10.5325/style.35.2.193 (Accessed: 6 October 2022).

———. (2007) *Jane Campion*. Urbana: University of Illinois Press.

———. (2009) 'Jane Campion: Adaptation, signature, autobiography', in Radner, H., Fox, A., and Bessière, I. (eds.) *Jane Campion: Cinema, nation, identity*. Detroit: Wayne State University Press, pp.139–56.

———. (2015) 'Giving credit to paratexts and parafeminism in *Top of the Lake* and *Orange is the New Black*', *Film Quarterly*, 68(3), Spring, pp. 17–25. https://doi.org/10.1525/fq.2015.68.3.17.

Maddox, G. (1996) 'A history of the Australian film finance corporation', *Media International Australia*, 80(1), May, pp. 75–83. https://doi.org/10.1177%2F1329878X9608000113.

Marks, L. U. (1998) 'Video haptics and erotics', *Screen*, 39(4), December, pp. 331–48. https://doi.org/10.1093/screen/39.4.331.
———. (2000) *The skin of the film: Intercultural cinema, embodiment, and the senses*. Durham: Duke University Press.
———. (2015) *Hanan al-cinema: Affections for the moving image*. Cambridge, MA; London, England: The MIT Press.
Marshall, L. (1996) 'What Jane Campion did next', *The Independent*, 22 September. Available at: https://www.independent.co.uk/arts-entertainment/what-jane-campion-did-next-1364490.html (Accessed: 22 March 2022).
Martin, K. H. (2017) 'NEW SCENE OF THE CRIME: Tone and tension in *Top of the Lake: China Girl*', *Digital Video Magazine*, September. Available at: https://web.archive.org/web/20200809113250/https://www.creativeplanetnetwork.com/news/news-features/tone-and-tension-top-lake-china-girl-619162 (Accessed: 3 August 2022).
Mayer, S. (2016) *Political animals: The new feminist cinema*. London & New York: I. B. Tauris.
———. (2017) 'Paradise, built in hell: Decolonising feminist utopias in *Top of the Lake* (2013)', *Feminist Review*, 116(1), July, pp. 102–17. https://doi.org/10.1057%2Fs41305-017-0066-7.
Mayne, J. (2005) *Claire Denis*. Urbana/Chicago: University of Illinois Press.
MIFF Talks Presents (2017) '*Top of the Lake: China Girl*, Sunday 6 August 2017, 12:30pm – 2:00pm, Comedy Theatre, 240 Exhibition Street, Melbourne'. Available at: https://miff.com.au/festival-archive/films/id/27230 (Accessed: 29 April 2022).
Milestone Films (1995) *Two Friends press kit*. Available at: https://cdn.shopify.com/s/files/1/0150/7896/files/2FriendsPK.pdf?1009 (Accessed: 29 April 2022).
Miller, N. K. (1988) *Subject to change: Reading feminist writing*. New York: Columbia University Press.
Modleski, T. (1998) *Old wives' tales and other women's stories*. New York: New York University Press.
Montpelier, R. (2019) 'Lina Wertmüller and Geena Davis call for change at the 2019 Governors Award', *Women and Hollywood*. Available at: https://womenandhollywood.com/lina-wertmuller-and-geena-davis-call-for-change-at-the-2019-governors-awards/ (Accessed: 27 April 2022).
Moore, S. (1995) *In the Cut*. New York: Plume Books.
Muir, K. (2018) 'Jane Campion: "Capitalism is such a macho force. I felt run over"', *The Guardian*, 20 May. Available at: https://www.theguardian.com/film/2018/may/20/jane-campion-unconventional-film-maker-macho-force (Accessed: 22 March 2022).
Mulvey, L. (1975) 'Visual pleasure and narrative cinema', *Screen* 16(3), Autumn, pp. 6–18.
———. (1987) 'Notes on Sirk and melodrama', in Gledhill, C. (ed.) *Home is where the heart is. Studies in melodrama and the woman's film*. London: BFI, pp. 75–9.
———. (1999a) 'Visual pleasure and narrative cinema', in Thornham, S. (ed.) *Feminist film theory: A reader*. New York: New York University Press, pp. 58–69.
———. (1999b) 'Afterthoughts on "visual pleasure and narrative cinema" inspired by King Vidor's *Duel in the Sun* (1946)', in Thornham, S. (ed.) *Feminist film theory: A reader*, pp. 122–30.
———. (2000) 'Visual pleasure and narrative cinema', in Kaplan, E. A. (ed.) *Feminism and film* Oxford: Oxford University Press, pp. 34–47.
Neroni, H. (2012) 'Following the impossible road to female passion: Psychoanalysis, the mundane, and the films of Jane Campion', *Discourse*, 34(2–3), pp. 294–310. https://doi.org/10.13110/discourse.34.2-3.0290.
———. (2017) 'Feminist filmmaking on television: Lacan, phallic enjoyment and Jane Campion's *Top of the Lake*', *Intertexts*, 21(1–2), Spring–Fall, pp. 115–35. doi:10.1353/itx.2017.0005.

Nyman, M. (2006) 'Interview with Michael Nyman', in *The Piano Special Edition* [DVD]. Optimum Releasing.
O'Connell, M. (2016) '*Game of Thrones* star joining Elisabeth Moss in *Top of the Lake* season 2', *The Hollywood Reporter*, 21 March. Available at: https://www.hollywoodreporter.com/live-feed/game-thrones-star-joining-elisabeth-877218 (Accessed: 3 August 2022).
Oliver, K. (1993) *Reading Kristeva: Unravelling the double bind*. Bloomington and Indianapolis: Indiana University Press.
Orr, B. (1999) 'Birth of a nation? From utu to the piano', in Coombs, F. and Gemmell, S. (eds) *Piano lessons: Approaches to The Piano*. Sydney, NSW: John Libbey Cinema and Animation, pp. 148–60.
Osterweil, A. (2016) 'Sophie Mayer's political animals', *Artforum International Magazine*, 1 June. Available at: https://www.artforum.com/print/201606/sophie-mayer-s-political-animals-the-new-feminist-cinema-60080 (Accessed: 3 August 2022).
Park, D. and Dietrich, D. (2005) 'In the Cut', *Film Quarterly*, 58(4), pp. 39–46. https://doi.org/10.1525/fq.2005.58.4.39.
Parliament of Australia (2008) '"Screen Australia act" Act No. 12 of 2008', 27 March. Available at: https://www.legislation.gov.au/Details/C2008A00012 (Accessed: 5 August 2022).
Peacock, S. (2014) *Swedish crime fiction*. Manchester: Manchester University Press.
Pihama, L. (1994) 'Are films dangerous? A Maori woman's perspective on *The Piano*', *Hecate*, 20(2), pp. 239–42.
——. (2000) 'Ebony and ivory: Constructions of Māori in *The Piano*' in Margolis, H. (ed.) *Jane Campion's The Piano*. Cambridge: Cambridge University Press, pp. 114–34.
Pinter, H. (1991). *Betrayal*. London: Faber and Faber.
Polan, D. (2001) *Jane Campion*. London: BFI.
Preston, Y. (1999) 'Getting it in the Cannes', in Wright Wexman, V. (ed.) *Jane Campion: Interviews*. Jackson: University Press of Mississippi, pp. 11–13.
Proulx, A. (1997) 'Brokeback Mountain', *The New Yorker*, 13 October. Available at: https://www.newyorker.com/magazine/1997/10/13/brokeback-mountain (Accessed: 22 March 2022).
Pulver, A. (2014) 'Jane Campion: "Life isn't a career"', *The Guardian*, 12 May. Available at: https://www.theguardian.com/film/2014/may/12/jane-campion-interview-cannes-the-piano (Accessed: 22 March 2022).
Rabiger, M. and Hurbis-Cherrier, M. (2013) *Directing: Film techniques and aesthetics*. New York: Focal Press.
Radner, H. (2009) '"In extremis": Jane Campion and the woman's film', in Radner, H., Fox, A., and Bessière, I. (eds) *Jane Campion: Cinema, nation, identity*. Detroit: Wayne State University Press, pp. 3–24.
Radstone, S. (2017) '*Top of the Lake*'s emotional landscape: Reparation at the edge of the world', *Critical Arts*, 31(5), pp. 87–94. https://doi.org/10.1080/02560046.2017.1348687.
Reuschmann, E. (2004) 'Out of place: Reading (post) colonial landscapes as gothic space in Jane Campion's films', *Post Script*, 24(2–3), Winter, pp. 8–21.
Reuters Staff (2019) 'Geena Davis calls Hollywood gender imbalance an "embarrassment"', *reuters.com*, 12 September. Available at: https://www.reuters.com/article/us-filmfestival-deauville-geenadavis-idUSKCN1VW2M1 (Accessed: 22 March 2022).
Rich, A. (1979) *On lies, secrets, and silence*. New York: W. W. Norton & Company.
Richard, D. E. (2018) 'Film phenomenology and adaptation: The fleshly dialogue of Jane Campion's *In the Cut*', *Adaptation*, 11(2), pp. 144–58. https://doi.org/10.1093/adaptation/apx028.
Rickey, C. (1999) 'A director strikes an intimate chord', in Wright Wexman, V. (ed.) *Jane Campion: Interviews*. Jackson: University Press of Mississippi pp. 50–3.
Ricks, C. (2009) 'Undermining Keats', *The New York Review*, 17 December. Available at: https://www.nybooks.com/articles/2009/12/17/undermining-keats/ (Accessed: 22 March 2022).

Robinson, N. (1999) 'With choices like these who needs enemies: *The Piano*, melodrama, and the woman's film', in Coombs, F. and Gemmell, S. (eds) *Piano lessons: Approaches to The Piano*. Sydney, NSW, Australia: John Libbey Cinema and Animation, pp. 19–43.

Rooney, D. (2021) 'Benedict Cumberbatch in Jane Campion's "*The Power of the Dog*": Film review', *The Hollywood Reporter*, 2 September. Available at: https://www.hollywoodreporter.com/movies/movie-reviews/power-of-the-dog-review-1235005112/ (Accessed: 22 March 2022).

Rowe, K. (1995) *The unruly woman: Gender and the genres of laughter*. Austin: University of Texas Press.

Rubin, G. (1975) 'The traffic in women: Notes on the "political economy" of sex', in Reiter, R. (ed.) *Toward an anthropology of women*. New York and London: Monthly Review Press, pp. 157–210.

Russell, C. (1999) *Experimental ethnography*. Durham: Duke University Press.

Russo, B. (1995) 'Email message to Dennis Doros (of Milestone Films)', 4 December, in contributor's possession.

Said, E. (1979) *Orientalism*. New York: Vintage.

Saraiya, S. (2017a) 'Jane Campion explains reasons behind "china girl" in new "*Top of the Lake*" season', *Variety*, 30 August. Available at: https://variety.com/2017/tv/features/jane-campion-top-of-the-lake-china-girl-1202541887/ (Accessed: 3 August 2022).

———. (2017b) 'Jane Campion on the ending of *Top of the Lake: China Girl*', *Variety*, 12 September. Available at: https://variety.com/2017/tv/news/jane-campion-top-of-the-lake-china-girl-finale-1202554618/ (Accessed: 3 August 2022).

———. (2017c) '"*Top of the Lake*: China Girl": Elisabeth Moss and Gwendoline Christie on the finale.' *Variety*, 12 September. Available at: https://variety.com/2017/tv/news/elisabeth-moss-gwendoline-christie-top-of-the-lake-china-girl-finale-1202554677/ (Accessed: 3 August 2022).

Scott, G. F. (2010) 'Review of *Bright Star*, by Jane Campion', *Studies in Romanticism*, 49(3), Fall, pp. 507–12. doi:10.1353/srm.2010.0020.

Sedgwick, E. K. (2015) *Between men: English literature and male homosocial desire*. New York: Columbia University Press.

Sellier, G. (2008) *Masculine singular: French new wave cinema*. Durham: Duke University Press.

Senn, N. (2017) 'Between innocence and adulthood: Telling *A Girl's Own Story*', *Senses of Cinema*, 20 September. Available at: https://www.sensesofcinema.com/2017/cteq/a-girls-own-story/ (Accessed: 3 August 2022).

Sharf, Z. (2018) 'Jane Campion: Why Debra Granik deserves Oscar nomination for "Leave No Trace" (exclusive)', *IndieWire*, 19 December. Available at: https://www.indiewire.com/2018/12/jane-campion-debra-granik-oscar-nom-best-director-leave-no-trace-1202029649/ (Accessed: 3 August 2022).

Showalter, E. (1982) *A literature of their own: From Charlotte Brontë to Doris Lessing*. London: Virago.

Silverman, K. (1988) *The acoustic mirror: The female voice in psychoanalysis and cinema*. Bloomington and Indianapolis: Indiana University Press.

Simmons, R. (2009) 'The suburb in Jane Campion's films', in Radner, H., Fox, A. and Bessière, I. (eds) *Jane Campion: Cinema, nation, identity*. Detroit: Wayne State University Press, pp. 175–86.

Simpson, C. (2000) 'Imagined geographies: Women's negotiation of space in contemporary Australian cinema, 1988–98', PhD diss. Murdoch University. Available at: https://researchrepository.murdoch.edu.au/id/eprint/312/ (Accessed: 3 August 2022).

ap Siôn, P. (2007) *The music of Michael Nyman: Texts, contexts and intertexts*. London: Routledge.

Smelik, A. (1998) *And the mirror cracked: Feminist cinema and film theory*. London: Macmillan Press Ltd.

Sobchack, V. (2004) *Carnal thoughts: Embodiment and moving image culture*. Berkeley: University of California Press.

Sontag, S. (1975) 'Fascinating fascism', *The New York Review*, 6 February. Available at: https://www.nybooks.com/articles/1975/02/06/fascinating-fascism/ (Accessed: 3 August 2022).

Soutphommasane, T. (2020) 'Elsewhere they get it but the Australian media is still living in White Australia', *The Guardian*, 18 August. Available at: https://www.smh.com.au/national/elsewhere-they-get-it-but-the-australian-media-is-still-living-in-white-australia-20200816-p55m73.html (Accessed: 3 August 2022).

Spender, D. (1980) *Man made language*. London and Boston: Routledge and Keegan Paul.

Spivak, G. C. (1981) 'French feminism in an international frame', *Yale French Studies* 62, pp. 156–7. https://doi.org/10.2307/2929898.

Stott, J. (1987) 'Independent feminist filmmaking and the Sydney filmmakers co-operative', in Blonski, A., Creed, B., and Freiberg, F. (eds) *Don't Shoot Darling!: Women's Independent Filmmaking in Australia*. Richmond, Australia: Greenhouse Publications, pp. 118–26.

Stratton, D. (1980) *The last new wave: The Australian film revival*. Sydney: Angus & Robertson.

Stynes, Y. (2020) '"Boat person, ladyboy or drug dealer": how Australian TV sidelines Asians', *The Guardian*, 30 January. Available at: https://www.theguardian.com/tv-and-radio/2020/jan/30/boat-person-ladyboy-or-drug-dealer-how-australian-tv-sidelined-asians (Accessed: 3 August 2022).

Tarr, C. and Rollet, B. (2001) *Cinema and the second sex: Women's filmmaking in France in the 1980s and 1990s*. London: Bloomsbury.

Taubin, A. (1996) 'Reversals of fortune', *The Village Voice*, 30 April, p. 51.

Thomas, K. (1996) 'Lives unfold in Campion's "Two Friends"', *Los Angeles Times*, 16 May. Available at: https://www.latimes.com/archives/la-xpm-1996-05-16-ca-4622-story.html (Accessed: 3 August 2022).

Thompson, A. O. (1996) 'Jane Campion's debut feature gets U.S. theatrical release', *American Cinematographer*, 77(7), July, pp. 14–24.

Thompson, K. and Bordwell, D. (2003) *Film history: An introduction*. New York: McGraw-Hill.

Thornham, S. (1997) *Passionate detachments: An introduction to feminist film theory*. London: Arnold.

———. (2012) *What if I had been the hero?: Investigating women's cinema*. London: BFI.

———. (2017) 'Beyond Bluebeard: feminist nostalgia and *Top of the Lake* (2013)', *Feminist Media Studies*, 19(1), pp. 102–17. https://doi.org/10.1080/14680777.2017.1396485.

———. (2019) *Spaces of women's cinema: Space, place and genre in contemporary women's filmmaking*. London: BFI.

Tims, A. (2012) 'How we made: Michael Nyman and Jane Campion on *The Piano*', *The Guardian*, 30 July. Available at: https://www.theguardian.com/film/2012/jul/30/how-we-made-the-piano (Accessed: 3 August 2022).

Tincknell, E. (2011) 'The time and the place: Music and costume and the "affect" of history in the New Zealand films of Jane Campion', in Fox, A., Grant, B. K., and Radner, H. (eds) *New Zealand Cinema: Interpreting the past*. Bristol, UK: Intellect Books Ltd, pp. 277–89.

———. (2013) *Jane Campion and adaptation: Angels, demons and unsettling voices*. Basingstoke: Palgrave.

Tobing Rony, F. (1996) *The third eye*. Durham: Duke University Press.

Trinh, T. M. (1991) *When the moon waxes red*. New York: Routledge.

Verhoeven, D. (2009) *Jane Campion*. New York: Routledge.

Vineyard, J. (2017) '"Top of the lake: China girl": Jane Campion on her "ovarian" series', *New York Times*, 12 September. Available at: https://www.nytimes.com/2017/09/12/arts/television/top-of-the-lake-china-girl-jane-campion.html (Accessed: 3 August 2022).

Waling, A. (2019) 'Problematising "toxic" and "healthy" masculinity for addressing gender inequalities', *Australian Feminist Studies*, 34(101), pp. 362–75. https://doi.org/10.1080/08164649.2019.1679021.

Wang, Y. (2000) 'Settlers and sojourners: Multicultural subjectivity of Chinese-Australian artists', in Ang, I., Law, L., Chalmers, S., and Mandy, T. (eds) *Alter/Asians: Asian-Australian identities in art, media and popular culture*. Sydney: Pluto Press, pp. 107–22.

Ward, S. (2022) 'Jane Campion breaks down four key scenes from *The Power of the Dog*', *Screen Daily*, 3 March. Available at: https://www.screendaily.com/features/jane-campion-breaks-down-four-key-scenes-from-the-power-of-the-dog/5168271.article (Accessed: 4 August 2022).

Warren, S. (2019) *Subject to reality*. Urbana: University of Illinois Press.

Watkins, L. (2013) 'Disharmonious designs: Colour, contrast and curiosity in Jane Campion's *In the Cut*', *NECSUS*, 2(1). doi: 10.5117/necsus2013.1.watk.

White, P. (2015) *Women's cinema, world cinema: Projecting contemporary feminisms*. Durham and London: Duke University Press.

Wielgus, A. (2019) '"The harder I swim, the faster I sink": *Top of the Lake*'s female detective in the global television economy', *Camera Obscura*, 34(2), pp. 71–101. doi:10.1215/02705346-7584916.

Williams, L. (1999) *Hard core*. Berkeley: University of California Press.

Williamson, K. (1999) 'The new filmmakers', in Wright Wexman, V. (ed.) *Jane Campion: Interviews*. Jackson: University Press of Mississippi, pp. 9–10.

Wilmington, M. (1996) '"*Two Friends*" marks turning point for girls, director Campion', *Chicago Tribune*, 10–16 May. Available at: https://www.chicagotribune.com/news/ct-xpm-1996 05 10 9605100302 story.html (Accessed: 3 August 2022).

Women and Hollywood (2022) 'Statistics: Facts to know about women in Hollywood', *WomenandHollywood.com*. Available at: https://womenandhollywood.com/resources/statistics/ (Accessed on: 28 April 2022).

Woolf, V. (1925) *To the Lighthouse*. London, Hogarth Press.

Young, I. M. (1980) 'Throwing like a girl: A phenomenology of feminine body comportment, motility and spatiality', *Human Studies*, 3(2), April, pp. 137–56. https://doi.org/10.1007/BF02331805.

Yue, G. (2015) 'The China girl on the margins of film', *October*, 153, pp. 96–116. https://doi.org/10.1162/OCTO_a_00228.

———. (2021) *Girl head: Feminism and materiality*. New York: Fordham University Press.

Zarzosa, A. (2010) 'Jane Campion's *The Piano*: Melodrama as mode of Exchange', *New Review of Film and Television Studies*, 8(4), December, pp. 396–411. https://doi.org/10.1080/17400309.2010.514664.

Filmography

FILMS AND TELEVISION SERIES DIRECTED BY JANE CAMPION

Tissues (1980).
Peel – An Exercise in Discipline (1982). 9 mins.
Passionless Moments (1983). 13 mins.
Mishaps of Seduction and Conquest (1984). 15 mins.
After Hours (1984). 26 mins.
A Girl's Own Story (1984) The Criterion Channel. 27 mins.
Dancing Daze (1986) ABC. 6 x 50 mins.
Two Friends (1986) Milestone Films. 76 mins.
Sweetie (1989) Avenue Pictures Productions. 97 mins.
An Angel at my Table (1989) Fine Line Features. 158 mins.
The Piano (1993) Miramax Films. 117 mins.
The Portrait of a Lady (1996) Gramercy Pictures. 142 mins.
Holy Smoke (1999) Miramax. 115 mins.
In the Cut (2003) Screen Gems. 119 mins.
The Lady Bug (2007) Dreamland Films. 3 mins.
The Water Diary (2008) The Criterion Channel. 17 mins.
Bright Star (2009) BBC Films. 119 mins.
Top of the Lake (2013) BBC. 6 x 60 mins.
Top of the Lake: China Girl (2017) BBC. 6 x 60 mins.
The Power of the Dog (2021) Netflix. 126 mins.

FILMS MENTIONED IN THIS VOLUME

Akerman, Chantal, director. *Jeanne Dielman 23 Quai du Commerce 1080 Bruxelles* (1975) Janus Films. 201 mins.
Armstrong, Gillian, director. *The Last Days of Chez Nous* (1992) Fine Line Features. 93 mins.

Arnold, Andrea, director. *Fish Tank* (2009) IFC Films. 123 mins.
Breillat, Catherine, director. *Romance* (1999) Trimark Pictures. 99 mins.
Davies, Garth, director. *Lion* (2016) The Weinstein Company. 118 mins.
Donahue, Tom, director. *This Changes Everything* (2018) Good Deed Entertainment. 97 mins.
Ducournau, Julia, director. *Titane* (2021) Neon. 108 mins.
Flaherty, Robert J., director. *Nanook of the North* (1922) Pathé Exchange. 79 mins.
Granik, Debra, director. *Leave No Trace* (2018) Bleecker Street Media. 109 mins.
Greenaway, Peter, director. *The Draughtsman's Contract* (1982) Curzon Artificial Eye. 104 mins.
Hicks, Scott, director. *Shine* (1998) Fine Line Features. 105 mins.
Lee, Ang, director. *Brokeback Mountain* (2005) Focus Features. 134 mins.
Leigh, Julia, director. *Sleeping Beauty* (2011) Paramount Pictures. 102 mins.
McKimmie, Jackie, director. *Stations* (1983) Umbrella Entertainment. 23 mins.
McQueen, Steve, director. *Widows* (2018) Twentieth Century Fox. 130 mins.
Noé, Gaspar, director. *Irréversible* (2002) Lionsgate Films. 97 mins.
Nolan, Christopher, director. *Memento* (2000) Newmarket Films. 113 mins.
Oldřich, Lipský, director. *Happy End* (1967) Continental Distributing. 71 mins.
Ophüls, Max, director. *Letter From An Unknown Woman* (1948) Universal Pictures. 86 mins.
Polanski, Roman, director. *The Pianist* (2002) Focus Features. 150 mins.
Potter, Sally, director. *Thriller* (1979) The Criterion Channel. 34 mins.
Rainer, Yvonne, director. *Film About a Woman Who. . .* (1974) The Criterion Channel. 90 mins.
Riefenstahl, Leni, director. *Triumph of the Will* (1935) IHF. 114 mins.
Schumacher, Joel, director. *Batman Forever* (1995) Warner Bros. 122 mins.
Varda, Agnès, director. *The Beaches of Agnès* (2008) PBS. 110 mins.
Various, directors. *To Each His Own Cinema (Chacun Son Cinema)* (2007) Dreamland Filmes. 119 mins.
Young, Claire, director. *From the Bottom of the Lake* (2013) BBC Worldwide. 52 mins.

TELEVISION SERIES MENTIONED IN THIS VOLUME

Neighbours (1985–2022) Seven.
Prime Suspect (1991–2006) BBC.
Changi (2001) ABC.
Curtin (2007) ABC.
The Fall (2013–2016) BBC.
The Family Law (2016–2019) SBS.
Big Little Lies (2017–2019) HBO.
The Handmaid's Tale (2017–present) Hulu.
Mystery Road (2018–present) ABC.
Little Fires Everywhere (2020) Hulu.
Mare of Easttown (2021) HBO.

Index

Note: n indicates 'note'

agency
   authorial, 37, 41, 52, 94, 109–10, 122, 125–6
   embodiment, 12, 59, 60–2, 67, 69
   female, 10, 41, 91, 106, 132
   feminist, 8, 57
   heterosexual relationships, 9
   in *A Girl's Own Story*, 32, 33
   in *Bright Star*, 96
   in *The Piano*, 75, 79, 80
   male, 107n
   #MeToo, 6–7
anthropology, 21–2, 144–5, 157
Antipodean
   cultural values, 164, 179
   feminist cinema, 2, 39, 40–1, 43, 52
   framework, 14, 50
   setting, 21, 30, 161, 183
   surrogacy, 169
approximation, 20, 29, 31
Asian
   Australian Asian, 166–7, 168
   Bowie's 'China Girl', 158n
   in prestige drama, 175
   modern slavery, 170, 175
   multiculturalism, 168–9, 170–1
   Orientalism, 158, 165–6, 168
   representation, 161, 164, 167–8, 171
   surrogacy trade, 162, 175
auteur, 15n, 37–8, 46, 52, 75, 94, 109–10, 114, 116, 142n
   Campion as, 3–5, 44, 110, 121, 125–6, 126n, 130, 142, 162
   cultural value of the, 8–9, 125–6
   death of the author, 37
   female, 3–5, 8, 42, 46, 50, 92–4, 107n, 109–10, 125, 142
   feminist, 3–5, 40–1, 142
   see also authorship
authorship
   collaborative, 38, 39, 52
   female, 4, 37, 106, 107n, 109, 110
   studies, 37
   see also agency and auteur

Bluebeard, 145, 146, 151, 158n
bodies, 12, 33, 57, 58, 59–63, 66–8, 71, 72n, 135, 136, 137, 142, 147, 148, 150, 171, 180–1, 183, 184
   as spectacle, 70, 104, 140, 142
   unruly, 59, 61, 67, 68

Campion, Jane
  After Hours, 4, 19, 40–1, 43, 62–3, 72, 129–30
  Angel at My Table, An, 1, 12, 15, 38, 43, 51, 52, 72, 81, 123, 162
  Bright Star, 1, 12, 29, 41, 76, 81, 91, 92, 93, 94, 95–8, 99, 100, 101, 103, 104, 106, 110
  Dancing Daze, 43, 162
  Girl's Own Story, A, 9, 20, 28–34, 46, 60, 62, 72, 91, 110, 149, 158n, 180
  Holy Smoke, 41, 57, 59, 60, 63–6, 68–9, 78, 87, 92, 182
  In the Cut, 1, 12, 32, 57, 59, 63–6, 70, 77, 81, 92–3, 103, 108, 110, 112–14, 116, 121, 156, 159, 180
  Lady Bug, The, 2–4
  Mishaps of Seduction and Conquest, 15n
  Passionless Moments, 9, 11, 20–8, 29, 30, 35, 46, 62, 181–2: 'Angela Eats Meat', 23, 25–7; 'Focal Lengths', 23; 'Ibhrahim Makes Sense of it All', 23; 'No Woodpeckers in Australia', 23–5, 28
  Peel – An Exercise in Discipline, 1, 42, 46, 60, 144
  Piano, The, 1, 12, 38–9, 41, 42, 46, 51, 73–89, 92, 94, 107n, 108, 110, 111–13, 114, 115, 117, 118–19, 120–4, 133, 135, 145, 147, 149, 150, 154, 163, 178–9, 180, 182
  Portrait of a Lady, The, 15, 38, 41, 76, 87, 92–4, 100, 110, 180
  Power of the Dog, The, 1, 7, 12–13, 91–6, 98–9, 100, 180: Elliot, Sam, 93; Cowboy, the, 93, 95, 98, 99, 102, 103, 104, 106; Netflix, 7, 105; Western, the, 7, 95, 98, 99, 183
  Sweetie, 38, 44, 50, 51, 57, 59, 60, 63–9, 70, 93, 110, 123, 149, 179, 182
  Tissues, 15n
  Top of the Lake, 1, 5, 7, 12, 92, 110, 112, 114, 129–43, 144, 146, 177, 179, 182
  Top of the Lake: China Girl, 2, 13, 19, 92, 112, 144–59, 160–77, 179, 181, 182
  Two Friends, 9, 10, 11, 37–52, 162
  Cannes Film Festival, 1, 3, 6, 39, 42–3, 93–4
    Palme d'Or, 1, 19, 34, 42, 94
Chapman, Jan
  Australian Academy of Cinema and Television Arts (AACTA), 41
  Sydney Women's Film Group, 41, 42
  Piano, The, 12, 89, 110–16, 119, 120–4
  Two Friends, 38, 39–41, 43, 44, 53n, 89n
colonial, 13, 20
  Campion as, 162
  colonialism, 181–4
  in *Passionless Moments*, 21, 24–5, 27–8
  in *The Piano*, 163
  Said, Edward, 21
  see also postcolonial
commentary (DVD), 89n, 109, 112–13, 116–17, 120–2, 125, 126n; *see also* paratext

Ducournau, Julia, 34–5
Dunst, Kirsten, 105

embodiment, 12–13, 59, 61, 63, 65–7, 69, 70–1, 83–4, 179, 180, 184
ethnography, 9, 11, 20, 21–5, 27–8, 35, 182

feminism
  collaboration, 33, 39, 41–2, 44–5, 52, 92, 125, 179, 182
  phenomenology, 61, 63, 66
  popular, 130–1
  postfeminism, 13, 107n, 130, 141
  poststructuralism, 95
Freud, Sigmund, 35
  family romance, 149
  incest, 145
  Oedipus myth, 145, 154
  on femininity, 140

Garner, Helen, 38–9, 40, 43–5, 47–51, 53n
gaze, the
  female, 29–30, 58–9, 64, 81, 126n, 139–41
  filmic, 81, 104, 182
  male, 30, 58–9, 62, 66–7, 69–70, 81, 107n, 140
Gillet, Sue, 74, 76–7, 86
gothic, 60, 120, 132–3, 145, 147, 148, 151, 157, 163

haptic, 63, 65, 71, 79, 82–3, 87–9, 89n, 104, 107n
  music, 75, 77–8, 82–3
  visuality, 73–4, 80, 83, 104
heterosexuality
  obligatory, 95–6
  relationships, 91, 95, 111–12, 114–15, 119, 126n
homophobia, 95, 104
homosexual, 93, 95, 97–9, 103
homosocial, 7, 12, 91–2, 95–9, 100–3
Hunter, Holly, 117, 135

incest, 31–2, 144–5, 148–51, 154–5, 157–8, 179, 181

Indigenous, 13, 24, 102, 183–4
  ethnographic film, 24
  filmmaker, 171
  masculinity, 102
  native, 21, 163, 182
  representation, 179, 183
Irigaray, Luce, 139, 152

Keitel, Harvey, 114, 122
kinship, 95–6, 98, 144, 145, 147–8, 150–4, 157, 158n, 181–2
Kristeva, Julia, 137, 140
  abject, 138, 172
  chora, 133–5, 138
  semiotic, 133–40
  Symbolic Order, 135, 143
Kushner, Rachel, 160, 177
  Flamethrowers, The, 160–2, 169, 176

Lacan, Jacques, 117
Lévi-Strauss, Claude *see* kinship

McHugh, Kathleen, 11, 21, 23, 30–1, 52n, 57, 81, 84–5, 132, 144, 150, 154, 166, 168
Marks, Laura U. *see* haptic
masculinity
  alternative, 92, 100, 107n
  competitive, 92, 98–103
  female, 97
  hegemonic, 91, 92, 99–100, 102, 104–6
  hypermasculinity, 95, 99, 101–3, 180, 184
  oppressive, 136
  toxic, 7, 91–2, 93, 107n
maternal, 133–8, 147, 148–9, 154
Mayer, So, 14, 31, 33, 106, 107n, 126n, 133, 175
  girl 'hood, 33

Milestone Films, 39–40, 45, 47, 50–1
misogyny, 27, 104, 113, 180
movements
  #BlackLivesMatter, 3
  #EverydaySexism, 3
  #MeToo, 3, 6–9, 12–13, 35, 91, 92, 130–2, 141–2, 178
  #TimesUp, 3, 6, 35
multiplicity, 11, 95, 141
Mulvey, Laura *see* visual pleasure

Neroni, Hilary, 21, 24, 80, 162
Nyman, Michael, 12, 73–4, 83, 122

Oedipal, 146, 149, 156
organisations
  Australian Academy of Cinema and Television Arts (AACTA), 41
  Australian Broadcasting Company (ABC), 39, 41–4, 51
  Australian Film Finance Corporation (FFC), 41–3
  Australian Film, Television and Radio School (AFTRS), 41–3
  Females First, 2
  Geena Davis Institute, 3
  Sydney Filmmakers Cooperative, 41–2
  Sydney Women's Film Group, 41–3
  Women's Film Unit (WFU), 4–5, 40, 129
Oscars, 1, 2, 92, 179
Other, the, 21–5, 27–8, 154, 171, 182–3

paratext, 12, 108–11, 115–19, 129, 124–5, 132–3, 144, 154, 166, 179
  Genette, Gérard, 109
  see also commentary (DVD)

Parker, Laurie, 12, 110, 112, 114–17, 119, 121
parler femme, 12, 108, 117–18, 120–1, 124–5; *see also* Irigaray
patriarchy, 2–3, 5–8, 10, 12–13, 25, 32, 61–2, 71, 75, 92, 95–7, 99, 101, 104, 108, 111–12, 114, 118, 129–34, 136–7, 139, 141–2, 144–6, 148, 151, 153, 157, 180
Patterson, Janet, 38–9, 43–4, 47–8
postcolonial, 24, 161, 163–4, 166, 177n; *see also* colonialism
postfeminism *see* feminism

queer, 33–4, 97–9, 103, 104–6

Rich, Adrienne, 20, 29
re-vision, 20, 29, 30–2, 34, 179
Rissient, Pierre, 42
Romantics, the, 109, 123
  Keats, John, 29, 76, 92–8, 100–1, 106
Rubin, Gayle, 139, 145, 157

Sedgwick, Eve Kosofsky, 95–7, 103
semiotic, 57, 149; *see also* Kristeva, semiotic
sexuality
  desire and sexuality, 111, 119, 125
  female sexuality, 30–2, 59, 68–9, 91, 114, 120–1, 125, 148–9, 157
  gender and sexuality, 93, 95, 98, 105–6, 180, 182, 184
Sobchack, Vivian, 74, 76–7, 111
subjectivity, 8–9, 12–13, 20, 23, 27, 30, 68, 74, 76, 82, 91, 111, 117, 120, 125, 129, 132–6, 138, 175

television, 5, 7–8, 13, 52, 132, 161–4, 168, 169–73
Thornham, Sue, 10–11, 14, 126n, 135, 139, 140, 146, 163
Tincknell, Estella, 5, 78, 94, 97
trauma, 32, 33, 86, 88–9, 131, 136, 139, 142, 144, 149, 171, 175
Trinh, T. Minh-ha, 24, 28

Verhoeven, Deb, 4, 52n, 94, 162
violence
    child abuse, 132, 136, 139–40, 142
    domestic, 165
    male, 6–7, 12, 14, 73, 82, 86–7, 129, 131, 133–4, 137–8, 140
    patriarchal, 6, 32, 105, 132, 135–7, 142, 173
    racial, 164, 171
    sexual violence, 4, 6, 40, 62, 75, 89n, 91–2, 129
visibility, 165,
    (hyper)visibility, 6, 130–2, 142
    (in)visibility, 131–3, 184
    spectacle, 134, 142
visual pleasure, 58–9, 67, 71
    post-visual pleasure, 12, 58–9, 63, 66, 71

Wegner, Ari, 105, 178
Weinstein, Harvey, 6, 9, 11, 131
White, Patricia, 3, 19

Yue, Genevieve, 25, 161, 163, 165–6, 171

EU representative:
Easy Access System Europe
Mustamäe tee 50, 10621 Tallinn, Estonia
Gpsr.requests@easproject.com

www.ingramcontent.com/pod-product-compliance
Lightning Source LLC
Chambersburg PA
CBHW051124160426
43195CB00014B/2335